Notary Signing Agent
Certification Training

STUDY GUIDE

Use this book to assist in passing the NSA
Certification Exam, and keep it as a reference
as you grow your Signing Agent business.

Published by:

National Notary Association
9350 De Soto Avenue
Chatsworth, CA 91311-4926
Telephone: (818) 739-4000
Fax: (818) 700-0920
Website: NationalNotary.org
Email: nna@NationalNotary.org

The information in this *Study Guide* is correct and current
at the time of its publication. This information is provided
to aid comprehension of Notary Signing Agent practices and
procedures and should not be construed as legal advice. Please
consult an attorney for inquiries relating to legal matters.

Third Edition, Second Printing ©2016
First Edition ©2015

ISBN: 978-1-59767-195-8

TABLE OF CONTENTS

Introduction

Congratulations on taking your first step toward becoming an NNA Certified Notary Signing Agent. Whether you are already a commissioned Notary or just getting started in this industry, this *Study Guide* is designed to help you review the information you need to pass the NSA certification exam and learn more about the critical role you will play as a Notary Signing Agent.

To achieve these goals, we have broken the information into three easy-to-follow Chapters:

❖ **Chapter One: Becoming a Notary Signing Agent**
This lesson reviews what a signing agent is, the steps to become one, details about the certification process, an overview of the NSA certification exam, and details about the NSA background screening.

❖ **Chapter Two: Getting Started as an NNA Certified Notary Signing Agent**
In lesson two, we take you through the major steps of an actual assignment: Landing the assignment, preparing for the appointment, conducting the signing, and post-appointment follow up.

❖ Chapter Three: Key Resource Documents

Here is where you will find three key Notary Signing Agent documents in their entirety: The *Notary Signing Agent Code of Conduct*, the *Notary Signing Agent Signing Presentation Guidelines*, and the *Code of Conduct Mapping Table*.

Each lesson will draw upon and quote from the Guiding Principles presented in the *Code of Conduct*, as well as highlighted excerpts from the *Signing Presentation Guidelines*, both of which we will introduce early in Lesson 1.

Again, we congratulate you on this important step toward becoming an NNA Certified Notary Signing Agent, and we thank you for choosing the National Notary Association as your educational source.

Chapter

1

Becoming a Notary Signing Agent

In this first lesson, we will review the role and responsibilities of the Notary Signing Agent and the process required for you to become one. We will also walk you through the NSA certification process, including an overview of the final certification exam and the background screening requirements. When you have completed this lesson, you will have a better understanding of what it means to be an NSA, what to expect and how to prepare for the certification exam, how long the certification process will take, and approximately how soon you can get started in your new NSA role.

THE ROLE OF THE NOTARY SIGNING AGENT

In simple terms, the Notary Signing Agent (NSA) is a Notary who is specifically trained to handle and notarize loan documents. But they often do much more. And given the fact that NSAs play a critical role in many mortgage transactions nationwide, their role is clearly a vitally important one.

When you work as an NSA, you are generally hired by a lender, title company or closing agent as an independent contractor. They need your services in order to complete the loan process, and they need to trust that you are qualified and competent in your role. Signing agents, in turn, earn income for delivering loan packages to borrowers and ensuring they signed, are returned to the lender in a safe and timely manner. For many NSAs, these services can translate into valuable income opportunities.

Notary Signing Agents generally have five primary responsibilities:
1. To coordinate and oversee the appointment at which loan documents are signed by a borrower
2. To receive or reproduce documents for the signing appointment, and to deliver the documents to the appointment
3. To ensure that real estate loan documents are properly executed
4. To ensure that the documents requiring notarization are properly notarized
5. To return the documents for processing

It is important to understand that Notary Signing Agents must follow federal and state regulations in order to protect a customer's personal and financial information. The information reviewed in this study guide, along with the Certification Course contents and accompanying NSA certification exam, is designed to further help ensure compliance with these regulations.

Given the critical responsibilities of the Notary Signing Agent, it should come as no surprise that there is a specific process required in order to carry out the role and become an NNA Certified NSA.

THE NNA NSA CERTIFICATION PROCESS

It should be first noted that before becoming an NNA Notary Signing Agent, you must already be a commissioned or appointed Notary Public. Once actively commissioned, any Notary may take the steps required to become a Notary Signing Agent.

In this section, we will focus on the five major requirements for becoming an NNA Certified Notary Signing Agent.

THE FIVE REQUIREMENTS

The created five standards required of all NNA NSA candidates:

1. Signing and adhering to the *Notary Signing Agent Code of Conduct*
2. Passing an annual certification examination
3. Submitting to an annual background screening
4. Using the *Signing Presentation Guidelines*
5. Owning Notary errors and omissions insurance coverage

1: Signing and Adhering to the *Code of Conduct*

To begin your certification process, the first document you will want to familiarize yourself with is the *Notary Signing Agent Code of Conduct*, particularly its 10 Guiding Principles, which we will cover in detail in Lesson 2 and is offered in its entirety in Lesson 3.

The *Code of Conduct* is so critical that it has become a requirement for certification that all NSAs read through it and sign, stating that he or she promises to abide by the *Code* in his or her professional practice. You will be provided online access to agree to the terms of the *Code* once you access the certification exam with the NNA.

The *Code* also provides much of the detailed information you will be tested on in the NNA's NSA certification exam, so it's important you understand it well.

2: Passing the Annual Certification Exam

Once you have agreed to the *Code of Conduct* terms, your next step is to take and pass the NSA certification exam. You are required to obtain a score of at least 80% to be considered as demonstrating competence of the proper procedures for conducting a loan document signing. The exam contains 45 questions, meaning you must correctly answer 36 of them to pass.

3: Submitting to a Background Screening

In addition to passing the Notary Signing Agent certification examination, all NNA Certified NSA candidates must undergo an annual background screening.

Why is a background screening required?

In order to guard borrowers' private financial information, the mortgage industry requires all persons involved in the lending process to undergo background screenings. Lenders, in turn, instruct title service companies to ensure that everyone with access to mortgage documents has been screened. This requirement applies to everyone handling loan documents, including Notary Signing Agents.

The NNA background screening includes the following:
- 10-Year Search of Criminal Records[1]
- Social Security Number Trace
- County Criminal Court Search[2]
- Motor Vehicle Records[3]
- National Sex Offender Database
- Nationwide Criminal Database
- Federal District Court Search
- USA Patriot Act including Terrorist Watch List

The NNA's comprehensive screening is the most widely recognized and accepted by the nation's leading lenders and title companies.

How does the background screening process work?

Within 24 hours of registration, you will receive an email directing you to the secure website of the NNA background screening provider. This is where you will submit the information required to initiate your screening process.

The entire background screening process is usually completed within five to 10 business days. However, certain states have additional requirements and may take longer. For the latest information on this and other state-specific NSA restrictions, please visit our website, *NationalNotary.org*.

1. California, Colorado, Kansas, Maryland, Massachusetts, Montana, New Hampshire, New Mexico, New York and Washington laws limit reporting to 7 years. Prior to June 10, 2015, Nevada law limited reporting to 7 years. Beginning June 10, 2015, Nevada reporting is limited to 10 years.
2. New York provided as a statewide search.
3. Unavailable in Washington and Pennsylvania.

You will be notified by email of whether or not your results meet the lending industry's compliance requirements. You will then be able to view your screening details on the provider's secure website. You have the right to dispute the accuracy or completeness of any information contained in your report and disputed information will be reinvestigated.

4: The *Signing Presentation Guidelines*

The *Signing Presentation Guidelines* include uniform talking points outlining how an NSA should open and close a signing appointment and introduce the documents. These guidelines cover 27 documents commonly found in a refinance loan package. The purpose of these guidelines is to help ensure a consistent, high-quality customer experience at every signing. To supplement this resource, the NNA has created **Loan Documents At-A-Glance**. This document provides additional facts and talking points for many common documents.

5: Notary Errors and Omissions Insurance Coverage

Many lenders, title companies and signing services require Notary Signing Agents to carry a Notary errors and omissions insurance policy, typically with a $25,000 coverage limit. Notary E&O insurance is your protection should you make an innocent mistake with a notarization or a false claim is filed against you stating that your notarization was in error.

A BRIEF OVERVIEW OF THE NSA CERTIFICATION EXAM

The Notary Signing Agent certification exam requires you to demonstrate your knowledge of sound mortgage signing practices as well as your solid understanding of *The Notary Signing Agent Code of Conduct* and *Signing Presentation Guidelines*. Here are some facts you need to know about the certification exam:

- ❖ **Online Accessibility Required.** The exam is taken fully online via a secure website provided by the NNA.

- ❖ **45 Questions.** It consists of a total of 45 rotating questions with a mix of both multiple-choice and true-false formats. As previously mentioned, a score of at least 80% is required to pass.

❖ **Open Book and Not Timed.** While the questions themselves are challenging, the test is not timed and is full "open-book format" so you are free to access any resources, including this NSA Course Study Guide, when taking it.

❖ **Annual Renewal.** To meet their service and compliance requirements, lenders and title companies generally require NSAs to renew their qualifications on an annual basis. This means you will need to take and pass the certification exam (as well as your background screening) annually. ■

Chapter

2

Getting Started as an NNA Certified Notary Signing Agent

In this lesson, we will take a deeper look at the specific guidelines and best practices when it comes to performing your role as a Notary Signing Agent. We will focus on how to present your business, including laws regulating fees and advertising, how to market your services, how to conduct a signing, and how to follow up once you have completed an assignment.

The information in this lesson will be pulled directly from two key documents: the *Notary Signing Agent Code of Conduct* and the associated *Signing Presentation Guidelines*.

This will be helpful for two reasons: First, the vast majority of the questions appearing in the NSA certification exam come from these two documents and, second, these are the guiding principles you will want to follow when conducting actual signings.

❖ **The *Code of Conduct*:** The *Code* is divided into nine distinct areas, each area represented by a key Guiding Principle. The document is designed to guide and educate both NSAs and the companies that hire them on standards of professionalism. It also offers specific guidelines on daily administrative tasks such as advertising one's services, the charging and collecting of fees, and how to demonstrate responsible conduct with contracting companies and borrowers. Much of this content will be covered in this lesson.

❖ **The *Signing Presentation Guidelines*:** This document provides specific guidance and suggestions as to the language you might use when performing an assignment.

Throughout this lesson, we will provide content from the *Code*'s Guiding Principles, as they pertain to each corresponding step in the NSA process. Again, both the *Code of Conduct* and the *Signing Presentation Guidelines* are offered in their entirety in Lesson 3 of this book, for you to review in more detail.

In this lesson, we will cover the following topics:
1. Standards of Practice and NSA Professionalism
2. Landing the Assignment
3. Preparing for the Assignment
4. Conducting the Assignment
   a. Meeting the borrowers
   b. Preparing the signing space
   c. Presenting and notarizing the documents
   d. Handling issues during the appointment
   e. Closing the meeting
5. Post-Assignment Follow Up

PART 1: STANDARDS OF PRACTICE AND NSA PROFESSIONALISM

In this section, we will focus on your qualifications, how you can market your services, confirming and collecting your fees, and maintaining standards of practice throughout each step of a loan signing.

Meeting NSA Qualifications

When it comes to NSA qualifications, you will find that the requirements for a Notary commission vary from state to state. Other qualifications are set by each contracting company, but many have similar requirements. The NNA's NSA Certification program reflects common standards and is widely accepted throughout the real estate finance industry. It is ultimately your responsibility to meet all the qualification requirements of your jurisdiction. Guiding Principle 1 of the *Code of Conduct* covers qualifications in great detail, but here are some key guidelines:

❖ **Professional Licenses:** NSAs must obtain and maintain all licenses and commissions required to perform signing services in your state or jurisdiction. This means you'll need to keep your Notary commission and any licenses required by your state to handle loan signings, such as a title producer license or license to practice law, current.

❖ **Background Screening:** As previously discussed, as an NSA, you are required to have background screenings of your identity, residence, record of state or federal criminal arrests and convictions, state motor vehicle records and a check of your name against pertinent lists as required by rules implementing the USA PATRIOT Act. Many lenders and title agencies require that this screening be on an annual basis. Passing a background screening on an annual basis qualifies you to work for the greatest number of contracting companies.

❖ **Notary and Federal Laws and Regulations:** To ensure compliance, it is your responsibility to keep current on all laws and regulations that affect the performance of notarial acts in your state or jurisdiction, especially as they pertain to the performance of signing services. This includes but is not limited to the:

> • Gramm-Leach-Bliley Act (GLBA)
>
> • Truth-in-Lending Act (TILA)
>
> • Real Estate Settlement Procedures Act (RESPA)
>
> • Fair and Accurate Credit and Transactions Act (FACTA)
>
> • Uniting and Strengthening America by Providing Appropriate Tools Required to Intercept and Obstruct Terrorism (USA PATRIOT) Act.

Take the time to access resources online to maintain a high level of understanding of the laws that impact your work.

❖ **Certification:** You must earn and maintain any certifications needed to service contracting companies and parties to the transaction. Find out what certifications your contracting companies require or certify on an annual basis. You will then be qualified for even the most stringent of contracting companies.

❖ **Closing Documents:** It's important to familiarize yourself with all closing documents for each assignment; however, as a Notary, you must be careful to never provide unauthorized counsel, or to advise signing parties, which could be construed as the unauthorized practice of law [the topic of Unauthorized Practice of Law is discussed in more detail in *Code of Conduct*, Guiding Principle 4]. This means that when you are asked a question that is inappropriate, such as: "is my interest rate a good one?", let the borrower know that you are not allowed by law to discuss this level of detail during the signing. The NNA Loan Documents At-A-Glance and the Presentation Guidelines are both resources that will help determine what questions you are able to answer.

❖ **Continued Education:** Stay informed on any technical matters, legal requirements and other developments that may affect your competence or responsibilities in rendering signing services. The NNA's NSA Annual Compliance is updated to keep NSAs current with new documents and regulations. Completing this course is noted on SigningAgent.com. This lets contracting companies know your knowledge is up to date.

❖ **Supervising Attorney:** If required by law or rule in your state or jurisdiction, you must submit to the supervision of an attorney. This simple rule in any regulated field is: follow the law.

Advertising Your Notary Signing Services

As a Notary Signing Agent, it is likely that you want to market or advertise your services; however, there are several important regulations regarding how Notaries are permitted to do so. For this reason, Guiding Principle 8 of the *Code* focuses entirely on laws and regulations regarding how a Notary Signing Agent may advertise services. The bottom line: When advertising or marketing your services or small business, you must never advertise in an unprofessional, false, misleading or deceptive way. Below is a detailed breakdown of advertising rules, as they apply to Notary Signing Agents.

❖ **Truthful Personal Assessment:** Never misrepresent your background, education, training or expertise in an application or interview, or post inaccurate claims on your company website or other promotional materials you distribute. This includes making exaggerated or excessive claims, promises or guarantees about the services you provide. It may be tempting to build up your resume when you are a beginner, promise a faster turnaround of documents or claim specialization in a unique area untruthfully. Take the time to build a real resume and you will grow important and fruitful relationships along the way.

❖ **Use of Professional or Improper Designation:** You cannot advertise or promote any services or make false, misleading, nonexistent or meaningless designations by using professional designations or certifications you have not received or earned.
A competitive advantage can be gained by building a strong reputation as an excellent NSA.

❖ **Observation of Rules of Use:** You must always comply with the requirements governing the use of membership and professional designations, logos and marks as may be required by the organizations that issued or certified the designations, logos, or marks. What this means is that you may not suggest to a borrower or contracting company that you are either an employee or a certified NSA if you are not, and therefore many not place a logo on a business card or name plate.

❖ **Solicitation of Outside Business:** When providing signing or Notary services on behalf of a signing service, you shouldn't directly or indirectly solicit signers for products or services other than the services you have been hired to perform. Many NSAs have additional lines of business, such as, tax preparation, equipment witnessing and mystery shopper services. When representing a contracting company at a signing appointment, maintain focus on the task at hand.

Confirming and Collecting Fees

Guiding Principle 7 of the *Code* addresses issues regarding fees, including when and how to confirm your fees, how to invoice and collect fees, and other rules you should be aware of before you begin taking on assignments. Below are some key guidelines with regards to NSA fees:

❖ **Establish Fees in Advance:** Be sure your fee is pre-determined with your contracting company and confirmed in your work contract before you head out to an assignment. This protects both parties, and ensures you earn the fee you are expecting. Often times, this contract will arrive via text or email. You should include the agreed-upon fee when you return the text or email.

❖ **Invoicing and Collection of Fees:** All invoices submitted to contracting companies should be completed in a way that's compliant with the contract you have established ahead of time with the company; furthermore, the invoice must match the agreed-upon amount. So, if a company's payment policy is 30 days after the close of the contract, you should wait the full 30 days before reaching out to the company about a late payment.

❖ **Collusion:** You must never collude or conspire with other Notary Signing Agents to set fees for signing services. Steer clear of joining social forums "discussion" groups where other Notaries are talking about banding together to set a standard fee in a specific area.

Maintaining High Standards of Professionalism

A major driving force of the SPW is to devise an industry-wide effort to elevate the standards of professional conduct for Notary Signing Agents nationwide. To this end, Guiding Principle 9 of the *Code of Conduct* offers guidelines pertaining to professionalism, including:

❖ **Refusing an Assignment:** If you are unable to meet all expectations of the contracting company, including but not limited to, prompt arrival at a set time, printing services, and providing copies of the closing documents, you must refuse the assignment. Keep in mind you may not ask someone else to print and prep a loan package while you are at another appointment.

- ❖ **Overbooking:** Exercise care in booking to ensure each appointment has ample time for completion. Make sure you have ample time to cross town at rush hour and give extra time to loan signings such as reverse mortgages for elderly borrowers.

- ❖ **Canceling/Rescheduling:** Avoid canceling or changing assignments whenever possible, but if you must do so, notify the contracting company rather than the signer. Things happen. If you are suddenly without transportation, contact your contracting company as soon as possible and make sure cancellations are few and far between.

- ❖ **Signing Scripts:** Follow any closing scripts provided by the contracting company, should that be a requirement of the company. Don't say more about a document than the Presentation Guidelines suggest.

- ❖ **Professional Communication and Attire:** As a representative of your contracting company, you should always maintain a level of professionalism in all of your verbal and written communications. Arrive to assignments promptly and dressed in an appropriate, professional manner. When in extreme weather, make sure your extra warm or extra light clothing is still business like.

Review the *Code's* Guiding Principle 9 for more ways in which Notary Signing Agents are expected to act towards contracting companies and parties to closing transactions.

PART 2: LANDING THE ASSIGNMENT

Once you have met all the qualifications to become a Notary Signing Agent, it is time to begin preparing for your first signing — starting with landing your first assignment. In this lesson, we will review the rules regarding how to advertise your services, the importance of confirming and communicating fees ahead of time, the need for impartiality in every transaction, and, finally, the importance of conducting your business signings with a high level of professionalism at all times.

Advertising Your Notary Signing Agent Services

Again, for many NSAs, one of the first steps in landing an assignment is advertising your services. There are many ways to successfully market yourself, such as registering with services that broker loan signing appointments, soliciting companies that provide direct work, and creating and distributing marketing materials, such as print brochures, business cards, and a business website. But as discussed in the previous section, when creating your marketing strategy, there are certain rules you must follow. Guiding Principle 8 of the *Code* covers this subject in more detail. Here are some highlights to consider when landing an assignment:

❖ **False or Misleading Claims:** Do not make exaggerated or excessive claims, promises or guarantees about the services you provide. When you reach out to a contracting company for business, don't pretend to have more experience than you do.

❖ **Observation of Rules for Use:** Always comply with the requirements governing the use of membership and professional designations, logos and marks as may be required by the issuing, certifying or accrediting entity. NNA members are allowed to use the NNA logo on business materials; however, you shouldn't use it if you are no longer a member of the association. The same applies for other memberships or professional designations.

Always Remain Impartial

As a Notary Public, it is your responsibility to act as a neutral, third-party witness to critical transactions. Therefore, it is crucial that you determine your impartiality before accepting any assignment. The *Code*'s Guiding Principle 3 discusses impartiality in detail, but here are some key points you should know before accepting any assignment:

❖ **Personal and Professional Interest:** Do not provide signing services for any transaction in which you or a close relative is directly or indirectly involved as a party, or in which the close relative is the loan officer, real estate agent, mortgage broker or a settlement services provider. Don't offer to notarize documents for old Aunt Mary's beach house if you stand to inherit the house when she dies.

❖ **Notary Signing Agent and Attorney in Fact:** You are not allowed to sign documents as both a Notary Signing Agent and attorney in fact for a principal in the same transaction. If you are attorney in fact for a business or property or other person, even if you will not be signing the document in a particular circumstance, hire a Notary.

❖ **Appearance of Partiality:** Refrain from performing signing services in any transaction that would raise the appearance of, or the potential for, a conflict of interest. Even if you aren't involved in the transaction, when taking care of friends and family, provide them with a referral rather than doing the work yourself.

Communicating and Confirming Fees

There are several rules you must keep in mind when it comes to the confirmation and communication of fees. The bottom line is that you must always follow all contractual obligations when charging and collecting fees for the services you have rendered. Review Guiding Principle 7 for more complete details regarding NSA fees, but here are some key points to remember:

❖ **Confirmation of Fee in Writing and Submission of Invoice:** Always confirm the fee to be paid by the contracting company for an assignment in writing prior to the appointment with the signer. Remember to submit those invoices for payment to the contracting company in a form that complies with the terms of the written agreement between you and contracting company. Make sure all your written records have the fee you agreed to when you accepted the assignment.

❖ **Performance and Referral for Fee:** You cannot refuse to perform services for an assignment that you had previously accepted due to a dispute over a negotiated fee. Never accept or charge an illegal referral fee, rebate, fee-split, unearned fee or kickback. And only charge and receive the fee for rendering signing services in connection with a transaction. Sometimes an agreed-upon fee doesn't seem to be enough for an appointment you agreed to oversee; the borrower lived much further away than you thought, for example, or you forgot to charge a printing fee. This happens to all of us in business. Let it go and learn from it.

Maintaining High Standards of Professionalism

Professionalism in this industry means always acting in a responsible manner towards contracting companies and all parties to the transaction. We discussed this topic in the previous section, and the *Code* offers the following guidelines in Guiding Principle 9:

❖ **Delegation of Duties:** You cannot authorize another Notary Signing Agent to perform signing services on your behalf without the prior approval of the contracting company providing the assignment. Having a partner NSA to pick up work for you in an emergency is a great idea. Just make sure the NSA has the same qualifications as yourself and get the switch approved before you do it.

❖ **Cancellation and Rescheduling of Appointments:** This one bears repeating: You must immediately notify the contracting company providing the assignment if an emergency will delay or prevent you from attending the appointment. **Do not contact the signer directly.** Keep your contracting agency advised if you are running late. If it keeps happening, take a look at your booking process.

❖ **Assignment Requirements:** Thoroughly review the requirements and expectations for each assignment ahead of time. Take careful note of what stipulated documents and payments you must receive from the signer and what documents and copies must be left with that individual. It's a good practice to make a note on a post-it and put it on the top document. Before leaving the borrower, double-check the note to make sure you haven't forgotten anything.

❖ **Contracting Company Instructions:** Make sure to study each lender and contracting company's instructions and signing scripts for each assignment prior to the signing appointment and follow such instructions and scripts as long as they do not violate any statute, regulation or official directive related to the performance of notarial acts. Lenders and title agencies tend to handle documents in a habitual manner. Once you get to know their pattern, make sure to check for changes to the system.

Exercise Diligence and Caution

The *Code's* Guiding Principle 5 focuses on the Notary Signing Agent's role when it comes to recognizing and reporting illegal and suspicious activity. While no one wants to believe they will be placed in a legally precarious position, NSAs are often privy to confidential data and responsible for critical documents. As such, it is essential to exercise care and caution at all times.

❖ **False Document or Certificate:** Be aware that a lender's representative, contracting company, closing agent, signer or any other person is not permitted to falsify information in a closing document or certificate of a notarial act. If you find numbers crossed out or information missing, call the contracting company and let them know.

- ❖ **Extra Certificate:** You cannot grant any request of a lender's representative, contracting company or closing agent to mail a signed and sealed notarial certificate that is not securely attached to an actual closing document notarized by you. Sometimes someone new or unaware at a contracting company may ask for something that is not legal like providing an extra certificate "just in case." Don't get offended; just remind them that this is prohibited by law.

PART 3: PREPARING FOR THE ASSIGNMENT

Once you have landed the assignment, the preparation process begins. In this lesson, we will review Guiding Principles related to preparing documents, including the importance of client confidentiality and other privacy concerns. We will also review ways to prepare a script to use when conducting a signing.

Focus on Privacy and Confidentiality

Before you begin to prepare the documents for your first signing, you will want to review, in detail, the *Code*'s Guiding Principle 6, which focuses on privacy and confidentiality. It is vital that you respect the privacy of each signer and protect loan documents from unauthorized disclosure. Here are some additional key concepts when it comes to ensuring the security and accuracy of all documents:

- ❖ **Nondisclosure of Signer Information:** Never disclose the transaction or personal information of a signer to any person not directly a party to the transaction. Don't leave documents out in a coffee shop or even at home and if a borrower wants to share their business, they will share the information themselves.

- ❖ **Scrutiny of Documents:** Do not inspect or examine the closing documents beyond what you need to in order to determine the requirements and conditions for the assignment and complete any journal entries. Once you have completed your journal entries and checked the documents to make sure there are no blank spaces, the dates and names are correct, and other details related to the notarization, stop there. It's not your responsibility to go beyond this level of review.

- ❖ **Reception, Delivery, Access and Printing of Documents:** Whenever practical, you should strive to receive and deliver all loan document packages in person or via secure means. Do not delegate the responsibility of downloading and printing all loan documents. Do not share access instructions, including passwords to websites for the purpose of viewing, downloading or printing loan documents. Don't ask family members to download and print documents in order to save time.

❖ **Compromised Security of Documents:** Always ensure that packages of loan documents are properly sealed upon reception and delivery; keep them under either personal control or lock and key. Immediately advise the contracting company of any circumstance leading you to believe the contents of the package have been compromised. If a package arrives unsealed, contact the contracting company and let them know.

❖ **Unprotected Network:** Never use a public or unsecured computer network or fax machine to retrieve or print communications in connection with a signing assignment, as they could be hacked or otherwise tampered with. If you have a portable printer, don't use the free wireless connection in your local mall or any public place to download your documents. This could compromise the safety of the data.

❖ **Transmission or Reception of Non-Public Personal Information:** Always use encryption, strong passwords and other secure delivery methods to send or receive closing documents or communications containing a signer's non-public personal information. Be smart about your passwords. Make sure they are not easy to figure out.

The biggest rule to remember when it comes to preparing for a signer is to pay attention to detail and deliver on all promises. Guiding Principle 9 focuses on Professionalism, and here are some key excerpts related specifically to preparation:

❖ **Review of Documents:** Review the loan documents prior to the signing appointment to confirm that the documents identify the correct signing party or parties and to determine which documents must be signed, dated, initialed and notarized. Remember that every stage of the loan process creates opportunity for errors. Even if you are pressed for time, always review the documents for potential errors that could arise during your signing appointment.

❖ **Notification of Missing Documents:** Immediately contact the closing agent prior to the appointment if you discover the Note, Mortgage or Deed of Trust, Truth-in-

Lending Disclosure or closing disclosure is either incomplete or missing from the document package. Arriving at the signing table with a document missing wastes your time and will be considered your error.

❖ **Appointment Confirmation:** Confirm the appointment to sign loan documents with the signer, ensuring that all parties and witnesses signing documents and checks (when applicable) will be available upon the Agent's arrival, unless expressly prohibited by the contracting company. Read the instructions carefully so you know what to ask the signer to have on hand. An inappropriate ID will stop the appointment in its tracks.

❖ **Professional Communications:** Always keep your verbal and written communications professional in both tone and demeanor. If you get angry, take a moment to compose yourself before reaching out to any business contact.

❖ **Notification of Late Arrival:** If you are running late, notify the signer and contracting company providing the assignment **at least 30 minutes** prior. If you hit an unexpected traffic jam on your way to an appointment, reach out sooner than later to let others know you may be later than scheduled. Don't let this become a habit.

Report Any Illegal or Suspicious Activity

As you prepare for your assignment, it is your responsibility to be aware of and report any potential illegal or suspicious activity that you encounter. The *Code's* Guiding Principle 5 focuses on this issue, and offers the following rules and guidelines:

❖ **False Document or Certificate:** Be aware that a lender's representative, contracting company, closing agent, signer or any other person is not permitted to falsify information in a closing document or certificate of a notarial act. If you see a certificate pre-printed with false information, do not use that certificate.

❖ **Approval of Power of Attorney Signing:** The Notary Signing Agent will not commence an appointment involving an attorney in fact signing for an absent principal unless specifically approved by the lender's representative or closing agent for the transaction. If the person appearing to sign before you is not the principal signer you are expecting, you should call the contracting agency right away.

❖ **Incomplete Documents:** Immediately contact the lender's representative and closing agent for the transaction if any loan document required to be notarized is incomplete or contains blank spaces. As with any notarization, blank spaces are always a cause for concern. Whether it's a missing date or name, be sure the absence is resolved before you offer your official notarization.

❖ **Presentation of Entire Document:** Present all pages of a document, not just the signature page, to a signer for signature. During the signing appointment is not the time to cut corners. Even if your signer asks to see only the signature pages, remind them that it's your job to present all documents for their review.

❖ **Evidence of Tampering:** Immediately contact the lender's representative and closing agent for the transaction if you believe that a document or notarial certificate has been tampered with or altered. If you spot any red flags — a suspicious cross-out, or information printed underneath other numbers, for example — halt the signing and contact the appropriate closing agent before proceeding.

❖ **Disclosure of Wrongdoing:** Never conceal knowledge of a criminal act committed in connection with a signing assignment. If you are aware that a criminal act has been committed, immediately notify a lawful authority. If you halt a signing due to suspicions of a fake ID, be sure to report the issue with the appropriate authorities.

One Final Note: Once you have already accepted an assignment, you must never refuse to perform the agreed-upon services over a dispute of a negotiated fee. This is why it is so important to confirm fees *prior* to the assignment. See the *Code*'s Guiding Principle 7 for more information on fees.

PART 4: CONDUCTING THE ASSIGNMENT

Now that you have landed the job and prepared for the appointment, it's time for you to conduct your first NSA assignment. But where do you start? From the clothing you wear, to the words you choose to help guide your signers through the signing process, it's clear that conducting your first signing begins before you even leave your office.

This lesson reviews several of the *Code's* Guiding Principles as they relate to the five major steps involved in closing assignments. It also reviews how to use the *Notary Signing Agent Signing Presentation Guidelines*, available in Lesson 3, to create your own signing script. You can also find listings and descriptions of key loan documents in Section 4, all of which we encourage you to familiarize yourself with on your own, as these are valuable resources you are likely to find yourself referencing often.

FIVE STEPS TO CONDUCTING THE ASSIGNMENT

We have broken the task of conducting the assignment into five main subsections:
1. Meeting the borrowers
2. Preparing the signing space
3. Presenting and notarizing the documents
4. Handling issues and challenges during the appointment
5. Closing the meeting

1. Meeting the Borrowers

Here is where you arrive, properly prepared, and borrowers get their first impression of you in person. It is important that you look professional and act professionally. In addition to dressing properly and arriving promptly, here are additional guidelines from Guiding Principle 9, focusing on professionalism:

❖ **Professional Communications:** Always keep your verbal and written communications professional in both tone and demeanor. Even if your signer is frustrated, angry or hostile, it's your job to maintain your composure and get through the signing in a professional manner.

❖ **Identifying Credentials:** You must present government-issued photo ID to the signer at the appointment prior to the signing of any documents. Proper ID can put your signers at ease, so it may be a good idea to bring your professional business cards in addition to your government-issued identification.

The first section of the *Signing Presentation Guidelines* offers an example script that you can use upon meeting with your borrowers:

> *"Hello, my name is (NAME) and I am here on behalf of (TITLE & CLOSING COMPANY), the title and closing company working with (LENDER) to conduct your loan signing. We spoke earlier on the phone. It is nice to meet you."*

Section 2 of the *Guidelines* further instructs you as to the proper steps you should take upon meeting with borrowers. It is important as you proceed into the closing transaction that you follow the closing instructions precisely.

- Provide the borrower with a state or federally issued photo ID.

- Wait for the borrower to invite you inside.

- Ask the borrower where he or she would like to conduct the signing, suggesting that all signers sit next to each other to facilitate the signing.

- Confirm that all parties that need to sign are present. Check copies of borrower identification at this time. ID should be a state or federally issued photo ID such as a passport or driver's license. If the borrower is unable to provide ID you should call your title company for instruction before proceeding with the closing.

2. Preparing the Signing Space

After introducing yourself and presenting your ID, take the lead in verifying that everyone who needs to be there is present, and arrange the space in an organized manner so as to avoid clutter, spills and distractions. Start by giving an overview of the entire appointment and set expectations for how the appointment will be conducted. The *Code's* Guiding Principle 4, focusing on Unauthorized Advice or Services, offers an important guideline on how to review your role and responsibility with all parties present:

- ❖ **Role and Limitations:** Clearly explain to the signing parties that you are solely responsible for providing signing services connected with the transaction and cannot answer specific questions about the transaction or the legal effect of the closing documents.

❖ **Response to Questions:** Explain that you are limited to the questions that you may answer. Your "answer" to any question will be the provision in the document that may answer the question or you will refer the individual to the contracting company's representative.

3. Presenting and Notarizing the Documents

This is one of the most important steps in the entire signing timeline. Here is where you provide an overview and instructions for signing the documents, and check IDs for all parties. You will also show the parties their copies, collect stipulations and complete your journal entries.

As you present loan documents, read each title, describe both the documents' purpose and signing requirements, and obtain any and all needed signatures. This part of the timeline ends with your notarizing required documents and performing a quality check once all documents are completed before you leave the appointment. Below we have outlined several key highlights from the *Code's* Guiding Principles focusing on notarial acts and the proper role of the NSA.

Performing the Notarizations

The *Code's* Guiding Principle 2 focuses on the notarization process itself, and offers these important guidelines:

❖ **Standard of Care:** Exercise reasonable care in the performance of all notarial acts and a high degree of care in verifying the identity of all parties during the closing. Signers may want to rush you through the process, but it's your job to pace the signing appropriately and ensure that everything is done correctly.

❖ **Improper Identification:** You cannot accept any unauthorized identification document as satisfactory evidence of identity during a closing for any reason, unless expressly authorized by law. Even if you know your signer on a personal basis, he or she must still present a satisfactory form of identification.

❖ **Undue Cause for Refusal:** You cannot refuse to perform a notarial act solely because a signer refuses to comply with any practice that is not a legal requirement for notarization in your state or jurisdiction. Be sure you know your state laws regarding thumbprints. If your state does not require them, then you cannot refuse the notarization based on a signer refusing to submit his or her thumbprint.

Acting as an Impartial, Third-Party Witness

The *Code*'s Guiding Principle 3, focusing on impartiality, offers these guidelines:

❖ **Personal Opinion:** Even if you have one, you must not offer any personal opinion to a signer about executing or not executing closing documents or consummating or not consummating a transaction. Even if you spot what seems to be a high interest rate or other loan detail, it is not your place to offer your opinion to the signer. Keep extraneous opinions to yourself.

❖ **Exercise of Rescission Option:** You will not:

- Recommend a borrower proceed with the signing of any closing document on the grounds that the rescission option provides three business days to thoroughly read loan documents.

- Ask questions of the borrower and decide whether to consummate the transaction. You will recommend that the borrower contact the lender's representative immediately before signing the documents. Reminding a nervous signer of the rescission option seems like an easy fix to move a signing forward but it can cause issues on the other end. Don't do it. Ask the borrower to reach out to the lender's rep instead.

Never Offer Unauthorized Advice or Services

It is critical that you adhere to the role to which you are assigned, and never offer advice or counsel to your signers. The *Code*'s Guiding Principle 4, focusing on Unauthorized Advice or Services, offers the following guidelines:

❖ **Legal Advice:** You will not offer legal advice to a signer during an assignment unless you are an attorney representing a party in the transaction. If you haven't gone to law school, passed the bar, and work as an attorney, don't offer legal advice.

- ❖ **Presentation of Documents:** Present each closing document to a signer in conformance with a signing script authorized by the contracting company. Then, naming and stating the general purpose of each document, specify the number of pages and indicate where signatures, dates or initials are to be placed. Present the Closing Disclosure or HUD-1 (whichever is in the loan package) first. Then keep the stacking order of the documents as the lender provided them to you. Use the At-A-Glance job aid to keep you on track.

- ❖ **Loan Term and Settlement Fees:** You may only identify and provide general descriptions of loan, payment amounts or any other loan terms, including settlement fees, to a borrower in the closing documents. However, you may not explain, interpret or provide legal advice about the loan terms or fees. If a signer has questions about the specific terms of the loan, or asks if you've seen better "deals", gently tell the borrower you are unable to comment and never offer advice on the actual loan details.

- ❖ **Disbursement or Funding Date:** Forecasting or disclosing actual disbursements or funding dates to a signer, unless expressly requested in writing by a lender's representative or closing agent, is not permitted. Leave all discussion of funding dates and disbursements to the lender's representative. This isn't your area of focus.

- ❖ **Disclosure of Contact Sources:** Provide the borrower with the contact information of the lender's representative and closing agent who can answer questions about the loan for them. If your signer needs more answers, give them the number of the appropriate contact so they can get the answers they need.

4. Handling Issues and Challenges

During any signing assignment, some issues will come up, from identification issues to a borrower who refuses to sign necessary documents. In such cases, you need to know how to respond professionally and be able to move forward with the assignment. A number of the more common issues are discussed in the *Code's* Guiding Principle 5, focusing on Standards of Practice:

- ❖ **Absent Signer:** You cannot comply with a request to notarize the signature of a signer who does not personally appear before you. Whether it's your boss, manager, or estranged sister-in-law, your signers MUST appear before you. No exceptions.

- ❖ **Falsification and Pre- or Post-Dated Notary Certificate:** Be aware that an NSA, lender's representative, contracting company, closing agent, signer or any other person is not permitted to falsify information, including pre- or post-dating a Notary certificate. A rushed closing agent who missed a deadline may try just about anything to get you to pre or post-date a certificate. Don't do it.

- ❖ **Signer Awareness, Willingness and Disability:** Immediately contact the lender's representative and closing agent for the transaction if you have a reasonable belief a signer is unaware of the loan, or the significance of the transaction, and is being overtly influenced or pressured, or possesses a physical disability requiring accommodation that you have not been trained or authorized to perform. If the signer seems "out of it" and/or doesn't seem to be responding appropriately to small talk or a brief explanation of the necessary documents, this could be a red flag. Pause the appointment and contact the appropriate representative to address your concerns.

- ❖ **Inconsistent Signatures or Handwriting:** Immediately contact the lender's representative and closing agent for the transaction if you have a reasonable belief that a signature or handwriting appears to be overtly inconsistent with any identification card, journal entry or document presented or signed in connection with the transaction. While you're not expected to be a professional handwriting analyst, major inconsistencies in signatures are a major red flag. If unsure, contact the appropriate representative.

- ❖ **Potential or Actual Misrepresentation:** Any potential or actual misrepresentation or falsehood must be immediately reported to the lender's representative and closing agent for the transaction. Sometimes, you have to trust your instincts. If something seems to be amiss, like a fake ID or problematic documentation, contact the contracting company. It's not worth the risk of making an incorrect judgment call.

The *Code's* Guiding Principle 6, focusing on privacy and confidentiality, offers this important guideline with regards to issues and challenges that may arise during an appointment:

- ❖ **Request for Electronic Documents:** Do not comply with any request from a signer to provide electronic closing documents. Instead, notify the lender's representative, contracting company or closing agent for the transaction. It makes sense to want an electronic copy of the loan package so a borrower might ask for one. If a signer asks you to email her the documents after the assignment, simply explain that the documents need to remain secure so you can't email but you will pass her request onto the contracting company.

❖ **Security of Documents:** Keep all documents under personal control or lock and key before, during and after the appointment. Secure the documents until they are securely passed on to the courier that will forward them to the appropriate party. Never leave them in your car, no matter how brief a time.

Maintaining High Standards of Professionalism

Finally, as with every step in the process, it's important you remain professional, even when issues and challenges occur. The following guidelines are offered in the *Code*'s Guiding Principle 9:

❖ **Changes to Documents:** Immediately inform the lender's representative and contracting company of any change to a closing document requested by a signer. Do not alter or add a document unless expressly authorized in writing by the lender's representative or contracting company. If a signer requests that a name on a document be changed (due to a recent marriage perhaps), let them know this is not something you are authorized to do.

❖ **Quality Assurance Review:** Before adjourning the signing appointment and delivering the package of documents for shipment to the closing agent, you must first check to see that the documents are properly completed, signed and notarized, and that all stipulations are present. Create a streamlined, end-of-appointment checklist that you can review to ensure all items are completed accurately. Catching an error while you're still at the signing table can save you a world of trouble.

5. Closing the Meeting

Once the documents are signed, it is time to wrap up the assignment and close the meeting. You will want to leave the appointment on a positive note, let the contracting company know you are finished and ship out the prepared loan package.

Properly Completing the Notarization

As with any notarization, you must properly complete the process following the guidelines discussed in the *Code's* Guiding Principle 2, focusing on notarization:

❖ **Journal of Notarial Acts and Notarial Evidence Form:** Record each notarial act performed on closing documents in your journal even if not required by law. Once completed, promptly return the Notarial Evidence Form for each assignment when requested or required by a lender, title company or contracting company. Complete the entire journal entry as part of the notarization while signers are still present, to ensure you gather all necessary information and signatures. Signers have little patience for what they might view as extraneous administrative work at the end of a long signing appointment.

Ending the Assignment

Section 5 of the *Signing Presentation Guidelines* provides NSAs with a detailed description of how to properly end an assignment.

❖ **Ending the Transaction:** Make sure the borrower has a hard copy of the closing package. If he or she asks for an electronic copy please direct him or her to the Title Company. Under no circumstances are you to email the documents to the borrower. If the borrower does not have the proper funds to give you as per the closing instructions, please contact your title or contracting company for Instructions.

Here is an example script: *"We have reviewed and you've signed all of the documents, which concludes the signing. Do you have any further questions? It was very nice to meet you (borrower name). I hope you feel this was a positive closing experience. Thank you very much for your time."*

PART 5: POST-ASSIGNMENT FOLLOW UP

Once you have completed the assignment, your work is not done. Besides leaving your appointment on a positive note, you need to ensure you alert the contracting company that the assignment is complete and return the completed loan package to each different contracting company in the way they ask so as to not delay loan processing.

And once that's all wrapped up, there are important considerations for guaranteeing that your new NSA business stays successful.

Collecting Fees

Once you've wrapped up the assignment, be sure to follow all of the *Code*'s Guiding Principle 7 regarding fees. First and foremost, follow all contractual obligations when charging and collecting fees for the services you have rendered.

❖ **Submission of Invoice for Contracted Fee and Separate Financial Records:** Follow the details of your agreement with the contracting company or closing agent when submitting your invoice, which should only reflect the exact, agreed-upon fee. Be sure to keep a separate and detailed record of all fees received and expenses incurred for each assignment. Even a minor discrepancy in the fee can become a major problem down the line. Be sure numbers match up exactly.

❖ **Collection of Fee from Signer or Contracting Company:** Do not attempt to collect a fee from the signer under any circumstances, and only attempt to collect from the contracting company if they have failed to fulfill their contractual obligations. If your contracting company is late on its payment, all interactions regarding fees **MUST** go through them, **NEVER** the signer.

Dealing with Illegal or Suspicious Activity

The end of an assignment offers one final opportunity to ensure that there is no illegal or suspicious activity present in the documents or the handling of the closing itself. The *Code*'s Guiding Principle 5 offers the following guideline to keep in mind when wrapping up an assignment:

❖ **Cooperation with Authorities:** Fully cooperate with law enforcement investigating any allegation of criminal activity of which you have knowledge. Take all law enforcement inquiries seriously, and respond diligently to all requests.

Ensuring Privacy and Confidentiality

Every stage of the closing process offers opportunities for you to ensure privacy and confidentiality of all documents and information, as thoroughly described in the *Code's* Guiding Principle 6. These include:

❖ **Journal Entries:** Take steps to prevent any other parties from viewing completed entries in your Notary journal. Never let signers peek at earlier journal entries. You can cover previous entries with a small piece of paper, or use a device such as the Notary Privacy Guard®, which is designed to cover the personal information of your clients. Show them you are serious about keeping their information safe by keeping other's information safe.

❖ **Compromised Security of Documents:** Always ensure that packages of closing documents are properly sealed upon reception and delivery; keep them under either personal control or lock and key. Don't leave important loan packages in unsecured places, such as in your car or on your desk. Invest in a lock-box or, even better, deliver all materials immediately.

❖ **Return of Documents:** In the event an assignment is postponed or canceled, be sure to return all documents, expected or not, to the appropriate contracting company or closing agent. Don't hold on to documents; it only increases your potential liability.

❖ **Handling of Electronic Documents and Non-Public Personal Information:** Always use encryption, strong passwords and other secure delivery methods to send or receive closing documents or communications containing a signer's non-public personal information. Remember to delete all associated files from your computer once the assignment is completed. Get into the habit of reviewing the files on your computer and deleting all documents related to loan packages as soon as the assignment is completed.

A Final Focus on Professionalism

As with every step in this process, the final stages of a closing offer an opportunity to focus on professionalism, as highlighted in the *Code*'s Guiding Principle 9:

* **Observance of Deadlines and Status Reporting:** Perform each assignment in a timely manner, including the return of all duly executed documents to the contracting company or closing agent according to the lender's requirements. You should also immediately inform the lender's representative and contracting company about any development. Allow yourself ample time for each assignment so you can return all completed documents promptly before heading out to your next assignment. ■

Chapter

3

Key Resource Documents

Welcome to the third and final lesson in this study guide, the Key Resource Documents. It contains annotated copies of key documents that are important for you to be familiar with if you want to pass the exam.

Included here are:

❖ **The *Notary Signing Agent Code of Conduct*:** This is, as we have mentioned numerous times throughout this book, one of the two key documents which the 45 questions in the NSA certification exam are based. You are asked to agree to the terms of this document when you access the NNA NSA Certification exam.

❖ **The *Signing Presentation Guidelines*:** The second document of which the certification exam is based on. This document helps you to know what information you are allowed to share with a borrower.

❖ **The NNA Loan Documents At-a-Glance:** This document contains the information from the Presentation Guidelines and additional documents not covered in the Guidelines. Use this document to identify in which specific document borrowers may find the answer to the questions they ask.

- ❖ **NSA Sample Loan Package:** This is an example of a set of standard loan documents annotated to help you remember important facts about each document. ■

Signing
Professionals
Workgroup

Notary
Signing Agent
Code of Conduct

January 21, 2016

CONTENTS

Notary Signing Agent Code of Conduct   ii

Notary Signing Agent Code of Conduct   iii

Version 1.01 was approved September 24, 2013.
Version 1.02 was approved October 9, 2013.
Version 2.0 approved June 3, 2014.
Version 3.0 was approved January 21, 2016.

For the list of amendments, visit www.signingprofessionalsworkgroup.org.

INTRODUCTION

Purpose of the Code

The Notary Signing Agent's pivotal role in lending integrity to mortgage finance and real property transactions necessitates sound standards for the performance of signing services.

While many occupations pose professional and ethical norms for their practitioners, the need for guidelines for Notary Signing Agents is necessary given the fact that the vocation of Notary Signing Agent is largely an unregulated profession. While state Notary Public laws and regulations apply to the notarial acts performed by NSAs, these laws offer no guidance to the non-notarial services rendered by NSAs.

The purpose of *The Notary Signing Agent Code of Conduct (Code)* is to enable Notary Signing Agents to operate according to the highest standards of practice expected of like professionals in the settlement services industry.

The *Code* Standards are of two types. Most are principles, policies and practices that have proven to be effective in helping Notary Signing Agents perform their primary function of witnessing the proper execution of loan and real estate documents. The rest address and guide the NSA's supportive duties, such as advertising services, charging and collecting fees, and demonstrating responsible conduct with contracting companies and customers.

Because the acts of Notary Signing Agents affect property, and most importantly, personal rights, it is imperative that standards of practice for NSAs be widely acknowledged as just, fair and well-developed. To that end, the Standards in this *Code* were drafted with input from representatives of occupational fields which employ NSAs, business professionals and NSAs themselves.

Organization of the Code

This *Notary Signing Agent Code of Conduct* is divided into ten sections or "Guiding Principles" to enumerate the essential roles of the Notary Signing Agent. They are general rules for responsible conduct.

Each Guiding Principle in turn sets forth particular "Standards of Practice" for the Notary Signing Agent. Each Standard clarifies the NSA's many duties.

Basis of the Code

The Guiding Principles and Standards of Practice are the distillation of interaction between the National Notary Association, thousands of Notary Signing Agents from every state and U.S. jurisdiction, lenders and the companies that employ NSAs. They address the common problems, issues and questions encountered by NSAs.

The Principles and Standards reflect the conviction that Notary Signing Agents must operate in a professional and businesslike fashion and always carefully document their official activities.

Statutory Requirements

In some jurisdictions, a particular Standard Practice may already be a requirement of statute, such as the universal legal mandate to identify document signers when performing notarial acts. For the overwhelming majority of Notary Signing Agents, no statute or administrative rule will prevent adherence to the Standards of Practice in the *Code*. If adherence to a Guiding Principle or Standard would result in violation of the law, the NSA should always comply with the law.

Contracting Company Expectations

The Standards may contradict the policies or expectations of the Notary Signing Agent's contracting company, especially with regard to notarial practices. The point of conflict often surfaces due to the unique pressures inherent in the settlement services industry to close loans and transactions as quickly as possible.

Notary Signing Agents should understand that the *Code* is a model for preferred conduct. A NSA should never violate the law if compliance with the law is against the wishes of the contracting company or any other party to the transaction.

Uses and Benefits of the Code

This *Code* may serve as a tool to guide and educate not only Notary Signing Agents, but also contracting companies employing NSAs and any users of NSA services.

Widespread implementation of the *Code* will reduce fraud and litigation.

Any Notary Signing Agent's adherence to the *Code's* Standards brings confidence that he or she is acting in accord with the highest standards of the vocation.

Widespread adherence to the Standards by Notary Signing Agents will engender heightened respect and recognition for NSAs.

Revision of the Code

The *Notary Signing Agent Code of Conduct* is not intended to be static and unchangeable. Its organization allows the separable Standards to be added, deleted or amended with little or no disruption of other elements in the *Code*.

While the 10 Guiding Principles of the *Code* are sufficiently general to embrace considerable change in the duties and practices of Notary Signing Agents without amendment to their current form, it is likely that the *Code's* Standards may in time need revision or supplement to accommodate technological developments.

Periodic review and revision of the *Code* is intended. The most current version of the *Code* and a list of version changes will be made available upon release.

DEFINITIONS

In this *Notary Signing Agent Code of Conduct* the following terms have the meaning ascribed:

D.1. Close Relative
"Close relative" means the Notary Signing Agent's spouse, domestic partner, parent, grandparent, sibling, child, stepchild, stepsibling, stepparent, step-grandparent, step-grandchild or in-law.

D.2. Closing
"Closing" means the consummation of a transaction involving the purchase, sale or financing of real property.

D.3. Closing Agent
"Closing agent" means a third party, including, but not limited to, an attorney, title agent or escrow officer, that performs duties incident to the consummation of a transaction involving the purchase, sale, or financing of an interest in real property.

D.4. Closing Documents
"Closing documents" mean the agreements, authorizations, contracts, disclosures, instructions, notices and statements executed to consummate the purchase, sale or financing of an interest in real property.

D.5. Contracting Company
"Contracting company" means an individual or entity that enters into an agreement with and hires Notary Signing Agents to perform signing services.

D.6. Critical Documents
"Critical documents" mean the Note, Deed of Trust or Mortgage, and, as applicable, the Truth in Lending Disclosure, HUD-1 Settlement Statement, Closing Disclosure and Notice of Right to Cancel form contained in the closing documents, and other documents specified by the lender.

D.7. Journal
"Journal" means a book or electronic medium to create and preserve a chronological record of notarizations maintained and retained by a Notary Signing Agent in his or her capacity as a Notary Public.

D.8. Lender's Representative
"Lender's representative" means an individual who acts on behalf of a lender, including, but not limited to, a loan officer, mortgage broker, banker, or loan closer or processor.

D.9. Non-Public Personal Information
"Non-public personal information" means personally identifiable data provided by a customer on a form or application, information about a customer's transactions, or any other information about a customer which is otherwise unavailable to the general public, and

includes a customer's first name or first initial and last name coupled with any of the following: Social Security number, driver's license number, state-issued ID number, credit card number, debit card number, or other financial account numbers.

D.10. Notarial Evidence Form

"Notarial Evidence Form" means a record of notarizations performed in a transaction involving the purchase, sale or financing of real estate that is completed by a Notary Signing Agent and retained by the lender or closing agent.

D.11. Notary Signing Agent or NSA

"'Notary Signing Agent' or 'NSA'" means an individual who has fulfilled all requirements to earn and maintain the Notary Signing Agent designation prescribed by the Signing Professionals Workgroup, and provides signing services as an independent contractor.

D.12. Settlement Services

"Settlement services" has the meaning ascribed in 12 USC § 2602, and includes any of the following when performed in connection with a real property closing: title searches, title examinations, the provision of title certificates, title insurance, services rendered by an attorney, the preparation of documents, property surveys, the rendering of credit reports or appraisals, pest and fungus inspections, services rendered by a real estate agent or broker, the origination of a federally related mortgage loan (including, but not limited to, the taking of loan applications, loan processing, and the underwriting and funding of loans), and the handling of the processing, and closing or settlement.

D.13. Signer

"Signer" means an individual who is a buyer, seller or borrower in a transaction to purchase, sell or finance an interest in real property.

D.14. Signing Assignment

"Signing assignment" means an engagement to provide signing services.

D.15. Signing Presentation Guidelines

"Signing presentation guidelines" means standardized written copy or answers used by a Notary Signing Agent in providing signing services.

D.16. Signing Services

"Signing services" means performance by a Notary Signing Agent of any of the following: coordination of the appointment at which closing documents are signed; receipt, duplication, transportation to the parties for signatures, transmission by fax, and delivery to a shipping carrier, of closing documents; care, custody, and control of closing documents while in the possession of a NSA; presentation of closing documents to the parties for signatures; notarization of closing documents; and supervision of the signing of documents by the parties.

THE GUIDING PRINCIPLES

1. Qualifications
The Notary Signing Agent will satisfactorily meet and maintain all qualifications necessary to perform signing services.

2. Notarization
The Notary Signing Agent will follow all laws, rules and best practices that apply to the notarizing of closing documents.

3. Impartiality
The Notary Signing Agent will remain impartial to the transaction at all times.

4. Unauthorized Advice or Services
The Notary Signing Agent will not provide legal, personal, financial or other advice or services to the signer in connection with a signing assignment nor explain the terms of any closing document presented to the signer.

5. Illegal and Suspicious Activity
The Notary Signing Agent will not perform an illegal, deceptive or harmful act in connection with a signing assignment and will report any suspicious activity to the NSA's contracting company.

6. Privacy and Confidentiality
The Notary Signing Agent will respect the privacy of each signer and protect closing documents from unauthorized disclosure.

7. Fees
The Notary Signing Agent will follow all contractual obligations in charging and collecting fees for services rendered.

8. Advertising
The Notary Signing Agent will not advertise signing services in a manner that is unprofessional, false, misleading or deceptive.

9. Professionalism
The Notary Signing Agent will always act in a responsible manner towards contracting companies and parties to the transaction.

10. Standards
The Notary Signing Agent will endeavor to maintain and raise standards of practice amongst practitioners in the signing services industry.

GUIDING PRINCIPLE 1: QUALIFICATIONS

The Notary Signing Agent will satisfactorily meet and maintain all qualifications necessary to perform signing services.

Standards of Practice

1.1. Background Screening
The Notary Signing Agent will submit to a background screening of the NSA's identity, residence, record of state or federal criminal arrests and convictions, and state motor vehicle record, and to a check of the NSA's name against pertinent lists as required by rules implementing the USA PATRIOT Act.

1.2. Professional Licenses
The Notary Signing Agent will obtain and maintain all licenses and commissions required to perform signing services in the NSA's state or jurisdiction.

1.3. Notary Laws and Rules
The Notary Signing Agent will keep current on all laws and official regulations that affect the performance of notarial acts in the NSA's state or jurisdiction.

1.4. Federal Laws
The Notary Signing Agent will demonstrate an understanding of the provisions of any relevant federal laws and official regulations that pertain to the performance of signing services, including, but not limited to, the Gramm-Leach-Bliley Act (GLBA), Truth in Lending Act (TILA), Real Estate Settlement Procedures Act (RESPA), Fair and Accurate Credit and Transactions Act (FACTA) and the Uniting and Strengthening America by Providing Appropriate Tools Required to Intercept and Obstruct Terrorism (USA PATRIOT) Act.

1.5. Certification
The Notary Signing Agent will earn and maintain any relevant certifications needed to service contracting companies and parties to the transaction.

1.6. Closing Documents
The Notary Signing Agent will become familiar with the closing documents for each assignment but will not use this knowledge to provide unauthorized counsel or advice to signing parties.

1.7. Ongoing Learning
The Notary Signing Agent will keep informed on any technical matters, legal requirements and other developments that affect the NSA's competence or responsibilities in rendering signing services.

1.8. Supervising Attorney

The Notary Signing Agent will willingly submit to the supervision of an attorney if required by law or rule in the NSA's state or jurisdiction.

GUIDING PRINCIPLE 2: NOTARIZATION

The Notary Signing Agent will follow all laws, rules and best practices that apply to the notarizing of closing documents.

Standards of Practice

2.1. Standard of Care
The Notary Signing Agent will exercise reasonable care in the performance of notarial duties generally and will exercise a high degree of care in verifying the identity of any person whose identity is the subject of a notarial act.

2.2. Improper Identification
The Notary Signing Agent will not accept an unauthorized identification document or other means of identification as satisfactory evidence of identity in order to expedite the closing of the transaction or for any other reason, and will ensure that any identification document presented has not expired, unless expressly authorized by law.

2.3. Discrepancies in Names
The Notary Signing Agent will not notarize the signature of a signing party whose name on the document cannot be verified with reasonable certainty by examining a written identification document or by the oaths of credible witnesses.

2.4. Notary Seal
The Notary Signing Agent will authenticate each notarial act performed on closing documents with the NSA's Notary seal, even if not required by law.

2.5. Seal Misuse
The Notary Signing Agent will not use the NSA's Notary seal for any purpose other than performing authorized notarial acts.

2.6. Journal of Notarial Acts
The Notary Signing Agent will record each notarial act performed on closing documents in a journal of notarial acts even if not required by law.

2.7. Notarial Evidence Form
The Notary Signing Agent will complete and promptly return a Notarial Evidence Form for each assignment when requested or required by a lender, title company, closing agent or contracting company.

2.8. Control of Seal and Journal
The Notary Signing Agent will keep the NSA's Notary seal and journal in a locked and secure area when not in use and not allow any other person to possess or use them.

2.9. Legibility

The Notary Signing Agent will ensure that the NSA's handwriting and Notary seal on all closing documents are legible and photographically reproducible.

2.10. Completion of Notarial Acts

The Notary Signing Agent will complete the notarial acts on all closing documents and the journal entries for the notarizations in the presence of the signer at the appointment when the documents are signed.

2.11. Notary Public Code of Professional Responsibility

The Notary Signing Agent will comply with all standards set forth in *The Notary Public Code of Professional Responsibility* as adopted and amended by the National Notary Association.

2.12. Undue Cause for Refusal

The Notary Signing Agent will not refuse to perform a notarial act solely because a signer refuses to comply with a practice that is not a legal requirement for notarization in the NSA's state or jurisdiction.

GUIDING PRINCIPLE 3: IMPARTIALITY

The Notary Signing Agent will remain impartial to the transaction at all times.

Standards of Practice

3.1. Personal Interest
The Notary Signing Agent will not provide signing services for a transaction in which the NSA or the NSA's close relative is directly or indirectly involved as a party.

3.2. Professional Interest
The Notary Signing Agent will not provide signing services for a transaction in which the NSA or NSA's close relative is the loan officer, real estate agent, mortgage broker, or a settlement services provider.

3.3. Notary Signing Agent and Attorney in Fact
The Notary Signing Agent will not sign documents in the capacity of Notary Signing Agent and as attorney in fact for a principal in the same transaction.

3.4. Notary Signing Agent and Witness
The Notary Signing Agent will not perform signing services in the capacity of Notary Signing Agent and witness to a deed, Deed of Trust or Mortgage in the same transaction unless expressly allowed by law.

3.5. Appearance of Partiality
The Notary Signing Agent will refrain from performing signing services in any transaction that would raise the appearance of or the potential for a conflict of interest.

3.6. Personal Opinion
The Notary Signing Agent will not offer a personal opinion to a signer about executing or not executing closing documents or consummating or not consummating a transaction.

3.7. Exercise of Rescission Option
The Notary Signing Agent will not recommend that a borrower proceed with the signing of any closing document on the grounds that the rescission option provides three business days to thoroughly read loan documents, ask questions of the lender and decide whether to consummate the transaction, but will recommend that the borrower contact the lender's representative immediately before signing the documents.

GUIDING PRINCIPLE 4: UNAUTHORIZED ADVICE OR SERVICES

The Notary Signing Agent will not provide legal, personal, financial or other advice or services to the signer in connection with a signing assignment nor explain the terms of any closing document presented to the signer.

Standards of Practice

4.1. Legal Advice

The Notary Signing Agent will not offer legal advice to a signer during an assignment to provide signing services unless the NSA is an attorney representing a party in the transaction.

4.2. Role and Limitations

The Notary Signing Agent will clearly explain to the signing parties that the NSA is solely responsible for providing signing services connected with the transaction and cannot answer specific questions about the transaction or the legal effect of the closing documents.

4.3. Response to Questions

The Notary Signing Agent may respond to a signer's specific question by directing the individual to read the provisions in the critical or other closing documents identified by the NSA that may answer the question or by referring the individual to the lender's representative or closing agent associated with the transaction.

4.4. Presentation of Documents

The Notary Signing Agent will present each closing document to a signer in conformance with a signing presentation guidelines authorized by the contracting company, and by naming and stating the general purpose of the document, specifying the number of pages and indicating where signatures, dates or initials are to be placed.

4.5. Loan Terms

The Notary Signing Agent may identify and provide a general description of a loan or payment amount, interest rate, annual percentage rate, finance charge, payment schedule, assumption option, prepayment penalty or any other loan term to a borrower in the closing documents, but may not explain, interpret or provide legal advice about the loan terms.

4.6. Settlement Fees

The Notary Signing Agent may identify and provide a general description of a fee or charge appearing on a signer's HUD-1, Closing Disclosure or other closing statement, as applicable, but may not explain, interpret or provide legal advice about the fee or charge.

4.7. Disbursement or Funding Date

The Notary Signing Agent will neither attempt to forecast nor disclose an actual disbursement or funding date to a signer unless expressly requested in writing by a lender's representative or closing agent or the date is clearly identified in a closing document the NSA can present to the individual.

4.8. Loan Programs and Professionals

The Notary Signing Agent will not advise a borrower on loan products, programs, competitive rates or mortgage loan professionals at a signing appointment or in any verbal or written communication in connection with an assignment.

4.9. Contact Sources

A Notary Signing Agent will not commence a signing appointment without having obtained the contact information of the lender's representative and closing agent associated with the transaction.

4.10. Disclosure of Contact Sources

The Notary Signing Agent will provide the borrower with the contact information of the lender's representative and closing agent who may answer questions about the loan and explain the terms of the loan or any closing document presented to the borrower.

GUIDING PRINCIPLE 5: ILLEGAL AND SUSPICIOUS ACTIVITY

The Notary Signing Agent will not perform an illegal, deceptive or harmful act in connection with a signing assignment and will report any suspicious activity to the NSA's contracting company.

Standards of Practice

5.1. Absent Signer
The Notary Signing Agent will not comply with a request to notarize the signature of a signer who does not personally appear before the NSA.

5.2. Pre- or Post-dated Certificate
The Notary Signing Agent will not pre- or post-date a notarial certificate in order to meet a funding deadline, avoid an expiring rate lock or for any other reason.

5.3. False Document or Certificate
The Notary Signing Agent will not comply with a request of a lender's representative, contracting company, closing agent, signer or any other person to falsify information in a closing document or certificate of a notarial act.

5.4. Extra Certificate
The Notary Signing Agent will not comply with a request of a lender's representative, contracting company or closing agent to mail a signed and sealed notarial certificate that is not securely attached to an actual closing document notarized by the NSA.

5.5. Approval of Power of Attorney Signing
The Notary Signing Agent will not commence an appointment involving an attorney in fact signing for an absent principal unless specifically approved by the lender's representative or closing agent for the transaction.

5.6. Signer Awareness, Willingness and Disability
The Notary Signing Agent will immediately contact the NSA's contracting company if the NSA has a reasonable belief that a signer is not aware of the loan or the significance of the transaction at the time closing documents are signed, possesses a physical disability requiring accommodation that the NSA has not been trained or authorized to perform, or the person is being overtly influenced or pressured into signing or not signing the documents.

5.7. Inconsistent Signatures or Handwriting
The Notary Signing Agent will immediately contact the NSA's contracting company if the NSA has a reasonable belief that a person's signature or handwriting appears to be overtly inconsistent with any identification card, journal entry or document presented or signed in connection with the transaction.

Notary Signing Agent Code of Conduct

13

5.8. Incomplete Documents

The Notary Signing Agent will immediately contact the NSA's contracting company if any closing document required to be notarized is incomplete or contains blank spaces.

5.9. Presentation of Entire Document

The Notary Signing Agent will present all pages of a closing document, and not just the signature page, to a signer for signature.

5.10. Potential or Actual Misrepresentation

The Notary Signing Agent will immediately report any potential or actual misrepresentation or falsehood known or witnessed by the NSA in connection with a transaction to the NSA's contracting company.

5.11. Unlawful Transaction

The Notary Signing Agent will immediately contact the NSA's contracting company if the NSA has knowledge or a reasonable belief that a transaction is unlawful.

5.12. Evidence of Tampering

The Notary Signing Agent will immediately contact the NSA's contracting company if the NSA has knowledge or a reasonable belief that a closing document or notarial certificate has been tampered with or altered.

5.13. Disclosure of Wrongdoing

The Notary Signing Agent will not conceal knowledge of a criminal act committed in connection with a signing assignment but will immediately notify a lawful authority as soon as the NSA becomes aware that a criminal act has been committed.

5.14. Cooperation with Authorities

The Notary Signing Agent will fully cooperate with law enforcement investigating an allegation of criminal activity of which the NSA has knowledge or that implicates the NSA.

GUIDING PRINCIPLE 6: PRIVACY AND CONFIDENTIALITY

The Notary Signing Agent will respect the privacy of each signer and protect closing documents from unauthorized disclosure.

Standards of Practice

6.1. Nondisclosure of Signer Information
The Notary Signing Agent will not disclose the transaction or personal information of a signer to any person not directly a party to the transaction.

6.2. Journal Entries
The Notary Signing Agent will take reasonable steps to prevent other parties from viewing completed entries in the NSA's Notary journal.

6.3. Scrutiny of Documents
The Notary Signing Agent will not inspect or examine the closing documents beyond what is needed to determine the requirements and conditions for the assignment and to complete any journal entries for notarizations on the documents.

6.4. Reception and Delivery of Documents
The Notary Signing Agent will reasonably attempt to receive and deliver all closing document packages in person or via secure means.

6.5. Printing of Documents
The Notary Signing Agent will personally download and print all closing documents and not assign this responsibility to any other person.

6.6. Compromised Documents
The Notary Signing Agent will ensure that any package of closing documents is properly sealed upon reception and delivery and will immediately report to the contracting company any circumstance leading the NSA to reasonably believe that the contents of the package have been compromised.

6.7. Security of Documents
The Notary Signing Agent will keep all closing documents committed to the NSA under personal control or lock and key before and during the appointment, and until delivering them via secure means to a reliable delivery service, including but not limited to a secured drop box location or hand delivery at a facility or office, or the closing agent for the transaction.

6.8. Request for Electronic Documents
The Notary Signing Agent will not comply with a request from a signer to provide electronic closing documents, but will notify the NSA's contracting company of the individual's request for documents.

6.9. Return of Documents

The Notary Signing Agent will return all executed or unexecuted closing documents in compliance with instructions from the contracting company or closing agent for the transaction in the event that an assignment is postponed or canceled.

6.10. Access Instructions

The Notary Signing Agent will not share with any person the logon credentials or access instructions to a website for the purpose of viewing, downloading or printing closing documents.

6.11. Unprotected Network

The Notary Signing Agent will not use a public or unsecured computer network to retrieve electronic communications in connection with a signing assignment, to access, download or print closing documents, or to fax signed documents to a lender's representative, contracting company or closing agent.

6.12. Transmission or Reception of Non-public Personal Information

The Notary Signing Agent will use encryption, strong passwords and other secure delivery methods to send or receive closing documents or communications containing a signer's non-public personal information, whether by fax, email or other means.

6.13. Deletion of Electronic Documents

The Notary Signing Agent will permanently erase any files containing electronic closing documents from the NSA's personal or a shared computer immediately upon conclusion of an assignment.

GUIDING PRINCIPLE 7: FEES

The Notary Signing Agent will follow all contractual obligations in charging and collecting fees for services rendered.

Standards of Practice

7.1. Confirmation of Fee in Writing
The Notary Signing Agent will confirm the fee to be paid by the contracting company for an assignment to provide signing services in writing prior to the appointment with the signer.

7.2. Performance for Fee
The Notary Signing Agent will not refuse to perform services for an assignment that the NSA has previously accepted in dispute over a negotiated fee unless the requirements for the assignment materially change after the NSA has accepted the assignment.

7.3. Referral Fee
The Notary Signing Agent will only charge and receive the fee for rendering signing services in connection with a transaction and will not accept, charge or pay an illegal referral fee, rebate, fee-split, unearned fee or kickback.

7.4. Collusion
The Notary Signing Agent will not collude with other NSAs to set fees for signing services.

7.5. Submission of Invoice
The Notary Signing Agent will submit an invoice for payment to the contracting company for each completed assignment in a form that complies with the terms of the written agreement between the NSA and contracting company.

7.6. Invoice for Contracted Fee
The Notary Signing Agent will invoice the contracting company for the exact fee negotiated between the NSA and company and will not over- or understate this fee.

7.7. Collection of Fee from Contracting Company
The Notary Signing Agent will not attempt to collect on a nonpaying account without first establishing that the contracting company has failed to fulfill its contractual obligations.

7.8. Collection of Fee from Signer
The Notary Signing Agent will not attempt to collect the signing fee from the signer in the event that the contracting company fails to remit timely payment.

7.9. Separate Financial Records
The Notary Signing Agent will keep a separate and detailed record of all fees received for each assignment.

GUIDING PRINCIPLE 8: ADVERTISING

The Notary Signing Agent will not advertise signing services in a manner that is unprofessional, false, misleading or deceptive.

Standards of Practice

8.1. Truthful Personal Assessment

The Notary Signing Agent will not misrepresent the NSA's background, education, training or expertise in an application or interview to provide signing services, on a website or in any promotional materials distributed by the NSA.

8.2. False or Misleading Claims

The Notary Signing Agent will not make exaggerated or excessive claims, promises or guarantees about the NSA's services.

8.3. Use of Professional Designation

The Notary Signing Agent will not advertise or promote the NSA's services by using professional designations or certifications the NSA has not received or earned.

8.4. Observation of Rules for Use

The Notary Signing Agent will comply with all requirements governing the use of membership and professional designations, logos and marks as may be required by the issuing, certifying or accrediting entity.

8.5. Use of Improper Designation

The Notary Signing Agent will not use any false, misleading, nonexistent or meaningless designation to lend credence to the NSA's background, education, expertise or services.

8.6. Solicitation of Outside Business

The Notary Signing Agent will not directly or indirectly solicit a signer for products or services other than as a Notary Signing NSA or Notary Public at an appointment to provide signing services or in any written, verbal or electronic communication in connection with the assignment.

GUIDING PRINCIPLE 9: PROFESSIONALISM

The Notary Signing Agent will always act in a responsible manner towards contracting companies and parties to the transaction.

Standards of Practice

9.1. Refusal of Assignment
The Notary Signing Agent will refuse to accept an assignment if the NSA reasonably foresees that he or she will be unable to meet the contracting company's expectations for the assignment, including, but not limited to, arriving at the appointment at the set time, and printing and providing copies of closing documents.

9.2. Overbooked Appointments
The Notary Signing Agent will schedule appointments with sufficient time to complete the assignment and not so closely schedule same-day appointments that the NSA cannot reasonably meet the expectations for any prior or subsequent assignment.

9.3. Delegation of Duties
The Notary Signing Agent will not authorize another Notary Signing Agent to perform signing services on the NSA's behalf without the express approval of the contracting company providing the assignment.

9.4. Cancellation and Rescheduling of Appointments
The Notary Signing Agent will not cancel or attempt to reschedule an appointment with a signer once the appointment has been set, but will immediately notify the contracting company providing the assignment if an emergency prohibits the NSA from attending the appointment.

9.5. Signing Presentation Guidelines
The Notary Signing Agent will follow any signing presentation guidelines in performing signing services as may be required by the contracting company.

9.6. Assignment Requirements
The Notary Signing Agent will thoroughly review the requirements and expectations for a given assignment, noting in particular what stipulated documents and payments the NSA must receive from the signer, and what documents and copies the NSA must leave with that individual.

9.7. Contracting Company Instructions
The Notary Signing Agent will review each lender's and contracting company's instructions and signing presentation guidelines for the assignment prior to the signing appointment and follow such instructions and guidelines provided they do not violate a statute, regulation or official directive related to the performance of notarial acts.

Notary Signing Agent Code of Conduct   19

9.8. Review of Documents

The Notary Signing Agent will review the closing documents prior to commencing the signing appointment to confirm the documents identify the correct signing party or parties and to determine which documents must be signed, dated, initialed and notarized.

9.9. Notification of Missing Documents

The Notary Signing Agent will immediately contact the closing agent for the transaction prior to the appointment if the NSA discovers that the Note, Mortgage or Deed of Trust, and, as applicable, the Truth in Lending Disclosure, Closing Disclosure, or other closing statement is either incomplete or missing from the closing package.

9.10. Appointment Confirmation

The Notary Signing Agent will confirm the appointment to sign closing documents with the signer, ensuring that all parties and witnesses signing documents, identification cards, stipulated documents and checks will be available upon the NSA's arrival, unless expressly prohibited by the contracting company.

9.11. Professional Communications

The Notary Signing Agent will ensure that the NSA's verbal and written communications, including, but not limited to, phone conversations, voicemail greetings, emails, faxes, Internet forum responses and social network postings, convey a professional tone and demeanor at all times.

9.12. Appropriate Attire

The Notary Signing Agent will dress for an assignment in a manner that conforms to the business requirements of the contracting company providing the assignment.

9.13. Notification of Late Arrival

The Notary Signing Agent will notify the signer and contracting company providing the assignment at least 30 minutes prior to the scheduled appointment time in the event that the NSA will arrive late to the appointment due to traffic, inclement weather or any other contingency.

9.14. Identifying Credentials

The Notary Signing Agent will present a government-issued identification document containing a photograph to identify the NSA upon meeting a signer at the appointment to sign closing documents.

9.15. Changes to Documents

The Notary Signing Agent will immediately inform the NSA's contracting company about any change to a closing document that is requested by a signer, and will not alter or add a document unless expressly authorized in writing by the lender's representative or contracting company; provided however, that a NSA may modify a notarial certificate on a document requiring notarization to comply with law in the NSA's state or jurisdiction.

9.16. Status Reporting

The Notary Signing Agent will immediately inform the NSA's contracting company about any development affecting the timely execution and return of the documents.

Notary Signing Agent Code of Conduct   20

9.17. Quality Assurance Review

The Notary Signing Agent will ensure that closing documents are properly completed, signed and notarized, and that all stipulations are present, before adjourning the signing appointment and delivering the package of closing documents for shipment to the closing agent or lender for the transaction.

9.18. Observance of Deadlines

The Notary Signing Agent will perform each assignment in a timely manner, and timely return all expected documents, duly executed, to the contracting company or closing agent for the transaction according to the requirements of the lender.

GUIDING PRINCIPLE 10: STANDARDS

The Notary Signing Agent will endeavor to maintain and raise standards of practice amongst practitioners in the signing services industry.

Standards of Practice

10.1. Association with Practitioners

The Notary Signing Agent is encouraged to join and participate in national and regional associations of Notaries Public, Notary Signing Agents and real property services professionals.

10.2. Encouragement of Practitioners

The Notary Signing Agent will encourage signing services practitioners to aspire to the highest standards of professional practice and enhance their professional competencies.

10.3. Dispensing Knowledge

The Notary Signing Agent will provide expertise to less experienced Agents and assist them in their professional advancement.

10.4. Higher Standards

The Notary Signing Agent will support the development and improvement of laws, regulations and standards of practice as will foster competence and ethical conduct among NSAs and will benefit contracting companies and parties to the transaction.

NOTARY SIGNING AGENT'S ACKNOWLEDGMENT

I have read *The Notary Signing Agent Code of Conduct* and agree to perform signing services in conformance with the Standards of Practice of this *Code*.

_____

Date

_____

Notary Signing Agent's Signature

_____

Notary Signing Agent's Printed Name

The *Notary Signing Agent Code of Conduct*
is published by the Signing Professionals Workgroup

Signing Professionals Workgroup
Notary Signing Agent
Signing Presentation Guidelines — Refinance

The Signing Presentation Guidelines provide signing professionals recommended descriptions of closing documents to present to borrowers. These are designed to assist the Notary Signing Agent, who as a notary public, is generally prohibited from explaining documents and from providing unauthorized legal or financial advice to borrowers.

Key:
Italics — Unspoken
Regular Font — Spoken
(Parentheses — Unspoken or Substitute data)

SECTION 1 — Pre-Signing Confirmation

As stated in the Code of Conduct, "The Notary Signing Agent will confirm the appointment to sign closing documents with the signer, ensuring that all parties and witnesses signing documents, identification cards, stipulated documents and checks will be available upon the NSA's arrival, unless expressly prohibited by the contracting company."

SECTION 2 — Introduction

Hello, my name is (NAME) and I am here on behalf of (TITLE & CLOSING COMPANY), the title and closing company working with (LENDER) to conduct your loan signing. We spoke earlier on the phone. It is nice to meet you.

SECTION 3 — Instructions

As the Notary Signing Agent, you should then provide the borrower with a state or federally issued photo ID. Wait for the borrower to invite you inside. Ask the borrower where he or she would like to conduct the signing, suggesting that all signers sit next to each other to facilitate the signing. Confirm that all parties that need to sign are present. Check copies of borrower identification at this time. ID should be a state or federally issued photo ID such as a passport or driver's license and must comply with state notary laws and regulations. If the borrower is unable to provide ID you should call your contracting company for instruction before proceeding with the closing.

It is important as you proceed with the signing of the loan package that you follow the closing instructions precisely.

1

SECTION 4 — Opening

I'd like to start by giving an overview of the signing process. The entire process typically takes about 45-60 minutes. We will move patiently and deliberately through these documents, at your pace, so do not feel rushed.

I have printed an entire copy of the loan package for your records. *(Hand borrower his or her copy.)*

You should sign your name exactly as your name appears on the signature line of the documents. Some of the documents must be notarized; I may also be required to administer an oath before completing the notarization on certain documents. As we review each document, I will describe to you the document's general purpose. Any questions beyond that related to fees, rates or other loan-specific items must be directed to your lender as I am not authorized to articulate beyond the general description of the documents. In addition, we must contact the lender or closing agent before making any changes or corrections to the documents.

Do you have any questions before we begin? *If the borrower requests an electronic copy, please direct him or her to contact (TITLE & CLOSING COMPANY).*

SECTION 5 — Closing Ceremony

As you walk through the documents with the borrower please find below definitions of the loan closing documents. It is suggested to use these descriptions as a guide as you walk the borrower through the loan closing documents. It is suggested as you go to the page to be signed you give the borrower the brief definition of the documents below. Please note packages will come in various stacking orders, so it is recommended you be familiar with these definitions. These definitions are in alphabetical order and will not be the order your document package comes in, so you should be familiar with the general description of the documents listed below and you may use these descriptions as a guide.

Borrower's Certification Authorization
This document certifies all of the information provided the loan application is true and complete.

Closing Disclosure — *combines and replaces the HUD/Settlement Statement and Truth in Lending (TIL) statement for most loans applied for beginning October 3, 2015*
The Closing Disclosure itemizes all closing costs. Page 1 includes loan amount, interest rate, projected monthly payments, closing costs and cash to close. The remaining pages include details of the closing cost, payoffs and payments, cash to close calculations, disclosures, loan calculations and contact information. Please note: The borrower should have received this document from his or her lender in advance of the closing.

Errors & Omissions (E&O) and Compliance Agreement
This states that if there are any typographical or clerical errors on the closing documents, the borrower would agree to sign any documents that had to be corrected.

Flood Hazard Notice
This indicates whether or not the property is in an area designated as a flood zone area.

2

Form 4506-T Request for Transcript of Tax Return
This form authorizes the lender to obtain transcripts of tax returns.

GFE/Good Faith Estimate — *replaced by the Loan Estimate for most loans applied for beginning October 3, 2015*
The Good Faith Estimate is an estimate of all closing fees including pre-paid and escrow items as well as lender charges.

HUD/Settlement Statement
The HUD/Settlement Statement itemizes all closing costs; on pages 1 and 2 items that appear on this statement include real estate commissions, loan fees, points, payoffs and escrow amounts. Page 3 of the Settlement Statement is a comparison of the fees disclosed on the Good Faith Estimate (GFE) to the actual costs as listed on the HUD/Settlement Statement.

The bottom portion of Page 3 shows the loan terms. The loan amount, rate, term, principal and interest payment as well as total payment are at the bottom. *(If the borrower has questions related to these amounts, direct the borrower to the lender.)*

Identification Verification Form
This form verifies identity of the borrower and should read exactly as their state or federal issued ID reads.

Impound Account Letter
This is the form authorizing the lender to collect real estate taxes and homeowner's insurance to be paid out of the borrower's escrow account when they are due and payable.

Initial Escrow Account Disclosure Statement
This is a one-year snapshot of the borrowers escrow account.

Insurance Requirements
This document states that homeowners insurance is required during the term of the loan.

Itemization of Amount Financed
This describes the items in detail that comprise the amounts necessary to calculate the annual percentage rate.

Loan Estimate — *replaces the Good Faith Estimate and initial Truth in Lending Disclosure for most loans applied for beginning October 3, 2015*
The Loan Estimate is an estimate of all closing fees including pre-paid, escrow items and lender charges. Please note: This document will be delivered to the borrower after the borower applies for the loan. It will typically not be included with the closing package.

Mortgage/Deed of Trust
This document is recorded in county land records as evidence of the lender's security interest in the property.

Note
The Note is a written promise to pay a sum of money at a stated interest rate during a specified term.

Notice of Right to Cancel

3

This is the borrower's notice of their right to cancel the transaction within a specified time frame.

Owner's Affidavit
This states that the borrower acknowledges no additional liens, judgments, encumbrances or claims against the property. It also states that no one else owns the property besides the borrower, there's no contract for sale, confirms marital status, no delinquent taxes and no zoning law violations.

Payment Letter
This is the borrower's principal, interest, real estate taxes and homeowner's insurance which total the monthly payment.

Riders (if applicable)

- **Planned Unit Development (PUD) Rider**
  This rider requires the borrower to pay fees or assessments that may be levied by a Homeowners Association (HOA) to prevent any liens by the association.

- **Second Home Rider**
  This rider states the borrower is not occupying the home as their primary residence.

- **1 - 4 Family Rider**
  This rider states the property is a multi-unit property.

- **Manufactured Home Rider**
  This rider states the property is a manufactured home.

- **Condominium Rider**
  This rider states the property is a condominium.

- **ARM Rider**
  This rider states this loan is an Adjustable Rate Mortgage (ARM) loan.

Servicing Disclosure Statement
This document discloses the fact that the lender has the right to sell, transfer or assign the servicing rights to the loan.

Signature and Name Affidavit
The Signature and Name Affidavit lists variations of the borrowers name such as "AKA's" that the lender may have located when checking their credit or when the title search was completed. The variations may differ from their name as it appears on the lender's loan documents.

Truth in Lending (TIL) — *replaced by the Loan Estimate for most loans applied for beginning October 3, 2015*
This is the Truth in Lending statement. It will include the following information:

- The annual percentage rate (APR)

- The finance charge

4

- The total of payments (the amount the borrower will have paid after they have made all of their scheduled mortgage payments)

Uniform Residential Loan Application/1003
This is the final, typed version of the loan application.

W-9
This form verifies the borrower's Social Security Number.

SECTION 6 — Ending the Transaction

Make sure the borrower has their printed copy of the closing package. If he or she asks for an electronic copy please direct them to contact (TITLE & CLOSING COMPANY), under no circumstances are you to email the documents to the borrower.

If borrower does not have the proper funds to give you as per the closing instructions, please contact your contracting company for instructions.

We have reviewed and you've signed all of the documents which conclude the signing. Do you have any further questions? It was very nice to meet you (borrower name). I hope you feel this was a positive closing experience. Thank you very much for your time.

5

CODE OF CONDUCT MAPPING TABLE

Timeline: Becoming an NSA

Guiding Principle – Main Principles	
1. Qualifications	The Notary Signing Agent will satisfactorily meet and maintain all qualifications necessary to perform signing services.
8. Advertising	The Notary Signing Agent will not advertise signing services in a manner that is unprofessional, false, misleading or deceptive.
10. Standards	The Notary Signing Agent will endeavor to maintain and raise standards of practice amongst practitioners in the signing services industry.

Guiding Principle 1: Qualifications	
1.1. Background Screening	The Notary Signing Agent will submit to a background screening of the Agent's identity, residence, record of state or federal criminal arrests and convictions, and state motor vehicle record, and to a check of the Agent's name against pertinent lists as required by rules implementing the USA PATRIOT Act.
1.2. Professional Licenses	The Notary Signing Agent will obtain and maintain all licenses and commissions required to perform signing services in the Agent's state or jurisdiction.
1.3. Notary Laws and Rules	The Notary Signing Agent will keep current on all laws and official regulations that affect the performance of notarial acts in the Agent's state or jurisdiction.

1.4. Federal Laws	The Notary Signing Agent will demonstrate an understanding of the provisions of any relevant federal laws and official regulations that pertain to the performance of signing services, including, but not limited to, the Gramm-Leach-Bliley Act (GLBA), Truth in Lending Act (TILA), Real Estate Settlement Procedures Act (RESPA), Fair and Accurate Credit and Transactions Act (FACTA) and the Uniting and Strengthening America by Providing Appropriate Tools Required to Intercept and Obstruct Terrorism (USA PATRIOT) Act.
1.5. Certification	The Notary Signing Agent will earn and maintain any relevant certifications needed to service contracting companies and parties to the transaction.
1.6. Closing Documents	The Notary Signing Agent will become familiar with the closing documents for each assignment but will not use this knowledge to provide unauthorized counsel or advice to signing parties.
1.7. Ongoing Learning	The Notary Signing Agent will keep informed on any technical matters, legal requirements and other developments that affect the Agent's competence or responsibilities in rendering signing services.
1.8. Supervising Attorney	The Notary Signing Agent will willingly submit to the supervision of an attorney if required by law or rule in the Agent's state or jurisdiction.

Guiding Principle 2: Notarization	
2.8. Control of Seal and Journal	The Notary Signing Agent will keep the Agent's Notary seal and journal in a locked and secure area when not in use and not allow any other person to possess or use them.

Guiding Principle 7: Fees	
7.4 Collusion	The Notary Signing Agent will not collude with other Agents to set fees for signing services.

Guiding Principle 8: Advertising	
8.1 Truthful Personal Assessment	The Notary Signing Agent will not misrepresent the Agent's background, education, training, or expertise in an application or interview, or when providing signing services on a website or in any promotional materials distributed by the Agent.
8.2 False or Misleading Claims	The Notary Signing Agent will not make exaggerated or excessive claims, promises, or guarantees about the Agent's services.
8.3 Use of Professional Designation	The Notary Signing Agent will not advertise or promote the Agent's services by using professional designations or certifications the Agent has not received or earned.
8.4 Observation of Rules for Use	The Notary Signing Agent will comply with all requirements governing the use of membership and professional designations, logos, and marks as may be required by the issuing, certifying, or accrediting entity.

8.5 Use of Improper Designation	The Notary Signing Agent will not use any false, misleading, nonexistent, or meaningless designation to lend credence to the Agent's background, education, expertise or services.
8.6. Solicitation of Outside Business	The Notary Signing Agent will not directly or indirectly solicit a signer for products or services other than as a Notary Signing Agent or Notary Public at an appointment to provide signing services or in any written, verbal or electronic communication in connection with the assignment.

Guiding Principle 9: Professionalism	
9.11. Professional Communications	The Notary Signing Agent will ensure that the Agent's verbal and written communications, including, but not limited to, phone conversations, voicemail greetings, emails, faxes, Internet forum responses and social network postings, convey a professional tone and demeanor at all times.

Guiding Principle 10: Standards	
10.1. Association with Practitioners	The Notary Signing Agent is encouraged to join and participate in national and regional associations of Notaries Public, Notary Signing Agents and real property services professionals.
10.2. Encouragement of Practitioners	The Notary Signing Agent will encourage signing services practitioners to aspire to the highest standards of professional practice and enhance their professional competencies.

Timeline: Landing the Assignment

Guiding Principle – Main Principles	
7. Fees	The Notary Signing Agent will follow all contractual obligations in charging and collecting fees for services rendered.
9. Professionalism	The Notary Signing Agent will always act in a responsible manner towards contracting companies and parties to the transaction.

Guiding Principle 3: Impartiality	
3.1 Personal Interest	The Notary Signing Agent will not provide signing services for a transaction in which the Agent or the Agent's close relative is directly or indirectly involved as a party.
3.2 Professional Interest	The Notary Signing Agent will not provide signing services for a transaction in which the Agent or Agent's close relative is the loan officer, real-estate agent, mortgage broker, or a settlement-services provider.
3.3 Notary Signing Agent and Attorney in Fact	The Notary Signing Agent will not sign documents in the capacity of Notary Signing Agent and as attorney in fact for a principal in the same transaction.
3.5 Appearance of Partiality	The Notary Signing Agent will refrain from performing signing services in any transaction that would raise the appearance of or the potential for a conflict of interest.

Guiding Principle 5: Illegal And Suspicious Activity	
5.3 False Document or Certificate	The Notary Signing Agent will not comply with a request of a lender's representative, contracting company, closing agent, signer, or any other person to falsify information in a closing document or certificate of a notarial act.
5.4 Extra Certificate	The Notary Signing Agent will not comply with a request of a lender's representative, contracting company or closing agent to mail a signed and sealed notarial certificate that is not securely attached to an actual closing document notarized by the Agent.

Guiding Principle 7: Fees	
7.1 Confirmation of Fee in Writing	The Notary Signing Agent will confirm the fee to be paid by the contracting company for an assignment to provide signing services in writing prior to the appointment with the signer.
7.2 Performance for Fee	The Notary Signing Agent will not refuse to perform services for an assignment that the Agent has previously accepted in dispute over a negotiated fee.
7.3 Referral Fee	The Notary Signing Agent will only charge and receive the fee for rendering signing services in connection with a transaction and will not accept or charge an illegal referral fee, rebate, fee-split, unearned fee, or kickback.
7.4 Collusion	The Notary Signing Agent will not collude with other Agents to set fees for signing services.

Guiding Principle 8: Advertising

8.1 Truthful Personal Assessment	The Notary Signing Agent will not misrepresent the Agent's background, education, training, or expertise in an application or interview, or when providing signing services on a website or in any promotional materials distributed by the Agent.
8.2 False or Misleading Claims	The Notary Signing Agent will not make exaggerated or excessive claims, promises, or guarantees about the Agent's services.
8.3 Use of Professional Designation	The Notary Signing Agent will not advertise or promote the Agent's services by using professional designations or certifications the Agent has not received or earned.
8.4 Observation of Rules for Use	The Notary Signing Agent will comply with all requirements governing the use of membership and professional designations, logos, and marks as may be required by the issuing, certifying, or accrediting entity.
8.5 Use of Improper Designation	The Notary Signing Agent will not use any false, misleading, nonexistent, or meaningless designation to lend credence to the Agent's background, education, expertise, or services.

Guiding Principle 9: Professionalism

9.1 Refusal of Assignment	The Notary Signing Agent will refuse to accept an assignment if the Agent reasonably foresees that he or she will be unable to meet the contracting company's expectations for the assignment, including, but not limited to, arriving at the appointment at the set time, and printing and providing copies of closing documents.

9.2 Overbooked Appointments	The Notary Signing Agent will schedule appointments with sufficient time to complete the assignment and not so closely schedule same-day appointments that the Agent cannot reasonably meet the expectations for any prior or subsequent assignment.
9.3 Delegation of Duties	The Notary Signing Agent will not authorize another Notary Signing Agent to perform signing services on the Agent's behalf without the express approval of the contracting company providing the assignment.
9.4 Cancellation and Rescheduling of Appointments	The Notary Signing Agent will not cancel or attempt to reschedule an appointment with a signer once the appointment has been set, but will immediately notify the contracting company providing the assignment if an emergency prohibits the Agent from attending the appointment.
9.6 Assignment Requirements	The Notary Signing Agent will thoroughly review the requirements and expectations for a given assignment, noting in particular what stipulated documents and payments the Agent must receive from the signer, and what documents and copies the Agent must leave with that individual.
9.7 Contracting Company Instructions	The Notary Signing Agent will review each lender's and contracting company's instructions and signing presentation guidelines for the assignment prior to the signing appointment and follow such instructions and guidelines provided they do not violate a statute, regulation or official directive related to the performance of notarial acts.

Timeline: Preparing for the Assignment

Guiding Principle – Main Principles	
3. Impartiality	The Notary Signing Agent will remain impartial to the transaction at all times.
6. Privacy and Confidentiality	The Notary Signing Agent will respect the privacy of each signer and protect closing documents from unauthorized disclosure.

Guiding Principle 4: Unauthorized Advice or Services	
4.9. Contact Sources	A Notary Signing Agent will not commence a signing appointment without having obtained the contact information of the lender's representative and closing agent associated with the transaction.

Guiding Principle 5: Illegal or Suspicious Activity	
5.3. False Document or Certificate	The Notary Signing Agent will not comply with a request of a lender's representative, contracting company, closing agent, signer or any other person to falsify information in a closing document or certificate of a notarial act.
5.4. Extra Certificate	The Notary Signing Agent will not comply with a request of a lender's representative, contracting company or closing agent to mail a signed and sealed notarial certificate that is not securely attached to an actual closing document notarized by the Agent.

5.5. Approval of Power of Attorney Signing	The Notary Signing Agent will not commence an appointment involving an attorney in fact signing for an absent principal unless specifically approved by the lender's representative or closing agent for the transaction.
5.8. Incomplete Documents	The Notary Signing Agent will immediately contact the NSA's contracting company if any closing document required to be notarized is incomplete or contains blank spaces.
5.9. Presentation of Entire Document	The Notary Signing Agent will present all pages of a closing document, and not just the signature page, to a signer for signature.
5.12. Evidence of Tampering	The Notary Signing Agent will immediately contact the NSA's contracting company if the NSA has knowledge or a reasonable belief that a closing document or notarial certificate has been tampered with or altered.
5.13. Disclosure of Wrongdoing	The Notary Signing Agent will not conceal knowledge of a criminal act committed in connection with a signing assignment but will immediately notify a lawful authority as soon as the Agent becomes aware that a criminal act has been committed.

Guiding Principle 6: Privacy and Confidentiality	
6.1. Nondisclosure of Signer Information	The Notary Signing Agent will not disclose the transaction or personal information of a signer to any person not directly a party to the transaction.

6.3. Scrutiny of Documents	The Notary Signing Agent will not inspect or examine the closing documents beyond what is needed to determine the requirements and conditions for the assignment and to complete any journal entries for notarizations on the documents.
6.4 Reception and Delivery of Documents	The Notary Signing Agent will reasonably attempt to receive and deliver all closing document packages in person or via secure means.
6.5. Printing of Documents	The Notary Signing Agent will personally download and print all closing documents and not assign this responsibility to any other person.
6.6. Compromised Documents	The Notary Signing Agent will ensure that any package of closing documents is properly sealed upon receipt and delivery and will immediately report to the contracting company any circumstance leading the Agent to reasonably believe that the contents of the package have been compromised.
6.7. Security of Documents	The Notary Signing Agent will keep all closing documents under personal control or lock and key before and during the appointment, and until delivering them via secure means to a reliable delivery service, including but not limited to a secured drop box location or hand delivery at a facility or office, or the closing agent for the transaction.

6.11. Unprotected Network	The Notary Signing Agent will not use a public or unsecured computer network to retrieve electronic communications in connection with a signing assignment, to access, download or print closing documents, or to fax signed documents to a lender's representative, contracting company or closing agent.
6.12. Transmission or Reception of Non-Public Personal Information	The Notary Signing Agent will use encryption, strong passwords and other secure delivery methods to send or receive closing documents or communications containing a signer's non-public personal information, whether by fax, email or other means.

Guiding Principle 7: Fees	
7.2. Performance for Fee	The Notary Signing Agent will not refuse to perform services for an assignment that the Agent has previously accepted in dispute over a negotiated fee.
7.3. Referral Fee	The Notary Signing Agent will only charge and receive the fee for rendering signing services in connection with a transaction and will not accept, charge or pay an illegal referral fee, rebate, fee-split, unearned fee or kickback.

Guiding Principle 9: Professionalism	
9.8. Review of Documents	The Notary Signing Agent will review the closing documents prior to commencing the signing appointment to confirm the documents identify the correct signing party or parties and to determine which documents must be signed, dated, initialed and notarized.

9.9. Notification of Missing Documents	The Notary Signing Agent will immediately contact the closing agent for the transaction prior to the appointment if the NSA discovers that the Note, Mortgage or Deed of Trust, and, as applicable, the Truth in Lending Disclosure, Closing Disclosure, or other closing statement is either incomplete or missing from the closing package.
9.10. Appointment Confirmation	The Notary Signing Agent will confirm the appointment to sign closing documents with the signer, ensuring that all parties and witnesses signing documents, identification cards, stipulated documents and checks will be available upon the Agent's arrival, unless expressly prohibited by the contracting company.
9.11. Professional Communications	The Notary Signing Agent will ensure that the Agent's verbal and written communications, including, but not limited to, phone conversations, voicemail greetings, emails, faxes, Internet forum responses and social network postings, convey a professional tone and demeanor at all times.
9.12. Appropriate Attire	The Notary Signing Agent will dress for an assignment in a manner that conforms to the business requirements of the contracting company providing the assignment.
9.13. Notification of Late Arrival	The Notary Signing Agent will notify the signer and contracting company providing the assignment at least 30 minutes prior to the scheduled appointment time in the event that the Agent will arrive late to the appointment due to traffic, inclement weather or any other contingency.

Guiding Principle 10: Standards of Practice	
10.2. Encouragement of Practitioners	The Notary Signing Agent will encourage signing services practitioners to aspire to the highest standards of professional practice and enhance their professional competencies.
10.3. Dispensing Knowledge	The Notary Signing Agent will provide expertise to less experienced Agents and assist them in their professional advancement.
10.4. Higher Standards	The Notary Signing Agent will support the development and improvement of laws, regulations and standards of practice as will foster competence and ethical conduct among Agents and will benefit contracting companies and parties to the transaction.

Timeline: Conducting the Assignment

Part 1: Meeting the Borrowers	
Guiding Principle 9: Professionalism	
9.11. Professional Communications	The Notary Signing Agent will ensure that the Agent's verbal and written communications, including, but not limited to, phone conversations, voicemail greetings, emails, faxes, Internet forum responses and social network postings, convey a professional tone and demeanor at all times.
9.12. Appropriate Attire	The Notary Signing Agent will dress for an assignment in a manner that conforms to the business requirements of the contracting company providing the assignment.

9.13. Notification of Late Arrival	The Notary Signing Agent will notify the signer and contracting company providing the assignment at least 30 minutes prior to the scheduled appointment time in the event that the Agent will arrive late to the appointment due to traffic, inclement weather or any other contingency.
9.14. Identifying Credentials	The Notary Signing Agent will present a government-issued identification document containing a photograph to identify the Agent upon meeting a signer at the appointment to sign closing documents.

Part 2: Preparing the Space

Guiding Principle 4: Unauthorized Advice or Services

4.2. Role and Limitations	The Notary Signing Agent will clearly explain to the signing parties that the Agent is solely responsible for providing signing services connected with the transaction and cannot answer specific questions about the transaction or the legal effect of the closing documents.

Part 3: Presenting the Documents

Guiding Principle 2: Notarization

2.1. Standard of Care	The Notary Signing Agent will exercise reasonable care in the performance of notarial duties generally and will exercise a high degree of care in verifying the identity of any person whose identity is the subject of a notarial act.

2.2. Improper Identification	The Notary Signing Agent will not accept an unauthorized identification document or other means of identification as satisfactory evidence of identity in order to expedite the closing of the transaction or for any other reason, and will ensure that any identification document presented has not expired, unless expressly authorized by law.
2.12. Undue Cause for Refusal	The Notary Signing Agent will not refuse to perform a notarial act solely because a signer refuses to comply with a practice that is not a legal requirement for notarization in the Agent's state or jurisdiction.

Guiding Principle 3: Impartiality

3.6. Personal Opinion	The Notary Signing Agent will not offer a personal opinion to a signer about executing or not executing closing documents or consummating or not consummating a transaction.
3.7. Exercise of Rescission Option	The Notary Signing Agent will not recommend that a borrower proceed with the signing of any closing document on the grounds that the rescission option provides three business days to thoroughly read loan documents, ask questions of the lender and decide whether to consummate the transaction, but will recommend that the borrower contact the lender's representative immediately before signing the documents.

Guiding Principle 4: Unauthorized Advice or Services	
4.1. Legal Advice	The Notary Signing Agent will not offer legal advice to a signer during an assignment to provide signing services unless the Agent is an attorney representing a party in the transaction.
4.3. Response to Questions	The Notary Signing Agent may respond to a signer's specific question by directing the individual to read the provisions in the critical or other closing documents identified by the Agent that may answer the question or by referring the individual to the lender's representative or closing agent associated with the transaction.
4.4. Presentation of Documents	The Notary Signing Agent will present each closing document to a signer in conformance with a signing presentation guidelines authorized by the contracting company, and by naming and stating the general purpose of the document, specifying the number of pages and indicating where signatures, dates or initials are to be placed.
4.5. Loan Terms	The Notary Signing Agent may identify and provide a general description of a loan or payment amount, interest rate, annual percentage rate, finance charge, payment schedule, assumption option, prepayment penalty or any other loan term to a borrower in the closing documents, but may not explain, interpret or provide legal advice about the loan terms.

4.6. Settlement Fees	The Notary Signing Agent may identify and provide a general description of a fee or charge appearing on a signer's HUD-1, Closing Disclosure or other closing statement, as applicable, but may not explain, interpret or provide legal advice about the fee or charge.
4.7. Disbursement or Funding Date	The Notary Signing Agent will neither attempt to forecast nor disclose an actual disbursement or funding date to a signer unless expressly requested in writing by a lender's representative or closing agent or the date is clearly identified in a closing document the Agent can present to the individual.
4.10. Disclosure of Contact Sources	The Notary Signing Agent will provide the borrower with the contact information of the lender's representative and closing agent who may answer questions about the loan and explain the terms of the loan or any closing document presented to the borrower.

Part 4: Handling Issues During the Appointment

Guiding Principle 5: Standards of Practice

5.1. Absent Signer	The Notary Signing Agent will not comply with a request to notarize the signature of a signer who does not personally appear before the Agent.
5.2. Pre- or Post-Dated Certificate	The Notary Signing Agent will not pre- or post-date a notarial certificate in order to meet a funding deadline, avoid an expiring rate lock or for any other reason.

5.3. False Document or Certificate	The Notary Signing Agent will not comply with a request of a lender's representative, contracting company, closing agent, signer or any other person to falsify information in a closing document or certificate of a notarial act.
5.4. Extra Certificate	The Notary Signing Agent will not comply with a request of a lender's representative, contracting company or closing agent to mail a signed and sealed notarial certificate that is not securely attached to an actual closing document notarized by the Agent.
5.5. Approval of Power of Attorney Signing	The Notary Signing Agent will not commence an appointment involving an attorney in fact signing for an absent principal unless specifically approved by the lender's representative or closing agent for the transaction.
5.6. Signer Awareness, Willingness and Disability	The Notary Signing Agent will immediately contact the NSA's contracting company if the NSA has a reasonable belief that a signer is not aware of the loan or the significance of the transaction at the time closing documents are signed, possesses a physical disability requiring accommodation that the NSA has not been trained or authorized to perform, or the person is being overtly influenced or pressured into signing or not signing the documents.

5.7. Inconsistent Signatures or Handwriting	The Notary Signing Agent will immediately contact the NSA's contracting company if the NSA has a reasonable belief that a person's signature or handwriting appears to be overtly inconsistent with any identification card, journal entry or document presented or signed in connection with the transaction.
5.8. Incomplete Documents	The Notary Signing Agent will immediately contact the NSA's contracting company if any closing document required to be notarized is incomplete or contains blank spaces.
5.9. Presentation of Entire Document	The Notary Signing Agent will present all pages of a closing document, and not just the signature page, to a signer for signature.
5.10. Potential or Actual Misrepresentation	The Notary Signing Agent will immediately report any potential or actual misrepresentation or falsehood known or witnessed by the NSA in connection with a transaction to the NSA's contracting company.

Guiding Principle 6: Privacy and Confidentiality	
6.8. Request for Electronic Documents	The Notary Signing Agent will not comply with a request from a signer to provide electronic closing documents, but will notify the NSA's contracting company of the individual's request for documents.

Guiding Principle 9: Professionalism

9.15. Changes to Documents	The Notary Signing Agent will immediately inform the NSA's contracting company about any change to a closing document that is requested by a signer, and will not alter or add a document unless expressly authorized in writing by the lender's representative or contracting company; provided however, that a NSA may modify a notarial certificate on a document requiring notarization to comply with law in the NSA's state or jurisdiction.
9.17. Quality Assurance Review	The Notary Signing Agent will ensure that closing documents are properly completed, signed and notarized, and that all stipulations are present, before adjourning the signing appointment and delivering the package of closing documents for shipment to the closing agent for the transaction.

Part 5: Closing the Meeting

Guiding Principle 2: Notarization

2.6. Journal of Notarial Acts	The Notary Signing Agent will record each notarial act performed on closing documents in a journal of notarial acts even if not required by law.
2.7. Notarial Evidence Form	The Notary Signing Agent will complete and promptly return a Notarial Evidence Form for each assignment when requested or required by a lender, title company or contracting company.

Timeline: Post Assignment

Guiding Principle – Main Principles	
7. Fees	The Notary Signing Agent will follow all contractual obligations in charging and collecting fees for services rendered.

Guiding Principle 5: Illegal and Suspicious Activity	
5.4. Extra Certificate	The Notary Signing Agent will not comply with a request of a lender's representative, contracting company or closing agent to mail a signed and sealed notarial certificate that is not securely attached to an actual closing document notarized by the Agent.
5.13. Disclosure of Wrongdoing	The Notary Signing Agent will not conceal knowledge of a criminal act committed in connection with a signing assignment but will immediately notify a lawful authority as soon as the Agent becomes aware that a criminal act has been committed.
5.14. Cooperation with Authorities	The Notary Signing Agent will fully cooperate with law enforcement investigating an allegation of criminal activity of which the Agent has knowledge or that implicates the Agent.

Guiding Principle 6: Privacy and Confidentiality	
6.1. Nondisclosure of Signer Information	The Notary Signing Agent will not disclose the transaction or personal information of a signer to any person not directly a party to the transaction.

6.2. Journal Entries	The Notary Signing Agent will take reasonable steps to prevent other parties from viewing completed entries in the Agent's Notary journal.
6.4. Reception and Delivery of Documents	The Notary Signing Agent will reasonably attempt to receive and deliver all closing document packages in person or via secure means.
6.6. Compromised Documents	The Notary Signing Agent will ensure that any package of closing documents is properly sealed upon receipt and delivery and will immediately report to the contracting company any circumstance leading the Agent to reasonably believe that the contents of the package have been compromised.
6.7. Security of Documents	The Notary Signing Agent will keep all closing documents under personal control or lock and key before and during the appointment, and until delivering them via secure means to a reliable delivery service, including but not limited to a secured drop box location or hand delivery at a facility or office, or the closing agent for the transaction.
6.9. Return of Documents	The Notary Signing Agent will return all executed or unexecuted closing documents in compliance with instructions from the contracting company or closing agent for the transaction in the event that an assignment is postponed or canceled.
6.12. Transmission or Reception of Non-Public Personal Information	The Notary Signing Agent will use encryption, strong passwords and other secure delivery methods to send or receive closing documents or communications containing a signer's non-public personal information, whether by fax, email or other means.

6.13. Deletion of Electronic Documents	The Notary Signing Agent will permanently erase any files containing electronic closing documents from the Agent's personal or a shared computer immediately upon conclusion of an assignment.

Guiding Principle 7: Fees	
7.5. Submission of Invoice	The Notary Signing Agent will submit an invoice for payment to the contracting company for each completed assignment in a form that complies with the terms of the written agreement between the Agent and contracting company.
7.7. Collection of Fee from Contracting Company	The Notary Signing Agent will not attempt to collect on a nonpaying account without first establishing that the contracting company has failed to fulfill its contractual obligations.
7.8. Collection of Fee from Signer	The Notary Signing Agent will not attempt to collect the signing fee from the signer in the event that the contracting company fails to remit timely payment.

Guiding Principle 9: Professionalism	
9.11. Professional Communications	The Notary Signing Agent will ensure that the Agent's verbal and written communications, including, but not limited to, phone conversations, voicemail greetings, emails, faxes, Internet forum responses and social network postings, convey a professional tone and demeanor at all times.

9.16. Status Reporting	The Notary Signing Agent will immediately inform the NSA's contracting company about any development affecting the timely execution and return of the documents.
9.18. Observance of Deadlines	The Notary Signing Agent will perform each assignment in a timely manner, and timely return all expected documents, duly executed, to the contracting company or closing agent for the transaction according to the requirements of the lender.

Borrower's Certification Authorization

Signing
Presentation
Guidelines

Borrower's Certification Authorization. This document certifies all of the information provided in the loan application is true and complete.

Additional Information

This is the Borrower's Certification and Authorization. By signing this document the borrower agrees and certifies that the information contained in the borrower's loan application is true and complete, without misrepresentation or omission of important facts.

The borrower also authorizes the lender to release loan-specific information to an investor looking to purchase the loan in the secondary market.

Information provided to the investor could include the borrower's employment history and income, bank account balances, credit history and copies of the borrower's income tax returns.

Compliance Agreement

Signing
Presentation
Guidelines

Compliance Agreement. This states that if there are any typographical or clerical errors on the closing documents, the borrower would agree to sign any documents that had to be corrected.

Additional Information

This is the Compliance Agreement. This document states that the borrower agrees to cooperate with the lender or lender's agent in fixing clerical errors on the documents after the property closes.

Depending upon the lender, this document may or may not be notarized.

Compliance Agreements may come in several forms:
- Errors & Omissions Agreement
- Document Correction Agreement
- Correction Agreement

Some variations (Correction Agreement – Limited Power of Attorney) give an agent of the lender permission to fix the clerical errors on the borrower's behalf. It speeds up the process of correcting the documents by giving someone who works for the lender the power to make corrections on the borrower's behalf.

Closing Disclosure

Signing
Presentation
Guidelines

n/a

Additional Information

Combines and replaces the HUD-1 and TIL statement for most loans October 3, 2015.

This is the Closing Disclosure. Your lender should have sent you this in advance. It itemizes all closing costs. Page 1 includes loan amount, interest rate, projected monthly payments, closing costs and cash to close. The remaining pages include closing cost details such as loan and other costs, payoffs and payments, cash to close calculations, disclosures, loan calculations and contact information.

In this document you can find:
- Loan terms
- Loan amount
- Interest rate
- Monthly principal and interest
- Cost at closing
- Loan disclosures
- Loan calculations
- Total of payments
- Finance charge
- Amount financed
- APR
- Total Interest Percentage

Deed of Trust

Signing Presentation Guidelines	**Deed of Trust.** This document is recorded in county land records as evidence of the lender's security interest in the property. *(Note: Any riders should also be signed at this time.)*
	Riders. (If applicable.) *(Note: even though the script only mentions the following riders, there are many more.)* • **Planned Unit Development (PUD) Rider.** This rider requires you to pay any fees or assessments that may be levied by a Homeowners Association to prevent any liens by the association. • **Second Home Rider.** This rider states you are not occupying the home as your primary residence. • **1-4 Family Rider.** This rider states that your property is a multi-unit property. • **Manufactured Home Rider.** *This rider states the property is a manufactured home.* • **Condominium Rider.** *This rider states the property is a condominium.* • **ARM Rider.** *This rider states this loan is an Adjustable Rate Mortgage (ARM) loan.*
Additional Information	This is a Deed of Trust. It is a security instrument whereby real property is pledged as a security for a debt. This is the one document in the package that is always notarized. Depending on the foreclosure law in the state where the borrower lives, a Deed of Trust or Mortgage is used. Foreclosure of a Mortgage must go through the court while a foreclosure for Deed of Trust goes through the title holder. With a Deed of Trust, the borrower receives title to the property but conveys title to a neutral third party – called a trustee – until the loan balance is paid in full. The "Assignment of Deed of Trust" that may be found in some loan packages is NOT the same as a Deed of Trust. A Notary should not notarize an Assignment of Deed of Trust that appears in the loan package.

Errors & Omissions (E&O) Agreement

Signing Presentation Guidelines	This states that if there are any typographical or clerical errors on the closing documents, the borrower would agree to sign any documents that had to be corrected.
Additional Information	This is the Errors & Omissions Agreement. This document states that the borrower agrees to cooperate with the lender or lender's agent in fixing clerical errors on the documents after the property closes. Depending upon the lender, this document may or may not be notarized. Errors & Omissions Agreement may come in several forms: • Compliance Agreement • Document Correction Agreement • Correction Agreement.

Flood Hazard Notice

Signing Presentation Guidelines	This indicates whether or not the property is in an area designated as a flood zone area.
Additional Information	This document also stipulates: • At minimum, how much flood insurance must be purchased • That flood insurance coverage is available under the National Flood Insurance Program (NFIP) • Whether federal disaster relief assistance may be available in the event of damage to the building caused by flooding in a federally declared disaster.

General Closing Instructions

Signing Presentation Guidelines	n/a

Additional Information

These are the General Closing Instructions. This document provides the lender's general requirements (conditions) to the settlement agent for the closing of all single-family residential mortgage loan transactions.

The General Closing Instructions provide the lender's conditions for executing and correcting documents, using a Power of Attorney and handling transactions with a rescission period.

GFE/Good Faith Estimate

Signing Presentation Guidelines	The **Good Faith Estimate** is an estimate of all closing fees including pre-paid and escrow items as well as lender charges.

Additional Information

Replaced by the Loan Estimate for most loans applied for beginning Ocotber 3, 2015.

Referred to as the GFE, this document must be provided by a lender or broker as provided by the Real Estate Settlement Procedures Act (RESPA). It is a disclosure in which the lender provides the borrower with the best estimate of settlement costs at the time of application.

It contains a summary of important loan terms and the total estimated costs for the loan. This information helps the borrower comparison shop from lender to lender.

Although the Good Faith Estimate is not signed, some lenders may include another document that asks borrowers to attest that they received and reviewed this document.

HUD-1 Settlement Statement

Signing Presentation Guidelines	The HUD/Settlement Statement itemizes all closing costs; on pages 1 and 2 items that appear on this statement include real estate commissions, loan fees, points, payoffs and escrow amounts. Page 3 of the Settlement Statement is a comparison of the fees disclosed on the Good Faith Estimate (GFE) to the actual costs as listed on the settlement statement/HUD.
	The bottom portion of Page 3 shows the loan terms. The loan amount, rate, term, principal and interest payment as well as total payment are at the bottom.

Additional Information

The HUD-1 Settlement Statement itemizes the actual settlement services provided and fees charged to the borrower. It's the cost of borrowing the money for the loan.

The following lines on the HUD-1 are of particular interest to signing professionals conducting a loan signing:
- Line 103 - Settlement charges to borrower
- Line 120 - Gross amount due from borrower
- Line 220 - Total amount paid by/for borrower
- Line 300 – Checkbox for borrower to provide/receive funds at closing
- Bottom half of page 3 summarizes loan terms (loan amount, term, interest rate)

The HUD-1 is the industry standard settlement statement adopted for use by the U.S. Department of Housing and Urban Development. The fully completed "HUD-1 Settlement Statement" generally must be delivered or mailed to the borrower at or before the settlement.

A borrower may request a preliminary HUD-1 24 hours before the closing.

In cases where there is no settlement meeting, the escrow agent will mail the final "HUD-1 Settlement Statement" after settlement.

HUD / VA Addendum to Uniform Residential Loan Application

Signing Presentation Guidelines   n/a

Additional Information   This is a common addendum to the Uniform Residential Loan Application that may appear in a loan package for both the Department of Veterans Affairs and the Department of Housing and Urban Development loans.

Both lenders and veterans complete certain sections of the form. Federal agencies must obtain approval for each collection of information they conduct or sponsor.

Impound Account Letter

Signing Presentation Guidelines

If the borrower IS escrowing funds:
Impound Account Letter. This is the form authorizing your lender to collect real estate taxes and homeowner's insurance to be paid out of your escrow account when they are due and payable.

If the borrower IS NOT escrowing funds:
You have not elected to have your real estate taxes and hazard insurance to be included in your monthly mortgage payment. It is important to note that you are responsible for making these payments outside of the mortgage payment.

Additional Information   This is the Impound Account Letter. This document informs the borrower if the lender requires him/her to set up an impound account to collect and manage Principal, Interest, Taxes and Insurance (PITI). On certain loans an impound account may be required if the principal amount exceeds 80% of the sales price or the appraised value, whichever is lower.

If not required by the lender, the borrower may elect to pay taxes and insurance as they are due or set up an impound account, in which case taxes and insurance are paid with the principal and interest charges each month. This document can sometimes be combined with the First Payment Letter and is called the **Impound Authorization and First Payment Notification**

Initial Escrow Account Disclosure Statement

Signing Presentation Guidelines   ***Initial Escrow Account Disclosure Statement.*** This is a one-year snapshot of your escrow account.

Additional Information   This is the Initial Escrow Account Disclosure. It outlines the activity in an escrow or impound account for the coming year. It also contains the information regarding the borrower's first payment for the loan. The escrow or impound account is where amounts for taxes and insurance paid as part of the monthly mortgage payment are deposited.

Insurance Requirements

Signing Presentation Guidelines   This document states that homeowners insurance is required during the term of the loan.

Additional Information   Also called the Hazard Insurance Disclosure. In this document, the lender outlines the policies and minimum requirements for a hazard insurance policy that must be provided to cover the subject property.

Itemization of Amount Financed

Signing Presentation Guidelines	This describes the items in detail that comprise the amounts necessary to calculate the annual percentage rate.
Additional Information	A separate written itemization of the good faith estimates of settlement costs provided for transactions subject to the Real Estate Settlement Procedures Act (RESPA). Specific amounts for costs on the form are assigned the corresponding line number on the HUD-1 in which the amounts would appear. This document includes: • The amount of any proceeds distributed directly to the borrower • The amount credited to the borrower's account with the lender • Any amounts paid to other persons by the lender on the borrower's behalf

IRS Form 4506-T

Signing Presentation Guidelines	n/a
Additional Information	This is the IRS Form 4506-T. This allows an auditor to request a copy of the borrower's tax return for auditing purposes. Loans are randomly chosen for audit to make sure that the borrowers / lender did not commit fraud by providing / altering false tax information. It is rarely used but kept in the borrower's file.

IRS Form W-9

Signing Presentation Guidelines	This form verifies the borrower's Social Security Number.
Additional Information	This is IRS Form W-9. It is used to verify the borrower's Social Security Number. Allows the lender to accurately report to the IRS the interest that the borrower paid on the mortgage during a particular tax year.

Limited Power of Attorney

Signing Presentation Guidelines	n/a
Additional Information	A Power of Attorney is a written authorization naming an agent to represent or act on another's behalf in private affairs, business or some other legal matter. A Limited Power of Attorney restricts power to perform only certain functions named in the document, such as the power to mortgage or sell real property. Some variations (Correction Agreement – Limited Power of Attorney) give an agent of the lender permission to fix the clerical errors on the borrower's behalf. It speeds up the process of correcting the documents by giving someone who works for the lender the power to make corrections on the borrower's behalf. This document commonly requires notarization.

Loan Estimate

Signing Presentation Guidelines	The *Loan Estimate* is an estimate of all closing fees including pre-paid and escrow items as well as lender charges.
Additional Information	Replaces the Good Faith Estimate for most loans October 3, 2015. This document must be provided by a lender or broker as provided by the Real Estate Settlement Procedures Act (RESPA). It is a disclosure in which the lender provides the borrower with the best estimate of settlement costs at the time of application. It contains a summary of important loan terms and the total estimated costs for the loan. This information helps the borrower comparison shop from lender to lender. Some lenders may include another document that asks borrowers to attest that they received and reviewed this document.

Loan Modification Agreement

Signing Presentation Guidelines

n/a

Additional Information

This is the Loan Modification Agreement. It permanently changes one or more of the terms on a home mortgage loan which can provide a way for a borrower to avoid foreclosure on the mortgage.

This document may:
- Lower the interest rate
- Extend the loan period
- Add/deletes fees due on the principal of the loan.

Mortgage

Signing Presentation Guidelines

Mortgage. This document is recorded in county land records as evidence of the lender's security interest in the property.

(Note: Any riders should also be signed at this time.)

Riders. (If applicable.)
(Note: Even though the script only mentions the following riders, there are many more)
- ***Planned Unit Development (PUD) Rider.*** This rider requires you to pay any fees or assessments that may be levied by a Homeowners Association to prevent any liens by the association.
- ***Second Home Rider.*** This rider states the borrower is not occupying the home as their primary residence.
- ***1-4 Family Rider.*** This rider states that the property is a multi-unit property.
- ***Manufactured Home Rider.*** *This rider states the property is a manufactured home.*
- ***Condominium Rider.*** *This rider states the property is a condominium.*
- ***ARM Rider.*** *This rider states this loan is an Adjustable Rate Mortgage (ARM) loan.*

Additional Information

This is a Mortgage. It is a security instrument whereby real property is pledged as a security for a debt. This is the one document in the package that is always notarized.

Depending on the foreclosure law in the state where the borrower lives, a Deed of Trust or Mortgage is used. Foreclosure of a Mortgage must go through the court while foreclosure of a Deed of Trust goes through the title holder. A Mortgage is also different from a Deed of Trust in another way. In a Deed of Trust a borrower receives title to the property but conveys title to a neutral third party until the loan balance is paid in full. With a Mortgage, there is no third party involved.

The "Assignment of Deed of Mortgage" that may be found in some loan packages is **NOT** the same as a Mortgage. A Notary should not notarize an Assignment of Mortgage that appears in a loan package.

Note

Signing Presentation Guidelines

The Note is a written promise to pay a sum of money at a stated interest rate during a specified term.

Additional Information

The Note is a legal document that obligates the borrower to repay a mortgage loan at a stated interest rate during a specified period.

This Note contains the following provisions:
- Loan amount
- Interest rate
- Terms of repayment
- Monthly payment amount and due date
- Prepayment provisions
- Late charges terms and conditions

Notice of Assignment, Sale or Transfer of Servicing Rights

Signing Presentation Guidelines	n/a

Additional Information

This document is required by RESPA. This document informs the borrower that the loan has been sold to another company that will service the borrower's loan.

It contains the name and contact information of the loan servicer and the date that the new loan servicer will begin accepting payments.

Notice of Right to Cancel

Signing Presentation Guidelines	This is the borrower's notice of their right to cancel the transaction within a specified time frame.

Additional Information

For qualifying loans, the Notice of Right to Cancel gives the borrower three business days to cancel the loan.

The Right to Cancel applies to the following types of loans made on a primary residence in which the property is pledged as security for the loan:
- Refinance loans
- First and second loans
- Home Equity Line of Credit (HELOC) loans
- Reverse mortgage loans

However, the Right to Cancel does not apply to purchase loans and loans on second residences, vacation homes and income properties.

Each borrower must receive two copies of the Right to Cancel. All copies of this document should be signed at the signing appointment. Some lenders calculate the rescission period; other lenders rely upon the SIGNING SPECIALIST to calculate this date.

Important Dates:
- Document preparation date
- Signing date
- End of the rescission period date

Calculating the rescission date:
- Count three (3) business days beginning with the first business day after the signing. The rescission period ends at midnight on the third business day
- "Business" days include any day of the week except Sunday and the following Federal Holidays:

New Year's Day	Memorial Day	Columbus Day
Martin Luther King, Jr. Day	Independence Day	Veterans Day
Presidents' Day	Labor Day	Thanksgiving Day
		Christmas Day

Occupancy Affidavit or Owner's Affidavit

Signing Presentation Guidelines	This states that the borrower acknowledges no additional liens, judgments, encumbrances or claims against the property. It also states that no one else owns the property besides the borrower, there's no contract for sale, confirms marital status, no delinquent taxes and no zoning law violations.
Additional Information	By signing this document the borrower declares that he/she as the purchaser or homeowner already occupies the property that is the subject of the loan or that he/she intends to occupy the property upon the close of escrow. The document also requires the borrower to certify that his/her financial condition has not materially changed since first applying for the loan. For example, that the borrower hasn't gone out and purchased a new car that could affect his or her credit score or expense requirements. Depending upon the loan package, the Occupancy Affidavit may be a separate document in and of itself, or there may be both a combined Occupancy Affidavit and Financial Status and Occupancy Affidavit in the package. This document commonly requires notarization.

PATRIOT ACT/Identification Verification Form

Signing Presentation Guidelines	This form verifies identity of the borrower and should read exactly as their state or federal issued ID reads.
Additional Information	The USA PATRIOT ACT requires all financial institutions to establish a Customer Identification Program (CIP) for all new account holders. The information supplied in the Customer Identification Verification Form is used to determine whether the borrower's name appears on a list of known or suspected terrorists who have engaged in terrorist acts against the United States. Following are key points about the CIP Form: • Signing Agent documents the identifying information from a borrower's ID card to help lenders, title offices and escrow companies comply with USA PATRIOT ACT. • One of few forms in a loan package that a Signing Agent may complete. • The Customer Identification Verification Form must include the signature, date and title of the person completing the form. • Signing Agents may enter the title Signing Agent in the relevant space on this form but should not use the title Notary Public.

Payment Letter

Signing Presentation Guidelines	This is the borrower's principal, interest, real estate taxes and homeowner's insurance which total the monthly payment.
Additional Information	In the Payment Letter to Borrower, the lender: • Informs the borrower what the borrower's monthly payment for the loan will be • Breaks down the costs for principal and interest, property taxes and fire, flood and mortgage insurance (when applicable) • Informs the borrower where to make payments for the loan When it is combined with the Impound Authorization, the first payment information is at the bottom. It restates the loan amount, indicates whether there are impounds, gives the date of the first payment, and provides the total monthly payment.

Payoff Statement

Signing Presentation Guidelines	n/a
Additional Information	This is the Payoff Statement. It allows the closing agent for the refinance transaction to disburse funds to pay off the current mortgage when the new loan is funded. The Payoff Statement is a document that is typically used in refinance transactions. The closing agent for the transaction relies on the loan payoff information provided by the borrower's current mortgage holder to itemize the amounts in the Payoff Statement.

Riders to Deed of Trust / Mortgage

Signing Presentation Guidelines

Riders.

(Note: even though the script only mentions the following riders, there are many more)

- ***Planned Unit Development (PUD) Rider.*** This rider requires you to pay any fees or assessments that may be levied by a Homeowners Association to prevent any liens by the association.
- ***Second Home Rider.*** This rider states you are not occupying the home as your primary residence.
- ***1-4 Family Rider.*** This rider states that your property is a multi-unit property.
- ***Manufactured Home Rider.*** This rider states the property is a manufactured home.
- ***Condominium Rider.*** This rider states the property is a condominium.
- ***ARM Rider.*** This rider states this loan is an Adjustable Rate Mortgage (ARM) loan.

Additional Information

This is a Rider to the Deed of Trust/Mortgage. The purpose of a rider is to include additional or special terms and conditions affecting the loan that are not present in the boilerplate text of the security instrument (Deed of Trust/Mortgage/Security Deed). Lenders attach riders when the loan has additional terms and provisions that must be explained in writing and that go beyond the standard provisions of the security instrument. Here are some additional examples:

- Adjustable Rate Rider
- Balloon Payment Rider
- Biweekly Payment Rider
- Condominium Rider

If marked on the Deed of Trust/Mortgage, the rider **must** be included in the **package and is considered incomplete without it.**

Servicing Disclosure Statement

Signing Presentation Guidelines

Servicing Disclosure Statement. This document discloses the fact that the lender has the right to sell, transfer or assign the servicing rights to the loan.

Additional Information

This is the Servicing Disclosure Statement. This statement informs the borrower that the servicing for the loan may be transferred to a different loan servicer.

Required by RESPA.

Signature Affidavit and Name Affidavit

Signing Presentation Guidelines

Signature Affidavit and Name Affidavit. The Signature & Name Affidavit lists variations of the borrowers name such as "AKA's" that the lender may have located when checking their credit or when the title search was completed. The variations may differ from their name as it appears on the lender's loan documents.

Additional Information

This is the Signature Affidavit and AKA ("Also Known As") statement. It ensures signature verification and uniformity on all documentation.

- The borrower is required to provide a sample signature for each of the names listed on the document. These names were generated from credit reports and title searches.
- A similar document called a **Name Affidavit** lists all names by which the borrower has been known but does not require sample signatures.
- Depending on the loan package, there may be separate or multiple Signature and Name Affidavits.

Specific Closing Instructions

Signing Presentation Guidelines   n/a

Additional Information   The Specific Closing Instructions are instructions from the lender to the closing agent. They provide the detailed closing stipulations and requirements for a specific residential mortgage loan transaction.

The Specific Closing Instructions list many of the loan documents appearing in the loan package. This list may be used as a reference to verify certain documents appear in the package. It also lists the terms for the loan, an estimate of closing costs, the party responsible for paying the costs and any impounds.

Truth In Lending Disclosure Statement

Signing Presentation Guidelines   ***Truth in Lending (TIL).*** This is the Truth in Lending statement. It will include the following information:

- The annual percentage rate (APR)
- The finance charge
- The total of payments (the amount the borrower will have paid after they have made all of their scheduled mortgage payments)

Additional Information   The federal Truth in Lending Act requires the lender to make disclosures on loans subject to the Real Estate Settlement Procedures Act within three days after receipt of a written application.

In this document, the borrower can find the following clearly stated:

- The Annual Percentage Rate (APR), which is the total cost of the loan, including loan fees, calculated into an annual rate. The APR will typically be higher than the interest rate for the loan.
- Finance charge – the dollar amount the loan will cost the borrower
- The amount financed
- Total payments and payment schedule
- Prepayment penalties, if any
- Assumption option, if allowed

Uniform Residential Loan Application/ 1003

Signing Presentation Guidelines   ***Uniform Residential Loan Application/1003.*** This is the final, typed version of the loan application.

Additional Information   This is the Uniform Residential Loan Application. Sometimes called the 1003, this document is the standardized loan application form for a residential mortgage loan required by Fannie Mae/Freddie Mac.

Mikos

CLOSING VENDOR ORDER

MIKOS ESCROW, INC.
555 N. JUNE ST
MODESTO, CA 95963
Phone: (555) 555-5555

Order Number: 08-5555555-C
Order Date: 05/06/20XX 09:39

Vendor Charge: $XXX.00
Vendor No: 00055555
Vendor Name: MEGAN BRADY
Vendor Address: 520 13TH ST
MODESTO, CA - 95354-2438
Vendor Phone: (555)555-5555   **Vendor Fax:** (000)000-0000
Assignment Type: Web Documents
Assigned Date: 06/14/20XX 13:10 PST
Closing Option: Agent's Office
Projected Closing Date: 06/17/20XX 18:00

Borrower: ROGERS, RICHARD WILLIAM
Home Phone: (555)322-7212
Borrower:

Work Phone: (555)555-5555   **Cell Phone:** (555)555-5555

Purchase: REFINANCE
Closing Location: 12345 GLORIETTA LANE, OAKDALE, CA - 95361-9258

Loan Number: 1234567890
Loan Amount: $205,631.00

COMMENTS:

FOR AFTER HOUR QUESTIONS, PLEASE CONTACT **LOC WATERS**, 555-555-5555.

Please read all instructions carefully before completing the signing appointment.

Borrower(s) should be contacted to confirm appointment date, time and location.

All documents should be printed and returned in the order they are attached. Do not shuffle pages in the package. Documents should not be cutoff. Most files are uploaded as mixed originals, when in doubt print on legal size paper. You will be contacted by a MIKOS representative when documents are ready to be printed.

All signed documents must be dropped within 4 hours of the closing using the courier label attached. After hours closings must be dropped by noon the next business day. After documents have been dropped, please login to www.**mikos**.com to confirm the signing has been completed.

Failure to comply with the instructions above could result in a reduction or waiver of your signing fee.

Closing Vendor Login Instructions:
- Go to www.**mikos**.com and go to Access Your Account
- User ID is your vendor number (DO NOT ENTER PRECEDING ZEROS)
- Password is: MIKOS (unless you have already changed)

****Please direct all billing and payment inquiries to accountspayable@MIKOS.com****

1

This email is your confirmation for the Jackson, for 5/16/20XX, @ 3:00 PM.

Questions before, during or after the appointment......Call 1-800-723-2408, Option 3.

****SPECIFIC SIGNING INSTRUCTIONS FOR THIS APPT****
****DOCS MUST BE DROPPED FOR DELIVERY TOMORROW***

PLEASE COLLECT COPY OF SIGNER'S PHOTO ID TO RETURN WITH THE DOCUMENTS. THE SIGNER(S) HAVE BEEN MADE AWARE TO HAVE THE COPY AVAILABLE TO GIVE TO YOU. IF FOR ANY REASON THEY WERE UNABLE TO GET A COPY MADE, PLEASE USE YOUR SMART PHONE (IF POSSIBLE) TO TAKE A CLEAR PICTURE OF THE ID, AND EMAIL IT TO US

BORROWER INFORMATION:

Richard William Rogers
8624 Oaklawn Ave.
Modesto , CA 95355

Day Phone: 626-335-7313
Evening Phone:
Other Phone:

Qty of Loans: 1
Loan #1: 5400234599-JA
Loan Types:
Refi

Docs Sent Via: E-Docs
  Shipping Co:
  Tracking #:

SHIPPING INSTRUCTIONS:

Shipper/Account:

Label included with docs.

If no label was included with docs, please contact Signings at 800-723-2408 (option 3) or via email at orders@signings.com.

FEE AGREEMENT
Loan Signing $XX.00   Qty: 1

If you have any questions during the signing please contact us before calling any other parties.

DO NOT INCLUDE THIS FORM, ANY INVOICE, OR CORRESPONDENCE WITH THE RETURNED DOCUMENTS

Thank you,
Signings Escrow & Lender Services
orders@signings.com

CLOSING INSTRUCTIONS:

*** PLEASE MAKE SURE TO CONFIRM WITH THE BORROWER ONCE YOU RECEIVE THIS CONFIRMATION ***
If you have ANY questions or problems, please contact the Service Signing CLOSING TEAM directly at 800-123-4567

CLOSING PREPARATION:
1. Please be sure to dress in BUSINESS OR BUSINESS CASUAL attire.
2. Please take TWO copies of the documents to the closing. One full set is to be given to the Borrower for their records.
NOTE
If the borrower requests an electronic copy of the closing documents, please inform your Service Signing representative. You as the Signing Agent should NEVER provide an electronic copy of documents to the Borrower. Inform the borrower you will submit their request and they will receive them from our office via Secured Email.
3. If for any reason you are going to be LATE to a signing, you MUST reach out to the Borrower(s) "and" the Service Signing Closing Coordinator listed on the Closing Instructions to advise of the situation. If you need to reschedule the original closing appointment, you MUST first inform your the Service Signing Closer prior to speaking with the Borrowers directly.
AT CLOSING:
Please make certain you review the Closing Instructions that you will receive with the closing package to ensure ALL documents are signed correctly.
1. Please use blue ink when signing the papers.
2. Please review each loan document signed to ensure that no signatures, initials, dates, etc. were omitted.
3. If the Borrower has any questions at the closing, and they cannot reach their Loan Officer please contact your Service Signing Closing Coordinator or Team Lead.
4. Customer Identification Form - If info is already filled in on page 2, 3, or 4, verify that info with one of the corresponding boxes and complete page 1.
**If there is no info checked to be verified then you MUST complete Name Verification on page 2, Address Verification on page 3, and Date of Birth Verification on page 3 - 4 all with one of the corresponding boxes.
5. Errors & Omissions - Please make sure that ALL parties on title are signing this form.
PLEASE PAY SPECIAL ATTENTION TO THE PAYPLAN ENROLLMENT AUTHORIZATION. DO NOT LEAVE IT BLANK. THEY MUST INDICATE THAT THEY ARE DECLINING OR ACCEPTING ENROLLMENT.
AFTER CLOSING:
1. You are REQUIRED to fax CRITICAL FUNDING DOCUMENTS to one of the following Service Signing fax numbers 800-123-4567
Please refer to the fax back checklist and requirements page for list of documents.
2. Please be sure to use the UPS label/account number provided and drop the package "after" you have faxed the critical documents and "Receive" a phone call or email from Service Signing confirming docs are "ok" to ship. If you don't hear from Service Signing please drop documents after 24 hrs of the closing.
3. PLEASE DO NOT update the signing completion status on the website. You are required to complete the e-billing but do not update STATUS via the website.
If you have ANY questions or problems, please contact the Service Signing CLOSING TEAM directly at 800-123-4567, Option #4.
Thank you!

NOTE: If you are in a "Witness State" (CT, FL, GA, LA*, MI, OH, SC, VT, WY), be sure you or the borrowers have arranged to have a witness present at the signing. ***LA requires two witnesses.**

Closing Disclosure

This form is a statement of final loan terms and closing costs. Compare this document with your Loan Estimate.

Closing Information

Date Issued	3/13/20XX
Closing Date	4/15/20XX
Disbursement Date	4/15/20XX
Settlement Agent	Stallwart Title
File #	12-3456
Property	8624 Oaklawn Ave. Modesto, CA 95355
Appraised Prop. Value	$280,000

Transaction Information

Borrower	Richard William Rogers 8624 Oaklawn Ave. Modesto, CA 95355
Lender	Tristar Finance Group

Lo___

Critical Document

Loan ID #	~~123-456789~~
MIC #	009874513

Loan Terms		**Can this amount increase after closing?**
Loan Amount	$205,631.00	NO
Interest Rate	3.25%	NO
Monthly Principal & Interest *See Projected Payments below for your Estimated Total Monthly Payment*	$894.92	NO

loan terms

		Does the loan have these features?
Prepayment Penalty		NO
Balloon Payment		NO

projected payments

Projected Payments		
Payment Calculation	**Years 1-4**	
Principal & Interest	$894.92	$894.92
Mortgage Insurance	+ —	+ —
Estimated Escrow *Amount can increase over time*	+ 445.23	+ 445.23
Estimated Total Monthly Payment	**$1,340.15**	**$944.04**

Estimated Taxes, Insurance & Assessments *Amount can increase over time* *See details on page 4*	$445.23 a month	**This estimate includes** ☒ Property Taxes ☒ Homeowner's Insurance ☒ Other: HOA Dues *See page 4 for escrowed property costs. You must pay for other property*	**In escrow?** YES YES NO

Borrower's cost (itemized on page 2)

Costs at Closing		
Closing Costs	$4,976.08	Costs + $2,762.07 in Other Costs – $500 *for details.*
Cash to Close	$2,666.92	Includes Closing Costs. *See Calculating Ca___* ☒ From ☐ To Borrower

Look and see if borrower needs to give you a check at the appointment

CLOSING DISCLOSURE

Closing Cost Details

Loan Costs	Borrower-Paid		Paid by Others
	At Closing	Before Closing	
A. Origination Charges	**$1,950.00**		
01 % of Loan Amount (Points)	$750.00		
02	$250.00		
03	$450.00		
04	$500.00		
05			
06			
07			
08			
B. Services Borrower Did Not Shop For	**$610.00**		
01		$405.00	
02		$30.00	
03	$20.00		
04	$45.00		
05	$65.00		
06	$45.00		
07			
08			
09			
10			
C. Services Borrower Did Shop For	**$935.50**		
01	$85.00		
02	$50.00		
03	$250.00		
04	$350.00		
05	$200.00		
06			
07			
08			
D. TOTAL LOAN COSTS (Borrower-Paid)	**$3,495.50**		
Loan Costs Subtotals (A + B + C)	$3,060.50	$435.00	

Other Costs	Borrower-Paid		Paid by Others
E. Taxes and Other Government Fees	**$60.00**		
01 Recording Fees Deed: Mortgage: $60.00	$60.00		
02			
F. Prepaids	**$2,125.12**		
01 Homeowner's Insurance Premium (12 mo.)	$1,209.96		
02 Mortgage Insurance Premium (mo.)			
03 Prepaid Interest ($17.71 per day from 4/15/20XX to 5/1/20XX)	$283.36		
04 Property Taxes (6 mo.) to Any County USA	$631.80		
05			
G. Initial Escrow Payment at Closing	**$576.95**		
01 Homeowner's Insurance $100.83 per month for mo.	$201.66		
02 Mortgage Insurance $82.35 per month for mo.	$164.70		
03 Property Taxes $105.30 per month for mo.	$210.60		
04			
05			
06			
07			
08 Aggregate Adjustment	−$0.01		
H. Other			
01			
02			
03			
04			
05			
06			
07			
08			
I. TOTAL OTHER COSTS (Borrower-Paid)	**$2,762.07**		
Other Costs Subtotals (E + F + G + H)	$2,762.07		
J. TOTAL CLOSING COSTS (Borrower-Paid)	**$4,976.08**		
Closing Costs Subtotals (D + I)	$5,822.57	$435.00	
Lender Credits	−$500.00		

CLOSING DISCLOSURE

PAGE 2 OF 5 • LOAN ID #

Payoffs and Payments

Use this table to see a summary of your payoffs and payments to others from your loan amount.

TO	AMOUNT
01 Payoff to XYZ Mortgage and Lending	$203,929.00
02	
03	
04	
05	
06	
07	
08	
09	
10	
11	
12	
13	
14	
15	
K. TOTAL PAYOFFS AND PAYMENTS	$115,000.00

Calculating Cash to Close

Use this table to see what has changed from your Loan Estimate.

	Loan Estimate	Final	Did this change?
Loan Amount	$150,000.00	$150,000.00	**NO**
Total Closing Costs (J)	–$5,099.00	–$5,757.57	**YES** · See **Total Loan Costs (D)** and **Total Other Costs (I)**
Closing Costs Paid Before Closing	$0	$435.00	**YES** · You paid these Closing Costs **before closing**
Total Payoffs and Payments (K)	–$120,000.00	–$115,000.00	**YES** · See **Payoffs and Payments (K)**
Cash to Close	$24,901.00 ☐ From ☒ To Borrower	$2,666.92 ☐ From ☒ To Borrower	Closing Costs Financed (Paid from your Loan Amount)

CLOSING DISCLOSURE

Additional Information About This Loan

Loan Disclosures

Assumption
If you sell or transfer this property to another person, your lender
- ☐ will allow, under certain conditions, this person to assume this loan on the original terms.
- ☒ will not allow assumption of this loan on the original terms.

Demand Feature
Your loan
- ☐ has a demand feature, which permits your lender to require early repayment of the loan. You should review your note for details.
- ☒ does not have a demand feature.

Late Payment
If your payment is more than ___ days late, your lender will charge a late fee of _____

Negative Amortization (Increase in Loan Amount)
Under your loan terms, you
- ☐ are scheduled to make monthly payments that do not pay all of the interest due that month. As a result, your loan amount will increase (negatively amortize), and your loan amount will likely become larger than your original loan amount. Increases in your loan amount lower the equity you have in this property.
- ☐ may have monthly payments that do not pay all of the interest due that month. If you do, your loan amount will increase (negatively amortize), and, as a result, your loan amount may become larger than your original loan amount. Increases in your loan amount lower the equity you have in this property.
- ☒ do not have a negative amortization feature.

Partial Payments
Your lender
- ☒ may accept payments that are less than the full amount due (partial payments) and apply them to your loan.
- ☐ may hold them in a separate account until you pay the rest of the payment, and then apply the full payment to your loan.
- ☐ does not accept any partial payments.

If this loan is sold, your new lender may have a different policy.

Security Interest
You are granting a security interest in _____

_____

_____

You may lose this property if you do not make your payments or satisfy other obligations for this loan.

Escrow Account
For now, your loan
- ☒ will have an escrow account (also called an "impound" or "trust" account) to pay the property costs listed below. Without an escrow account, you would pay them directly, possibly in one or two large payments a year. Your lender may be liable for penalties and interest for failing to make a payment.

Escrow		
Escrowed Property Costs over Year 1		Estimated total amount over year 1 for your escrowed property costs:
Non-Escrowed Property Costs over Year 1		Estimated total amount over year 1 for your non-escrowed property costs: You may have other property costs.
Initial Escrow Payment		A cushion for the escrow account you pay at closing. See Section G on page 2.
Monthly Escrow Payment		The amount included in your total monthly payment.

- ☐ will not have an escrow account because ☐ you declined it ☐ your lender does not offer one. You must directly pay your property costs, such as taxes and homeowner's insurance. Contact your lender to ask if your loan can have an escrow account.

No Escrow		
Estimated Property Costs over Year 1		Estimated total amount over year 1. You must pay these costs directly, possibly in one or two large payments a year.
Escrow Waiver Fee		

In the future,
Your property costs may change and, as a result, your escrow payment may change. You may be able to cancel your escrow account, but if you do, you must pay your property costs directly. If you fail to pay your property taxes, your state or local government may (1) impose fines and penalties or (2) place a tax lien on this property. If you fail to pay any of your property costs, your lender may (1) add the amounts to your loan balance, (2) add an escrow account to your loan, or (3) require you to pay for property insurance that the lender buys on your behalf, which likely would cost more and provide fewer benefits than what you could buy on your own.

Loan Calculations

Total of Payments. Total you will have paid after you make all payments of principal, interest, mortgage insurance, and loan costs, as scheduled.	$334,211.11
Finance Charge. The dollar amount the loan will cost you.	$134,516.19
Amount Financed. The loan amount available after paying your upfront finance charge.	$199,694.92
Annual Percentage Rate (APR). Your costs over the loan term expressed as a rate. This is not your interest rate.	3.940%
Total Interest Percentage (TIP). The total amount of interest that you will pay over the loan term as a percentage of your loan amount.	67.36%

Loan details including finance charge and amount financed

Questions? If you have questions about the loan terms or costs on this form, use the contact information below. To get more information or make a complaint, contact the Consumer Financial Protection Bureau at **www.consumerfinance.gov/mortgage-closing**

O[...]

App[...]
If th[...] our lender is required to give [...] 3 days before closing. If you[...] your lender at the information [...]

Contract Details
See your note and security instrument for information about
• what happens if you fail to make your payments,
[...] e early repayment of the
[...] ey are due.

APR may be higher than interest rate because it reflects cost of financing

Liab[...]
If yo[...] the foreclosure does not cove[...] an,
☐ sta[...] he unpaid balance. If you refinance or take on any additional debt on this property, you may lose this protection and have to pay any debt remaining even after foreclosure. You may want to consult a lawyer for more information.
☐ state law does not protect you from liability for the unpaid balance.

Refinance
Refinancing this loan will depend on your future financial situation, the property value, and market conditions. You may not be able to refinance this loan.

Tax Deductions
If you borrow more than this property is worth, the interest on the loan amount above this property's fair market value is not deductible from your federal income taxes. You should consult a tax advisor for more information.

Contact Information

	Lender	Mortgage Broker	Settlement Agent
Name	Tristar Finance Group		Stallwart Title
Address	1000 Main Street Los Angeles, CA 91301		5555 Casandia Dr., Suite 2 Modesto, CA 95822
NMLS ID			
ST License ID			P76821
Contact	Amir Kumar		Joan Taylor
Contact NMLS ID	12345		
Contact __ License ID			
Email	akumar@tristarfg.com		joan@stallwarttitle.com
Phone	123-456-7890		555-321-9876

Confirm Receipt

By signing, you are only confirming that you have received this form. You do not have to accept this loan because you have signed or received this form.

_____   _____   _____   _____
Applicant Signature   Date   Co-Applicant Signature   Date

CLOSING DISCLOSURE   PAGE 5 OF 5 • LOAN ID #

US Department of Housing and Urban Development

SETTLEMENT STATEMENT

OMB No. 2502-0265

A.

B. Type of Loan			
1. [X] FHA 2. [] RHS 3. [] Conv. Unins. 4. [] VA 5. [] Conv. Ins. 6. [] Other	6. File Number: 000-55555-000	7. Loan Number: 1234567890	8. Mortgage Ins. Case #: 55-55-5-12345678

C. NOTE: This form is furnished to give you a statement of actual settlement costs. Amounts paid to and by the settlement agent are shown. Items marked 'POC' were paid outside the closing; they are shown here for information purposes and are note included in the totals.

D. NAME AND ADDRESS OF BORROWER: RICHARD WILLIAM ROGERS,   8624 OAKLAWN, MODESTO, CA 95355

E. NAME AND ADDRESS OF SELLER:

F. NAME AND ADDRESS OF LENDER: TRISTAR FINANCE GROUP 1000 MAIN STREET LOS ANGELES, CA 91301

G. PROPERTY LOCATION   8624 OAKLAWN, MODESTO, CA 95355

H. SETTLEMENT AGENT: Stallwart Title, 5555 Casandra Blvd. Ste 2, Modesto, CA 95822 (222) 222-2222
   PLACE OF SETTLEMENT: Stallwart Title, 5555 Casandra Blvd. Ste 2, Modesto, CA 95822 (222) 222-2222

I. SETTLEMENT DATE: 03-18-20XX   DISBURSEMENT DATE: 03-21-20XX

J. SUMMARY OF BORROWER(S) TRANSACTION		K. SUMMARY OF SELLER(S) TRANSACTION	
100. GROSS AMOUNT DUE FROM BORROWER:		**400. GROSS AMOUNT DUE TO SELLER:**	
101. Contract Sales Price		401.	
102. Personal Property		402.	
103. Settlement charges to borrower (line 1400)	$4,976.08	403.	
104. PAYOFF	$203,924.00	404.	
105.		405.	
Adjustments for items paid by Seller in advance		Adjustments for items paid by Seller in advance	
106. City Property Tax		406. City Property Tax	
107. County Property Tax		407. County Property Tax	
108. Annual Assessment		408. Annual Assessment	
109. School Property Tax		409. School Property Tax	
110. MUD Tax		410. MUD Tax	
111. Other Tax		411. Other Tax	
112.		412.	
120. Gross Amount Due From Borrower	$208,900.08	**420. Gross Amount Due To Seller**	$0.00
200. AMOUNTS PAID BY OR IN BEHALF OF BORROWER:		**500. REDUCTIONS IN AMOUNT DUE TO SELLER:**	
201. Deposit of Earnest Money		501. Excess Deposit	
202. Principal Amount of New Loan(s)	$205,631.00	502. Settlement charges to seller (line 1400)	$0.00
203.		503. Existing Loan(s) Taken Subject to	
204. Application Deposit		504.	
205.		505.	
206.		506.	
207.		507.	
208.		508.	
209.		509.	
Adjustments for items unpaid by Seller		Adjustments for items unpaid by Seller	
210. City Property Tax		510. City Property Tax	
211. County Property Tax		511. County Property Tax	
212. Annual Assessment		512. Annual Assessment	
213. School Property Tax		513. School Property Tax	
214. MUD Tax		514. MUD Tax	
215. Other Tax		515. Other Tax	
216. Prepaid Finance Charge	$5,936.08	516.	
217.		517.	
218.		518.	
219.		519.	
220. Total Paid By/For Borrower	$211,567.00	**520. Total Reduction Amount Due Seller**	$0.00
300. CASH AT SETTLEMENT FROM/TO BORROWER:		**600. CASH AT SETTLEMENT TO/FROM SELLER:**	
301. Gross Amount due from borrower (line 120)	$208,900.08	601. Gross amount due to seller (line 420)	$0.00
302. Less amounts paid by/for borrower (line 220)	$211,567.00	602. Less reductions in amount due seller (line 520)	$0.00
303. Cash [X] From [] To Borrower	$ 2,666.92	**603. Cash [] From [] To Seller**	$0.00

...ated at 35 minutes per response for collecting, reviewing, and reporting the data. This agency may not collect this information, and you are ... OMB control number. No confidentiality is assured; this disclosure is mandatory.This is designed to provide the parties to a RESPA covered

US Department of Housing and Urban Development

OMB No. 2502-0265

L.

SETTLEMENT CHARGES

			Paid From Borrower's Funds at Settlement	Paid From Seller's Funds at Settlement
700. Total Real Estate Broker fees Division of commission as follows:				
701.				
702.				
703. Commission paid at settlement				
704.				
800. ITEMS PAYABLE IN CONNECTION WITH LOAN				
801. Our origination charge		(from GFE #1)		
802. Your credit or charge points for the specific interest rate chosen	($4,112.62)	(from GFE #2)	$3984.77	
803. Your adjusted origination charges		(from GFE A)	($0.00)	
804. Appraisal Fee		(from GFE #3)		
805. Credit Report		(from GFE #3)	$29.85	
806. Tax Service		(from GFE #3)		
807. YIELD SPREAD PREMIUM		(from GFE #3)	$1028.16	
808.				
809.				
810.				
900. ITEMS REQUIRED BY LENDER TO BE PAID IN ADVANCE 901.				
Daily Interest 03/18/20XX TO 04/01/20XX 14 DAYS @$18.3096/DAY		(from GFE #10)	$256.33	
902. Mortgage Insurance Premium		(from GFE #3)		
903. Homeowners Insurance		(from GFE #11)		
904.				
905.				
1000. RESERVES DEPOSITED WITH LENDER				
1001. Initial Deposit for your escrow account		(from GFE #9)	$2,011.50	
1002. Homeowners Insurance 5 months @ $48.33 per month	241.65			
1003. Mortgage Insurance				
1004. Property Taxes 5 months @ $157.32 per month	$786.60			
1005.				
1006.				
1007. Aggregate Adjustment	($293.27)			
1008.				
1009.				
1100. TITLE CHARGES				
1101. Title Services and lenders title insurance		(from GFE #4)	$1,260.00	
1102. Settlement or Closing Fee	$400.00			
1103. Owners title Insurance		(from GFE #5)		
1104. Lenders Title Insurance	$385.00			
1105. Lenders Title Policy Limit				
1106. Owners title policy limit				
1107. Agents Portion of the total title insurance premium				
1108. Underwriters portion of the total title insurance premium				
1109. Tax Research Fee				
1110. NOTARY FEE			$175.00	
1111. OVERNIGHT AND WIRE FEE			$55.00	
1112.				
1113.				
1200. GOVERNMENT RECORDING AND TRANSFER CHARGES				
1201. Government Recording charges DEED $110.00		(from GFE #7)	$110.00	
1202.				
1203. Transfer taxes		(from GFE #8)	$1,179.90	
1204.				
1205.				
1300. ADDITIONAL SETTLEMENT CHARGES				
1301. Required services that you can shop for		(from GFE #6)		
1302.				
1303.			$525.00	
1304.				
1305.				
1400. Total Settlement Charges (enter on lines 103, Section J and 502, Section K)			$4976.08	$0.00

I have carefully reviewed the HUD-1 Settlement Statement and to the best of my knowledge and belief, it is a true and accurate statement of all receipts and disbursements made on my account or by me in this transaction. I further certify that I have received a copy of HUD-1 Settlement Statement.

BORROWER(S):

X_____   X_____
RICHARD WILLIAM ROGERS

The HUD-1 Settlement Statement which I have prepared is a true and accurate account of this transaction. I have caused or will cause the funds to be disbursed in accordance with this statement.

_____
Stallworth Title of Modesto Settlement Agent

_____
Date

ADDENDUM TO HUD-1

Loan Number: 1234567890
File Number: 000-55555-000
Borrower: RICHARD WILLIAM ROGERS

	Paid From Borrower's Funds at Settlement	Paid From Seller's Funds at Settlement
---------------PAYOFFS---------------		
PAYOFF TO XYZ MORTAGE AND LENDING		
Total	$203,929.00 $203,929.00	

X_____
Signature   RICHARD WILLIAM ROGERS   Date

X_____
Signature   Date

X_____
Signature   Date

X_____
Signature   Date

X_____
Signature   Date

X_____
Signature   Date

Comparison of Good Faith Estimate (GFE) and HUD-1 Charges.		Good Faith Estimate	HUD-1 Amt
Charges That Cannot Increase	**HUD Line Number**		
Our origination charge	801	$0.00	$0.00
Your credit or charge points for the specific interest rate chosen	802	($5,936.08)	($4,112.62)
Your adjusted origination charges	803	($0.00)	($0.00)
Transfer taxes	1203	$1,179.90	$1,179.90
Charges That in Total Cannot Increase More Than 10%	**HUD Line Number**		
Government Recording charges DEED $110	1201	$110.00	$110.00
Appraisal Fee	804	$0.00	$0.00
Credit Report	805	$50.00	$29.85
YIELS SPREAD PREMIUM	807	$1,028.16	$1,028.16
	808		
Title Services and lenders title insurance	1101	$1,210.00	$1,260.00
Required services that you can shop for	1301	$0.00	$0.00
Total		$10,315.64	$8,472.03
Increase between GFE and HUD-1 Charges		$1,843.61	0.71%
Charges That Can Change	**HUD Line Number**		
Initial Deposit for your escrow account	1001	$5,936.08	$4,976.08
Daily Interest 03/18/20XX TO 04/01/20XX @$18.3096/DAY	901	$256.33	$256.33
Homeowners Insurance	903	$0.00	$0.00

Loan Terms

Your initial loan amount is	$205,631.00
Your loan term is	30 years
Your initial interest rate is	3.25 %
Your initial monthly amount owed for principal, interest, and any mortgage insurance	$894.92 includes ☑ Principal ☑ Interest ☐ Mortgage Insurance
Can your interest rate rise?	☑ No ☐ Yes, it can rise to a maximum of 0.0 %. The first change will be on and can change again every after . Every charge date, your interest rate can increase or decrease by 0.0 %. Over the life of the loan, your interest rate is guaranteed to never be lower than 0.0 % or higher than 0.0 %.
Even if you make payments on time, can your loan balance rise?	☑ No ☐ Yes, it can rise to a maximum of
Even if you make payments on time, can your monthly amount owed for principal, interest, and mortgage insurance rise?	☑ No ☐ Yes, the first increase can be on and the monthly amount owed can rise to $0.00 The maximum it can ever rise to $0.00
Does your loan have a prepayment penalty?	☑ No ☐ Yes, your maximum prepayment penalty is $0.00
Does your loan have a balloon payment?	☑ No ☐ Yes, you have a balloon payment of $0.00 due in 0 years on
Total monthly amount owed including escrow account payments.	☐ You do not have a monthly escrow payment for items, such as property taxes and homeowner's insurance. You must pay these items directly yourself. ☑ You have an additional monthly escrow payment of $445.23 that results in a total initial monthly amount owed of $1,340.15 This includes principal, interest, any mortgage insurance and any items checked below. ☑ Property Taxes ☑ Homeowner's Insurance ☐ Flood Insurance ☐ ☐ ☐

Note: If you have any questions about the Settlement Charges and Loan Terms listed on this form, please contact your lender.

Loan terms spelled out. Ask borrower to confirm terms are correct

NOTICE OF RIGHT TO CANCEL

Loan Number: 1234567890

Borrowers: RICHARD WILLIAM ROGERS

Property Address: 8624 OAKLAWN AVENUE, MODESTO, CALIFORNIA 95355

YOUR RIGHT TO CANCEL

You are entering into a transaction that will result in a mortg[...] our home. You hav[...] a legal right under federal law to cancel this transaction, wit[...] om whichever of th[...] following events occurs last:

Date of signing appointment

1. the date of the transaction, which is MARCH 13, 20XX   ; or
2. the date you receive your Truth in Lending disclosures; or
3. the date you receive this notice of your right to cancel.

Each borrower must receive two executed copies

If you cancel the transaction, the mortgage, lien or security interest is also cancelled. Within 20 calendar days after we receive your notice, we must take the steps necessary to reflect the fact that the mortgage, lien or security interest on or in your home has been cancelled, and we must return to you any money or property you have given to us or to anyone else in connection with this transaction.

You may keep any money or property we have given you until we have done the things mentioned above, but you must then offer to return the money or property. If it is impractical or unfair for you to return the property, you must offer its reasonable value. You may offer to return the property at your home or at the location of the property. Money must be returned to the address below. If we do not take possession of the money or property within 20 calendar days of your offer, you may keep it without further obligation.

HOW TO CANCEL

If you decide to cancel this transaction, you may do so by notifying us in writing, at

TRISTAR FINANCE GROUP, INC
1000 MAIN STREET
LOS ANGELES, CALIFORNIA 91301

You may use any written statement that is signed and dated by you and states your intention to cancel, or you m[...] notice by dating and signing below. Keep one copy of this notice because it contains important information [...] rights.

Rescission Date goes here

If you cancel by mail or telegram, you must send the notice no later than midnight of MARCH 16, 20XX (or midnight of the third business day following the latest of the three events listed above). If you send or deliver your written notice to cancel some other way, it must be delivered to the above address no later than that time.

I WISH TO CANCEL

Do not sign here

_____
Consumer's Signature   Date
RICHARD WILLIAM ROGERS

ACKNOWLEDGMENT OF RECEIPT

EACH OF THE UNDERSIGNED HEREBY ACKNOWLEDGES THE RECEIPT OF TWO (2) COMPLETED COPIES OF THIS NOTICE OF RIGHT TO CANCEL.

_____   _____
RICHARD WILLIAM ROGERS   Date

NOTICE OF RIGHT TO CANCEL/RESCISSION MODEL FORM H-8 (GENERAL)
15 U.S.C. 1635(a); 12 CFR 1026.23; Model Form H-8
NORTC.MSC 12/30/11

FEDERAL TRUTH-IN-LENDING DISCLOSURE STATEMENT
(THIS IS NEITHER A CONTRACT NOR A COMMITMENT TO LEND)

Loan Number: 1234567890   Date: MARCH 13, 20XX

Creditor: TRISTAR FINANCE GROUP, INC

Address: 1000 MAIN STREET, LOS ANGELES, CALIFORNIA 91301

Borrower(s): RICHARD WILLIAM ROGERS

Address: 8624 OAKLAWN AVENUE, MODESTO, CALIFORNIA 95355

Disclosures marked with an "x" are applicable:

ANNUAL PERCENTAGE RATE	FINANCE CHARGE	Amount Financed	Total of Payments	☐ Total Sale Price
The cost of your credit as a yearly rate	The dollar amount the credit will cost you.	The amount of credit provided to you or on your behalf.	The amount you will have paid after you have made all payments as scheduled.	The total cost of your purchase on credit including your down-payment of $
3.940 %	$134,516.19	$199,694.92	$334,211.11	$N/A

INTEREST RATE AND PAYMENT SUMMARY

	Rate & Monthly Payment
Interest Rate	3.250%
Principal + Interest Payment	$ 894.92
☒ Est. Taxes + Insurance (Escrow) ☒ Includes Mortgage Insurance	$ 445.23
Total Est. Monthly Payment	$ 1,340.15

There is no guarantee that you will be able to refinance to lower your rate and payments.

☐ **DEMAND FEATURE:** This obligation has a demand feature.
☐ **VARIABLE RATE FEATURE:** Your loan contains a variable rate feature. Disclosures about the variable rate feature have been provided to you earlier.

FEDERAL TRUTH-IN-LENDING DISCLOSURE STATEMENT
MODEL FORM H-4(E)
TILFL.DSC 09/26/12   Page 1 of 2

PROPERTY INSURANCE: You may obtain fire and other hazard insurance from anyone you want that is acceptable to the Creditor.

SECURITY: You are giving a security interest in: 8624 OAKLAWN AVENUE, MODESTO, CALIFORNIA 95355

☐ The goods or property being purchased   ☒ Real property you already own.

FILING FEES: $ 110.00

LATE CHARGE: If payment is more than ___15___ days late, you will be charged ___4.000___ % of the payment.

PREPAYMENT: If you pay off early, you

☐ may   ☒ will not   have to pay a penalty.

☒ may   ☐ will not   be entitled to a refund of part of the finance charge.

ASSUMPTION: Someone buying your property

☐ may   ☒ may, subject to conditions   ☐ may not   assume the remainder of your loan on the original terms.

See your contract documents for any additional information about nonpayment, default, any required repayment in full before the scheduled date and prepayment refunds and penalties.

☐ "e" means an estimate   ☐ all dates and numerical disclosures except the late payment disclosures are estimates.

Each of the undersigned acknowledge receipt of a complete copy of this disclosure. The disclosure does not constitute a contract or a commitment to lend.

Applicant   RICHARD WILLIAM ROGERS _____   Date _____

Applicant _____   Date _____

Applicant _____   Date _____

Applicant _____   Date _____

Applicant _____   Date _____

Applicant _____   Date _____

FEDERAL TRUTH-IN-LENDING DISCLOSURE STATEMENT
MODEL FORM H-4(E)
TILFL.DSC 09/26/12   Page 2 of 2

MIN: 123456789123454564 **NOTE** Loan Number: 1234567890

FHA CASE NO.

000-5555555-000

MARCH 13, 20XX   LOS ANGELES   CALIFORNIA
[Date]   [City]   [State]

8624 OAKLAWN AVENUE, MODESTO, CALIFORNIA 95355
[Property Address]

1. PARTIES

"Borrower" means each person signing at the end of this Note, and the person's successors and assigns. "Lender" means TRISTAR FINANCE GROUP, INC., CALIFORNIA CORPORATION   and its successors and assigns.

2. BORROWER'S PROMISE TO PAY; INTEREST

In return for a loan received from Lender, Borrower promises to pay the principal sum of TWO HUNDRED FIVE THOUSAND SIX HUNDRED THIRTY-ONE AND 00/100 Dollars (U.S.$ 205,631.00   ), plus interest, to the order of Lender. Interest will be charged on unpaid principal, from the date of disbursement of the loan proceeds by Lender, at the rate of THREE AND 250/1000   percent (3.250 %) per year until the full amount of principal has been paid.

3. PROMISE TO PAY SECURED

Borrower's promise to pay is secured by a mortgage, deed of trust or similar security instrument that is dated the same date as this Note and called the "Security Instrument." The Security Instrument protects the Lender from losses which might result if Borrower defaults under this Note.

4. MANNER OF PAYMENT

(A) Time

Borrower shall make a payment of principal and interest to Lender on the first day of each month beginning on MAY 1, 20XX   . Any principal and interest remaining on the first day of APRIL, 2043   , will be due on that date, which is called the "Maturity Date."

(B) Place

Payment shall be made at 5555 MODESTO POINTE COURT, SUITE 301, Modesto, CALIFORNIA 92879   or at such other place as Lender may designate in writing by notice to Borrower.

(C) Amount

Each monthly payment of principal and interest will be in the amount of U.S. $ 894.92   .
This amount will be part of a larger monthly payment required by the Security Instrument, that shall be applied to principal, interest and other items in the order described in the Security Instrument.

(D) Allonge to this Note for Payment Adjustments

If an allonge providing for payment adjustments is executed by Borrower together with this Note, the covenants of the allonge shall be incorporated into and shall amend and supplement the covenants of this Note as if the allonge were a part of this Note. (Check applicable box.)

☐ Growing Equity Allonge   ☐ Graduated Payment Allonge
☐ Other [specify]

CALIFORNIA - FHA FIXED RATE NOTE
CAFHA.NTE 03/01/10   Page 1 of 4

5. BORROWER'S RIGHT TO PREPAY

Borrower has the right to pay the debt evidenced by this Note, in whole or in part, without charge or penalty, on the first day of any month. Lender shall accept prepayment on other days provided that Borrower pays interest on the amount prepaid for the remainder of the month to the extent required by Lender and permitted by regulations of the Secretary. If Borrower makes a partial prepayment, there will be no changes in the due date or in the amount of the monthly payment unless Lender agrees in writing to those changes.

6. BORROWER'S FAILURE TO PAY

(A) Late Charge for Overdue Payments

If Lender has not received the full monthly payment required by the Security Instrument, as described in Paragraph 4(C) of this Note, by the end of fifteen calendar days after the payment is due, Lender may collect a late charge in the amount of FOUR AND 000/1000   percent (4.000 %) of the overdue amount of each payment.

(B) Default

If Borrower defaults by failing to pay in full any monthly payment, then Lender may, except as limited by regulations of the Secretary in the case of payment defaults, require immediate payment in full of the principal balance remaining due and all accrued interest. Lender may choose not to exercise this option without waiving its rights in the event of any subsequent default. In many circumstances regulations issued by the Secretary will limit Lender's rights to require immediate payment in full in the case of payment defaults. This Note does not authorize acceleration when not permitted by HUD regulations. As used in this Note, "Secretary" means the Secretary of Housing and Urban Development or his or her designee.

(C) Payment of Costs and Expenses

If Lender has required immediate payment in full, as described above, Lender may require Borrower to pay costs and expenses including reasonable and customary attorneys' fees for enforcing this Note to the extent not prohibited by applicable law. Such fees and costs shall bear interest from the date of disbursement at the same rate as the principal of this Note.

7. GROUNDS FOR ACCELERATION OF DEBT

(A) Default

Lender may, except as limited by regulations issued by the Secretary in the case of payment defaults, require immediate payment in full of all sums secured by the Security Instrument and due under this Note if:

(i)   Borrower defaults by failing to pay in full any monthly payment required by this Note and the Security Instrument prior to or on the due date of the next monthly payment, or

(ii) Borrower defaults by failing, for a period of thirty days, to perform any other obligations contained in the Security Instrument securing this Note.

(B) Sale Without Credit Approval

Lender shall, if permitted by applicable law (including section 341 (d) of the Garn-St. Germain Depository Institutions Act of 1982, 12 U.S.C. 1701j - 3(d)) and with the prior approval of the Secretary, require immediate payment in full of all the sums due under this Note and secured by the Security Instrument if:

(i)   All or part of the Property, or a beneficial interest in a trust owning all or part of the Property, is sold or otherwise transferred (other than by devise or descent), and

(ii) The Property is not occupied by the purchaser or grantee as his or her principal residence, or the purchaser or grantee does so occupy the Property, but his or her credit has not been approved in accordance with the requirements of the Secretary.

(C) No Waiver

If circumstances occur that would permit Lender to require immediate payment in full, but Lender does not require such payments, Lender does not waive its rights with respect to subsequent events.

(D) Regulations of HUD Secretary

In many circumstances regulations issued by the Secretary will limit Lender's rights, in the case of payment defaults, to require immediate payment in full and foreclose if not paid. This Note and the Security Instrument do not authorize acceleration or foreclosure if not permitted by regulations of the Secretary.

(E)   Mortgage Not Insured

Borrower agrees that if the Security Instrument and this Note are not determined to be eligible for insurance under the National Housing Act within 60 DAYS   from the date hereof, Lender may, at its option require immediate payment in full of all sums secured by the Security Instrument. A written statement of any authorized agent of the Secretary dated subsequent to 60 DAYS from the date hereof, declining to insure the Security Instrument and this Note, shall be deemed conclusive proof of such ineligibility.   Notwithstanding the foregoing, this option may not be exercised by Lender when the unavailability of insurance is solely due to Lender's failure to remit a mortgage insurance premium to the Secretary.

8.   WAIVERS

Borrower and any other person who has obligations under this Note waive the rights of presentment and notice of dishonor.   "Presentment" means the right to require Lender to demand payment of amounts due.   "Notice of dishonor" means the right to require Lender to give notice to other persons that amounts due have not been paid.

9.   GIVING OF NOTICES

Unless applicable law requires a different method, any notice that must be given to Borrower under this Note will be given by delivering it or by mailing it by first class mail to Borrower at the property address above or at a different address if Borrower has given Lender a notice of Borrower's different address.

Any notice that must be given to Lender under this Note will be given by first class mail to Lender at the address stated in Paragraph 4(B) or at a different address if Borrower is given a notice of that different address.

10. OBLIGATIONS OF PERSONS UNDER THIS NOTE

If more than one person signs this Note, each person is fully and personally obligated to keep all of the promises made in this Note, including the promise to pay the full amount owed.   Any person who is a guarantor, surety or endorser of this Note is also obligated to do these things.   Any person who takes over these obligations, including the obligations of a guarantor, surety or endorser of this Note, is also obligated to keep all of the promises made in this Note.   Lender may enforce its rights under this Note against each person individually or against all signatories together.   Any one person signing this Note may be required to pay all of the amounts owed under this Note.

CALIFORNIA - FHA FIXED RATE NOTE
CAFHA.NTE 03/01/10   Page 3 of 4

BY SIGNING BELOW, Borrower accepts and agrees to the terms and covenants contained in pages 1 through 4 of this Note.

_____ (Seal)
RICHARD WILLIAM ROGERS   -Borrower

_____ (Seal)
                             -Borrower

The word seal
means signature,
no Notary seal
used here

_____ (Seal)
                             -rrower

_____ (Seal)
                             -Borrower

_____ (Seal)
                             -Borrower

_____ (Seal)
                             -Borrower

[Sign Original Only]

CALIFORNIA - FHA FIXED RATE NOTE
CAFHA.NTE 03/01/10   Page 4 of 4

Recording Requested By:
TRISTAR FINANCE GROUP

And After Recording Return To:
TRISTAR FINANCE GROUP
1000 MAIN STREET
LOS ANGELES, CALIFORNIA 90025
Loan Number: 1234567890

—— [Space Above This Line For Recording Data] ——

DEED OF TRUST

MIN: 1234567890-123456778

DEFINITIONS

Words used in multiple sections of this document are defined below and other words are defined in Sections 3, 11, 13, 18, 20 and 21. Certain rules regarding the usage of words used in this document are also provided in Section 16.

(A) "**Security Instrument**" means this document, which is dated   MARCH 13, 20XX   , together with all Riders to this document.
(B) "**Borrower**" is   RICHARD WILLIAM ROGERS, AN UNMARRIED MAN

Borrower is the trustor under this Security Instrument.
(C) "**Lender**" is TRISTAR FINANCE GROUP

Lender is a   CALIFORNIA CORPORATION   organized
and existing under the laws of   CALIFORNIA
Lender's address is   1000 MAIN STREET, LOS ANGELES, CALIFORNIA 91301

(D) "**Trustee**" is   STALLWART TITLE OF MODESTO
5555 CASANDRA BLVD. SUITE 2, MODESTO, CALIFORNIA 95822

(E) "**MERS**" is Mortgage Electronic Registration Systems, Inc. MERS is a separate corporation that is acting solely as a nominee for Lender and Lender's successors and assigns. **MERS is the beneficiary under this Security Instrument.** MERS is organized and existing under the laws of Delaware, and has an address and telephone number of P.O. Box 2026, Flint, MI 48501-2026, tel. (888) 679-MERS.
(F) "**Note**" means the promissory note signed by Borrower and dated   MAY 1, 20XX   .
The Note states that Borrower owes Lender TWO HUNDRED FIVE THOUSAND, SIX HUNDRED THIRTY ONE AND 00/100   Dollars (U.S. $205, 631.00) plus interest.

Borrower: ____

CALIFORNIA--Single Family--Fannie Mae/Freddie Mac UNIFORM INSTRUMENT - MERS
Form 3005 01/01   Page 1 of 14

Borrower has promised to pay this debt in regular Periodic Payments and to pay the debt in full not later than APRIL 1, 2043 .

(G) "**Property**" means the property that is described below under the heading "Transfer of Rights in the Property."

(H) "**Loan**" means the debt evidenced by the Note, plus interest, any prepayment charges and late charges due under the Note, and all sums due under this Security Instrument, plus interest.

(I) "**Riders**" means all Riders to this Security Instrument that are executed by Borrower. The following Riders are to be executed by Borrower [check box as applicable]:

☐ Adjustable Rate Rider	☐ Planned Unit Development Rider
☐ Balloon Rider	☐ Biweekly Payment Rider
☐ 1-4 Family Rider	☐ Second Home Rider
☒ Condominium Rider	☐ Other(s) [specify]

If any boxes are checked, make sure the riders are in the package

(J) "**Applicable Law**" means all controlling applicable federal, state and local statutes, regulations, ordinances and administrative rules and orders (that have the effect of law) as well as all applicable final, non-appealable judicial opinions.

(K) "**Community Association Dues, Fees, and Assessments**" means all dues, fees, assessments and other charges that are imposed on Borrower or the Property by a condominium association, homeowners association or similar organization.

(L) "**Electronic Funds Transfer**" means any transfer of funds, other than a transaction originated by check, draft, or similar paper instrument, which is initiated through an electronic terminal, telephonic instrument, computer, or magnetic tape so as to order, instruct, or authorize a financial institution to debit or credit an account. Such term includes, but is not limited to, point-of-sale transfers, automated teller machine transactions, transfers initiated by telephone, wire transfers, and automated clearinghouse transfers.

(M) "**Escrow Items**" means those items that are described in Section 3.

(N) "**Miscellaneous Proceeds**" means any compensation, settlement, award of damages, or proceeds paid by any third party (other than insurance proceeds paid under the coverages described in Section 5) for: (i) damage to, or destruction of, the Property; (ii) condemnation or other taking of all or any part of the Property; (iii) conveyance in lieu of condemnation; or (iv) misrepresentations of, or omissions as to, the value and/or condition of the Property.

(O) "**Mortgage Insurance**" means insurance protecting Lender against the nonpayment of, or default on, the Loan.

(P) "**Periodic Payment**" means the regularly scheduled amount due for (i) principal and interest under the Note, plus (ii) any amounts under Section 3 of this Security Instrument.

(Q) "**RESPA**" means the Real Estate Settlement Procedures Act (12 U.S.C. §2601 et seq.) and its implementing regulation, Regulation X (24 C.F.R. Part 3500), as they might be amended from time to time, or any additional or successor legislation or regulation that governs the same subject matter. As used in this Security Instrument, "RESPA" refers to all requirements and restrictions that are imposed in regard to a "federally related mortgage loan" even if the Loan does not qualify as a "federally related mortgage loan" under RESPA.

(R) "**Successor in Interest of Borrower**" means any party that has taken title to the Property, whether or not that party has assumed Borrower's obligations under the Note and/or this Security Instrument.

TRANSFER OF RIGHTS IN THE PROPERTY

The beneficiary of this Security Instrument is MERS (solely as nominee for Lender and Lender's successors and assigns) and the successors and assigns of MERS. This Security Instrument secures to Lender: (i) the repayment of the Loan, and all renewals, extensions and modifications of the Note; and (ii) the performance of Borrower's

```
Borrower: ____
```

CALIFORNIA--Single Family--Fannie Mae/Freddie Mac UNIFORM INSTRUMENT - MERS
Form 3005 01/01   Page 2 of 14

covenants and agreements under this Security Instrument and the Note. For this purpose, Borrower irrevocably grants and conveys to Trustee, in trust, with power of sale, the following described property located in the
COUNTY of STANISLAUS :
[Type of Recording Jurisdiction]   [Name of Recording Jurisdiction]

LOT 10, BLOCK 55555 OF VILLAGE HIGHLANDS PHASE III, AS PER MAP FILED DECEMBER 9, 19XX IN VOLUME 02 OF MAPS, PAGE 55 STANISLAUS COUTY RECORDS.

A.P.N.: 0088-002-155
which currently has the address of   8624 OAKLAWN AVENUE
                                  [Street]

may be filled in or may refer to exhibit 'A', a separate document

MODESTO   , California   95355   ("Property A...
[City]   [Zip Code]

TOGETHER WITH all the improvements now or hereafter erected on the property, and all easements, appurtenances, and fixtures now or hereafter a part of the property. All replacements and additions shall also be covered by this Security Instrument. All of the foregoing is referred to in this Security Instrument as the "Property." Borrower understands and agrees that MERS holds only legal title to the interests granted by Borrower in this Security Instrument, but, if necessary to comply with law or custom, MERS (as nominee for Lender and Lender's successors and assigns) has the right: to exercise any or all of those interests, including, but not limited to, the right to foreclose and sell the Property; and to take any action required of Lender including, but not limited to, releasing and canceling this Security Instrument.

BORROWER COVENANTS that Borrower is lawfully seised of the estate hereby conveyed and has the right to grant and convey the Property and that the Property is unencumbered, except for encumbrances of record. Borrower warrants and will defend generally the title to the Property against all claims and demands, subject to any encumbrances of record.

THIS SECURITY INSTRUMENT combines uniform covenants for national use and non-uniform covenants with limited variations by jurisdiction to constitute a uniform security instrument covering real property.

UNIFORM COVENANTS. Borrower and Lender covenant and agree as follows:

1. **Payment of Principal, Interest, Escrow Items, Prepayment Charges, and Late Charges.** Borrower shall pay when due the principal of, and interest on, the debt evidenced by the Note and any prepayment charges and late charges due under the Note. Borrower shall also pay funds for Escrow Items pursuant to Section 3. Payments due under the Note and this Security Instrument shall be made in U.S. currency. However, if any check or other instrument received by Lender as payment under the Note or this Security Instrument is returned to Lender unpaid, Lender may require that any or all subsequent payments due under the Note and this Security Instrument be made in one or more of the following forms, as selected by Lender: (a) cash; (b) money order; (c) certified check, bank check, treasurer's check or cashier's check, provided any such check is drawn upon an institution whose deposits are insured by a federal agency, instrumentality, or entity; or (d) Electronic Funds Transfer.

Payments are deemed received by Lender when received at the location designated in the Note or at such other location as may be designated by Lender in accordance with the notice provisions in Section 15. Lender may return any payment or partial payment if the payment or partial payments are insufficient to bring the Loan current. Lender may accept any payment or partial payment insufficient to bring the Loan current, without waiver of any rights hereunder or prejudice to its rights to refuse such payment or partial payments in the future, but Lender is not

Borrower: ____

CALIFORNIA--Single Family--Fannie Mae/Freddie Mac UNIFORM INSTRUMENT - MERS
Form 3005 01/01   Page 3 of 14

obligated to apply such payments at the time such payments are accepted. If each Periodic Payment is applied as of its scheduled due date, then Lender need not pay interest on unapplied funds. Lender may hold such unapplied funds until Borrower makes payment to bring the Loan current. If Borrower does not do so within a reasonable period of time, Lender shall either apply such funds or return them to Borrower. If not applied earlier, such funds will be applied to the outstanding principal balance under the Note immediately prior to foreclosure. No offset or claim which Borrower might have now or in the future against Lender shall relieve Borrower from making payments due under the Note and this Security Instrument or performing the covenants and agreements secured by this Security Instrument.

2. Application of Payments or Proceeds. Except as otherwise described in this Section 2, all payments accepted and applied by Lender shall be applied in the following order of priority: (a) interest due under the Note; (b) principal due under the Note; (c) amounts due under Section 3. Such payments shall be applied to each Periodic Payment in the order in which it became due. Any remaining amounts shall be applied first to late charges, second to any other amounts due under this Security Instrument, and then to reduce the principal balance of the Note.

If Lender receives a payment from Borrower for a delinquent Periodic Payment which includes a sufficient amount to pay any late charge due, the payment may be applied to the delinquent payment and the late charge. If more than one Periodic Payment is outstanding, Lender may apply any payment received from Borrower to the repayment of the Periodic Payments if, and to the extent that, each payment can be paid in full. To the extent that any excess exists after the payment is applied to the full payment of one or more Periodic Payments, such excess may be applied to any late charges due. Voluntary prepayments shall be applied first to any prepayment charges and then as described in the Note.

Any application of payments, insurance proceeds, or Miscellaneous Proceeds to principal due under the Note shall not extend or postpone the due date, or change the amount, of the Periodic Payments.

3. Funds for Escrow Items. Borrower shall pay to Lender on the day Periodic Payments are due under the Note, until the Note is paid in full, a sum (the "Funds") to provide for payment of amounts due for: (a) taxes and assessments and other items which can attain priority over this Security Instrument as a lien or encumbrance on the Property; (b) leasehold payments or ground rents on the Property, if any; (c) premiums for any and all insurance required by Lender under Section 5; and (d) Mortgage Insurance premiums, if any, or any sums payable by Borrower to Lender in lieu of the payment of Mortgage Insurance premiums in accordance with the provisions of Section 10. These items are called "Escrow Items." At origination or at any time during the term of the Loan, Lender may require that Community Association Dues, Fees, and Assessments, if any, be escrowed by Borrower, and such dues, fees and assessments shall be an Escrow Item. Borrower shall promptly furnish to Lender all notices of amounts to be paid under this Section. Borrower shall pay Lender the Funds for Escrow Items unless Lender waives Borrower's obligation to pay the Funds for any or all Escrow Items. Lender may waive Borrower's obligation to pay to Lender Funds for any or all Escrow Items at any time. Any such waiver may only be in writing. In the event of such waiver, Borrower shall pay directly, when and where payable, the amounts due for any Escrow Items for which payment of Funds has been waived by Lender and, if Lender requires, shall furnish to Lender receipts evidencing such payment within such time period as Lender may require. Borrower's obligation to make such payments and to provide receipts shall for all purposes be deemed to be a covenant and agreement contained in this Security Instrument, as the phrase "covenant and agreement" is used in Section 9. If Borrower is obligated to pay Escrow Items directly, pursuant to a waiver, and Borrower fails to pay the amount due for an Escrow Item, Lender may exercise its rights under Section 9 and pay such amount and Borrower shall then be obligated under Section 9 to repay to Lender any such amount. Lender may revoke the waiver as to any or all Escrow Items at any time by a notice given in accordance with Section 15 and, upon such revocation, Borrower shall pay to Lender all Funds, and in such amounts, that are then required under this Section 3.

Lender may, at any time, collect and hold Funds in an amount (a) sufficient to permit Lender to apply the Funds at the time specified under RESPA, and (b) not to exceed the maximum amount a lender can require under RESPA. Lender shall estimate the amount of Funds due on the basis of current data and reasonable estimates of expenditures of future Escrow Items or otherwise in accordance with Applicable Law.

The Funds shall be held in an institution whose deposits are insured by a federal agency, instrumentality, or entity (including Lender, if Lender is an institution whose deposits are so insured) or in any Federal Home Loan Bank. Lender shall apply the Funds to pay the Escrow Items no later than the time specified under RESPA. Lender

Borrower: _____

CALIFORNIA--Single Family--Fannie Mae/Freddie Mac UNIFORM INSTRUMENT - MERS
Form 3005 01/01   Page 4 of 14

shall not charge Borrower for holding and applying the Funds, annually analyzing the escrow account, or verifying the Escrow Items, unless Lender pays Borrower interest on the Funds and Applicable Law permits Lender to make such a charge. Unless an agreement is made in writing or Applicable Law requires interest to be paid on the Funds, Lender shall not be required to pay Borrower any interest or earnings on the Funds. Borrower and Lender can agree in writing, however, that interest shall be paid on the Funds. Lender shall give to Borrower, without charge, an annual accounting of the Funds as required by RESPA.

If there is a surplus of Funds held in escrow, as defined under RESPA, Lender shall account to Borrower for the excess funds in accordance with RESPA. If there is a shortage of Funds held in escrow, as defined under RESPA, Lender shall notify Borrower as required by RESPA, and Borrower shall pay to Lender the amount necessary to make up the shortage in accordance with RESPA, but in no more than 12 monthly payments. If there is a deficiency of Funds held in escrow, as defined under RESPA, Lender shall notify Borrower as required by RESPA, and Borrower shall pay to Lender the amount necessary to make up the deficiency in accordance with RESPA, but in no more than 12 monthly payments.

Upon payment in full of all sums secured by this Security Instrument, Lender shall promptly refund to Borrower any Funds held by Lender.

4. Charges; Liens. Borrower shall pay all taxes, assessments, charges, fines, and impositions attributable to the Property which can attain priority over this Security Instrument, leasehold payments or ground rents on the Property, if any, and Community Association Dues, Fees, and Assessments, if any. To the extent that these items are Escrow Items, Borrower shall pay them in the manner provided in Section 3.

Borrower shall promptly discharge any lien which has priority over this Security Instrument unless Borrower: (a) agrees in writing to the payment of the obligation secured by the lien in a manner acceptable to Lender, but only so long as Borrower is performing such agreement; (b) contests the lien in good faith by, or defends against enforcement of the lien in, legal proceedings which in Lender's opinion operate to prevent the enforcement of the lien while those proceedings are pending, but only until such proceedings are concluded; or (c) secures from the holder of the lien an agreement satisfactory to Lender subordinating the lien to this Security Instrument. If Lender determines that any part of the Property is subject to a lien which can attain priority over this Security Instrument, Lender may give Borrower a notice identifying the lien. Within 10 days of the date on which that notice is given, Borrower shall satisfy the lien or take one or more of the actions set forth above in this Section 4.

Lender may require Borrower to pay a one-time charge for a real estate tax verification and/or reporting service used by Lender in connection with this Loan.

5. Property Insurance. Borrower shall keep the improvements now existing or hereafter erected on the Property insured against loss by fire, hazards included within the term "extended coverage," and any other hazards including, but not limited to, earthquakes and floods, for which Lender requires insurance. This insurance shall be maintained in the amounts (including deductible levels) and for the periods that Lender requires. What Lender requires pursuant to the preceding sentences can change during the term of the Loan. The insurance carrier providing the insurance shall be chosen by Borrower subject to Lender's right to disapprove Borrower's choice, which right shall not be exercised unreasonably. Lender may require Borrower to pay, in connection with this Loan, either: (a) a one-time charge for flood zone determination, certification and tracking services; or (b) a one-time charge for flood zone determination and certification services and subsequent charges each time remappings or similar changes occur which reasonably might affect such determination or certification. Borrower shall also be responsible for the payment of any fees imposed by the Federal Emergency Management Agency in connection with the review of any flood zone determination resulting from an objection by Borrower.

If Borrower fails to maintain any of the coverages described above, Lender may obtain insurance coverage, at Lender's option and Borrower's expense. Lender is under no obligation to purchase any particular type or amount of coverage. Therefore, such coverage shall cover Lender, but might or might not protect Borrower, Borrower's equity in the Property, or the contents of the Property, against any risk, hazard or liability and might provide greater or lesser coverage than was previously in effect. Borrower acknowledges that the cost of the insurance coverage so obtained might significantly exceed the cost of insurance that Borrower could have obtained. Any amounts disbursed by Lender under this Section 5 shall become additional debt of Borrower secured by this Security Instrument. These amounts shall bear interest at the Note rate from the date of disbursement and shall be payable, with such interest, upon notice from Lender to Borrower requesting payment.

Borrower: _____

CALIFORNIA--Single Family--Fannie Mae/Freddie Mac UNIFORM INSTRUMENT - MERS
Form 3005 01/01   Page 5 of 14

All insurance policies required by Lender and renewals of such policies shall be subject to Lender's right to disapprove such policies, shall include a standard mortgage clause, and shall name Lender as mortgagee and/or as an additional loss payee and Borrower further agrees to generally assign rights to insurance proceeds to the holder of the Note up to the amount of the outstanding loan balance. Lender shall have the right to hold the policies and renewal certificates. If Lender requires, Borrower shall promptly give to Lender all receipts of paid premiums and renewal notices. If Borrower obtains any form of insurance coverage, not otherwise required by Lender, for damage to, or destruction of, the Property, such policy shall include a standard mortgage clause and shall name Lender as mortgagee and/or as an additional loss payee and Borrower further agrees to generally assign rights to insurance proceeds to the holder of the Note up to the amount of the outstanding loan balance.

In the event of loss, Borrower shall give prompt notice to the insurance carrier and Lender. Lender may make proof of loss if not made promptly by Borrower. Unless Lender and Borrower otherwise agree in writing, any insurance proceeds, whether or not the underlying insurance was required by Lender, shall be applied to restoration or repair of the Property, if the restoration or repair is economically feasible and Lender's security is not lessened. During such repair and restoration period, Lender shall have the right to hold such insurance proceeds until Lender has had an opportunity to inspect such Property to ensure the work has been completed to Lender's satisfaction, provided that such inspection shall be undertaken promptly. Lender may disburse proceeds for the repairs and restoration in a single payment or in a series of progress payments as the work is completed. Unless an agreement is made in writing or Applicable Law requires interest to be paid on such insurance proceeds, Lender shall not be required to pay Borrower any interest or earnings on such proceeds. Fees for public adjusters, or other third parties, retained by Borrower shall not be paid out of the insurance proceeds and shall be the sole obligation of Borrower. If the restoration or repair is not economically feasible or Lender's security would be lessened, the insurance proceeds shall be applied to the sums secured by this Security Instrument, whether or not then due, with the excess, if any, paid to Borrower. Such insurance proceeds shall be applied in the order provided for in Section 2.

If Borrower abandons the Property, Lender may file, negotiate and settle any available insurance claim and related matters. If Borrower does not respond within 30 days to a notice from Lender that the insurance carrier has offered to settle a claim, then Lender may negotiate and settle the claim. The 30-day period will begin when the notice is given. In either event, or if Lender acquires the Property under Section 22 or otherwise, Borrower hereby assigns to Lender (a) Borrower's rights to any insurance proceeds in an amount not to exceed the amounts unpaid under the Note or this Security Instrument, and (b) any other of Borrower's rights (other than the right to any refund of unearned premiums paid by Borrower) under all insurance policies covering the Property, insofar as such rights are applicable to the coverage of the Property. Lender may use the insurance proceeds either to repair or restore the Property or to pay amounts unpaid under the Note or this Security Instrument, whether or not then due.

6. Occupancy. Borrower shall occupy, establish, and use the Property as Borrower's principal residence within 60 days after the execution of this Security Instrument and shall continue to occupy the Property as Borrower's principal residence for at least one year after the date of occupancy, unless Lender otherwise agrees in writing, which consent shall not be unreasonably withheld, or unless extenuating circumstances exist which are beyond Borrower's control.

7. Preservation, Maintenance and Protection of the Property; Inspections. Borrower shall not destroy, damage or impair the Property, allow the Property to deteriorate or commit waste on the Property. Whether or not Borrower is residing in the Property, Borrower shall maintain the Property in order to prevent the Property from deteriorating or decreasing in value due to its condition. Unless it is determined pursuant to Section 5 that repair or restoration is not economically feasible, Borrower shall promptly repair the Property if damaged to avoid further deterioration or damage. If insurance or condemnation proceeds are paid in connection with damage to, or the taking of, the Property, Borrower shall be responsible for repairing or restoring the Property only if Lender has released proceeds for such purposes. Lender may disburse proceeds for the repairs and restoration in a single payment or in a series of progress payments as the work is completed. If the insurance or condemnation proceeds are not sufficient to repair or restore the Property, Borrower is not relieved of Borrower's obligation for the completion of such repair or restoration.

Lender or its agent may make reasonable entries upon and inspections of the Property. If it has reasonable cause, Lender may inspect the interior of the improvements on the Property. Lender shall give Borrower notice at the time of or prior to such an interior inspection specifying such reasonable cause.

Borrower: _____

CALIFORNIA--Single Family--Fannie Mae/Freddie Mac UNIFORM INSTRUMENT - MERS
Form 3005 01/01   Page 6 of 14

8. Borrower's Loan Application. Borrower shall be in default if, during the Loan application process, Borrower or any persons or entities acting at the direction of Borrower or with Borrower's knowledge or consent gave materially false, misleading, or inaccurate information or statements to Lender (or failed to provide Lender with material information) in connection with the Loan. Material representations include, but are not limited to, representations concerning Borrower's occupancy of the Property as Borrower's principal residence.

9. Protection of Lender's Interest in the Property and Rights Under this Security Instrument. If (a) Borrower fails to perform the covenants and agreements contained in this Security Instrument, (b) there is a legal proceeding that might significantly affect Lender's interest in the Property and/or rights under this Security Instrument (such as a proceeding in bankruptcy, probate, for condemnation or forfeiture, for enforcement of a lien which may attain priority over this Security Instrument or to enforce laws or regulations), or (c) Borrower has abandoned the Property, then Lender may do and pay for whatever is reasonable or appropriate to protect Lender's interest in the Property and rights under this Security Instrument, including protecting and/or assessing the value of the Property, and securing and/or repairing the Property. Lender's actions can include, but are not limited to: (a) paying any sums secured by a lien which has priority over this Security Instrument; (b) appearing in court; and (c) paying reasonable attorneys' fees to protect its interest in the Property and/or rights under this Security Instrument, including its secured position in a bankruptcy proceeding. Securing the Property includes, but is not limited to, entering the Property to make repairs, change locks, replace or board up doors and windows, drain water from pipes, eliminate building or other code violations or dangerous conditions, and have utilities turned on or off. Although Lender may take action under this Section 9, Lender does not have to do so and is not under any duty or obligation to do so. It is agreed that Lender incurs no liability for not taking any or all actions authorized under this Section 9.

Any amounts disbursed by Lender under this Section 9 shall become additional debt of Borrower secured by this Security Instrument. These amounts shall bear interest at the Note rate from the date of disbursement and shall be payable, with such interest, upon notice from Lender to Borrower requesting payment.

If this Security Instrument is on a leasehold, Borrower shall comply with all the provisions of the lease. Borrower shall not surrender the leasehold estate and interests herein conveyed or terminate or cancel the ground lease. Borrower shall not, without the express written consent of Lender, alter or amend the ground lease. If Borrower acquires fee title to the Property, the leasehold and the fee title shall not merge unless Lender agrees to the merger in writing.

10. Mortgage Insurance. If Lender required Mortgage Insurance as a condition of making the Loan, Borrower shall pay the premiums required to maintain the Mortgage Insurance in effect. If, for any reason, the Mortgage Insurance coverage required by Lender ceases to be available from the mortgage insurer that previously provided such insurance and Borrower was required to make separately designated payments toward the premiums for Mortgage Insurance, Borrower shall pay the premiums required to obtain coverage substantially equivalent to the Mortgage Insurance previously in effect, at a cost substantially equivalent to the cost to Borrower of the Mortgage Insurance previously in effect, from an alternate mortgage insurer selected by Lender. If substantially equivalent Mortgage Insurance coverage is not available, Borrower shall continue to pay to Lender the amount of the separately designated payments that were due when the insurance coverage ceased to be in effect. Lender will accept, use and retain these payments as a non-refundable loss reserve in lieu of Mortgage Insurance. Such loss reserve shall be non-refundable, notwithstanding the fact that the Loan is ultimately paid in full, and Lender shall not be required to pay Borrower any interest or earnings on such loss reserve. Lender can no longer require loss reserve payments if Mortgage Insurance coverage (in the amount and for the period that Lender requires) provided by an insurer selected by Lender again becomes available, is obtained, and Lender requires separately designated payments toward the premiums for Mortgage Insurance. If Lender required Mortgage Insurance as a condition of making the Loan and Borrower was required to make separately designated payments toward the premiums for Mortgage Insurance, Borrower shall pay the premiums required to maintain Mortgage Insurance in effect, or to provide a non-refundable loss reserve, until Lender's requirement for Mortgage Insurance ends in accordance with any written agreement between Borrower and Lender providing for such termination or until termination is required by Applicable Law. Nothing in this Section 10 affects Borrower's obligation to pay interest at the rate provided in the Note.

Mortgage Insurance reimburses Lender (or any entity that purchases the Note) for certain losses it may incur if Borrower does not repay the Loan as agreed. Borrower is not a party to the Mortgage Insurance.

    Borrower: ____

CALIFORNIA--Single Family--Fannie Mae/Freddie Mac UNIFORM INSTRUMENT - MERS
Form 3005 01/01   Page 7 of 14

Mortgage insurers evaluate their total risk on all such insurance in force from time to time, and may enter into agreements with other parties that share or modify their risk, or reduce losses. These agreements are on terms and conditions that are satisfactory to the mortgage insurer and the other party (or parties) to these agreements. These agreements may require the mortgage insurer to make payments using any source of funds that the mortgage insurer may have available (which may include funds obtained from Mortgage Insurance premiums).

As a result of these agreements, Lender, any purchaser of the Note, another insurer, any reinsurer, any other entity, or any affiliate of any of the foregoing, may receive (directly or indirectly) amounts that derive from (or might be characterized as) a portion of Borrower's payments for Mortgage Insurance, in exchange for sharing or modifying the mortgage insurer's risk, or reducing losses. If such agreement provides that an affiliate of Lender takes a share of the insurer's risk in exchange for a share of the premiums paid to the insurer, the arrangement is often termed "captive reinsurance." Further:

(a) Any such agreements will not affect the amounts that Borrower has agreed to pay for Mortgage Insurance, or any other terms of the Loan. Such agreements will not increase the amount Borrower will owe for Mortgage Insurance, and they will not entitle Borrower to any refund.

(b) Any such agreements will not affect the rights Borrower has - if any - with respect to the Mortgage Insurance under the Homeowners Protection Act of 1998 or any other law. These rights may include the right to receive certain disclosures, to request and obtain cancellation of the Mortgage Insurance, to have the Mortgage Insurance terminated automatically, and/or to receive a refund of any Mortgage Insurance premiums that were unearned at the time of such cancellation or termination.

11. Assignment of Miscellaneous Proceeds; Forfeiture. All Miscellaneous Proceeds are hereby assigned to and shall be paid to Lender.

If the Property is damaged, such Miscellaneous Proceeds shall be applied to restoration or repair of the Property, if the restoration or repair is economically feasible and Lender's security is not lessened. During such repair and restoration period, Lender shall have the right to hold such Miscellaneous Proceeds until Lender has had an opportunity to inspect such Property to ensure the work has been completed to Lender's satisfaction, provided that such inspection shall be undertaken promptly. Lender may pay for the repairs and restoration in a single disbursement or in a series of progress payments as the work is completed. Unless an agreement is made in writing or Applicable Law requires interest to be paid on such Miscellaneous Proceeds, Lender shall not be required to pay Borrower any interest or earnings on such Miscellaneous Proceeds. If the restoration or repair is not economically feasible or Lender's security would be lessened, the Miscellaneous Proceeds shall be applied to the sums secured by this Security Instrument, whether or not then due, with the excess, if any, paid to Borrower. Such Miscellaneous Proceeds shall be applied in the order provided for in Section 2.

In the event of a total taking, destruction, or loss in value of the Property, the Miscellaneous Proceeds shall be applied to the sums secured by this Security Instrument, whether or not then due, with the excess, if any, paid to Borrower.

In the event of a partial taking, destruction, or loss in value of the Property in which the fair market value of the Property immediately before the partial taking, destruction, or loss in value is equal to or greater than the amount of the sums secured by this Security Instrument immediately before the partial taking, destruction, or loss in value, unless Borrower and Lender otherwise agree in writing, the sums secured by this Security Instrument shall be reduced by the amount of the Miscellaneous Proceeds multiplied by the following fraction: (a) the total amount of the sums secured immediately before the partial taking, destruction, or loss in value divided by (b) the fair market value of the Property immediately before the partial taking, destruction, or loss in value. Any balance shall be paid to Borrower.

In the event of a partial taking, destruction, or loss in value of the Property in which the fair market value of the Property immediately before the partial taking, destruction, or loss in value is less than the amount of the sums secured immediately before the partial taking, destruction, or loss in value, unless Borrower and Lender otherwise agree in writing, the Miscellaneous Proceeds shall be applied to the sums secured by this Security Instrument whether or not the sums are then due.

If the Property is abandoned by Borrower, or if, after notice by Lender to Borrower that the Opposing Party (as defined in the next sentence) offers to make an award to settle a claim for damages, Borrower fails to respond to Lender within 30 days after the date the notice is given, Lender is authorized to collect and apply the Miscellaneous Proceeds either to restoration or repair of the Property or to the sums secured by this Security Instrument, whether

Borrower: _____

or not then due. "Opposing Party" means the third party that owes Borrower Miscellaneous Proceeds or the party against whom Borrower has a right of action in regard to Miscellaneous Proceeds.

Borrower shall be in default if any action or proceeding, whether civil or criminal, is begun that, in Lender's judgment, could result in forfeiture of the Property or other material impairment of Lender's interest in the Property or rights under this Security Instrument. Borrower can cure such a default and, if acceleration has occurred, reinstate as provided in Section 19, by causing the action or proceeding to be dismissed with a ruling that, in Lender's judgment, precludes forfeiture of the Property or other material impairment of Lender's interest in the Property or rights under this Security Instrument. The proceeds of any award or claim for damages that are attributable to the impairment of Lender's interest in the Property are hereby assigned and shall be paid to Lender.

All Miscellaneous Proceeds that are not applied to restoration or repair of the Property shall be applied in the order provided for in Section 2.

12. Borrower Not Released; Forbearance By Lender Not a Waiver. Extension of the time for payment or modification of amortization of the sums secured by this Security Instrument granted by Lender to Borrower or any Successor in Interest of Borrower shall not operate to release the liability of Borrower or any Successors in Interest of Borrower. Lender shall not be required to commence proceedings against any Successor in Interest of Borrower or to refuse to extend time for payment or otherwise modify amortization of the sums secured by this Security Instrument by reason of any demand made by the original Borrower or any Successors in Interest of Borrower. Any forbearance by Lender in exercising any right or remedy including, without limitation, Lender's acceptance of payments from third persons, entities or Successors in Interest of Borrower or in amounts less than the amount then due, shall not be a waiver of or preclude the exercise of any right or remedy.

13. Joint and Several Liability; Co-signers; Successors and Assigns Bound. Borrower covenants and agrees that Borrower's obligations and liability shall be joint and several. However, any Borrower who co-signs this Security Instrument but does not execute the Note (a "co-signer"): (a) is co-signing this Security Instrument only to mortgage, grant and convey the co-signer's interest in the Property under the terms of this Security Instrument; (b) is not personally obligated to pay the sums secured by this Security Instrument; and (c) agrees that Lender and any other Borrower can agree to extend, modify, forbear or make any accommodations with regard to the terms of this Security Instrument or the Note without the co-signer's consent.

Subject to the provisions of Section 18, any Successor in Interest of Borrower who assumes Borrower's obligations under this Security Instrument in writing, and is approved by Lender, shall obtain all of Borrower's rights and benefits under this Security Instrument. Borrower shall not be released from Borrower's obligations and liability under this Security Instrument unless Lender agrees to such release in writing. The covenants and agreements of this Security Instrument shall bind (except as provided in Section 20) and benefit the successors and assigns of Lender.

14. Loan Charges. Lender may charge Borrower fees for services performed in connection with Borrower's default, for the purpose of protecting Lender's interest in the Property and rights under this Security Instrument, including, but not limited to, attorneys' fees, property inspection and valuation fees. In regard to any other fees, the absence of express authority in this Security Instrument to charge a specific fee to Borrower shall not be construed as a prohibition on the charging of such fee. Lender may not charge fees that are expressly prohibited by this Security Instrument or by Applicable Law.

If the Loan is subject to a law which sets maximum loan charges, and that law is finally interpreted so that the interest or other loan charges collected or to be collected in connection with the Loan exceed the permitted limits, then: (a) any such loan charge shall be reduced by the amount necessary to reduce the charge to the permitted limit; and (b) any sums already collected from Borrower which exceeded permitted limits will be refunded to Borrower. Lender may choose to make this refund by reducing the principal owed under the Note or by making a direct payment to Borrower. If a refund reduces principal, the reduction will be treated as a partial prepayment without any prepayment charge (whether or not a prepayment charge is provided for under the Note). Borrower's acceptance of any such refund made by direct payment to Borrower will constitute a waiver of any right of action Borrower might have arising out of such overcharge.

15. Notices. All notices given by Borrower or Lender in connection with this Security Instrument must be in writing. Any notice to Borrower in connection with this Security Instrument shall be deemed to have been given to Borrower when mailed by first class mail or when actually delivered to Borrower's notice address if sent by other means. Notice to any one Borrower shall constitute notice to all Borrowers unless Applicable Law expressly requires

Borrower: _____

CALIFORNIA--Single Family--Fannie Mae/Freddie Mac UNIFORM INSTRUMENT - MERS
Form 3005 01/01   Page 9 of 14

otherwise. The notice address shall be the Property Address unless Borrower has designated a substitute notice address by notice to Lender. Borrower shall promptly notify Lender of Borrower's change of address. If Lender specifies a procedure for reporting Borrower's change of address, then Borrower shall only report a change of address through that specified procedure. There may be only one designated notice address under this Security Instrument at any one time. Any notice to Lender shall be given by delivering it or by mailing it by first class mail to Lender's address stated herein unless Lender has designated another address by notice to Borrower. Any notice in connection with this Security Instrument shall not be deemed to have been given to Lender until actually received by Lender. If any notice required by this Security Instrument is also required under Applicable Law, the Applicable Law requirement will satisfy the corresponding requirement under this Security Instrument.

16. Governing Law; Severability; Rules of Construction. This Security Instrument shall be governed by federal law and the law of the jurisdiction in which the Property is located. All rights and obligations contained in this Security Instrument are subject to any requirements and limitations of Applicable Law. Applicable Law might explicitly or implicitly allow the parties to agree by contract or it might be silent, but such silence shall not be construed as a prohibition against agreement by contract. In the event that any provision or clause of this Security Instrument or the Note conflicts with Applicable Law, such conflict shall not affect other provisions of this Security Instrument or the Note which can be given effect without the conflicting provision.

As used in this Security Instrument: (a) words of the masculine gender shall mean and include corresponding neuter words or words of the feminine gender; (b) words in the singular shall mean and include the plural and vice versa; and (c) the word "may" gives sole discretion without any obligation to take any action.

17. Borrower's Copy. Borrower shall be given one copy of the Note and of this Security Instrument.

18. Transfer of the Property or a Beneficial Interest in Borrower. As used in this Section 18, "Interest in the Property" means any legal or beneficial interest in the Property, including, but not limited to, those beneficial interests transferred in a bond for deed, contract for deed, installment sales contract or escrow agreement, the intent of which is the transfer of title by Borrower at a future date to a purchaser.

If all or any part of the Property or any Interest in the Property is sold or transferred (or if Borrower is not a natural person and a beneficial interest in Borrower is sold or transferred) without Lender's prior written consent, Lender may require immediate payment in full of all sums secured by this Security Instrument. However, this option shall not be exercised by Lender if such exercise is prohibited by Applicable Law.

If Lender exercises this option, Lender shall give Borrower notice of acceleration. The notice shall provide a period of not less than 30 days from the date the notice is given in accordance with Section 15 within which Borrower must pay all sums secured by this Security Instrument. If Borrower fails to pay these sums prior to the expiration of this period, Lender may invoke any remedies permitted by this Security Instrument without further notice or demand on Borrower.

19. Borrower's Right to Reinstate After Acceleration. If Borrower meets certain conditions, Borrower shall have the right to have enforcement of this Security Instrument discontinued at any time prior to the earliest of: (a) five days before sale of the Property pursuant to any power of sale contained in this Security Instrument; (b) such other period as Applicable Law might specify for the termination of Borrower's right to reinstate; or (c) entry of a judgment enforcing this Security Instrument. Those conditions are that Borrower: (a) pays Lender all sums which then would be due under this Security Instrument and the Note as if no acceleration had occurred; (b) cures any default of any other covenants or agreements; (c) pays all expenses incurred in enforcing this Security Instrument, including, but not limited to, reasonable attorneys' fees, property inspection and valuation fees, and other fees incurred for the purpose of protecting Lender's interest in the Property and rights under this Security Instrument; and (d) takes such action as Lender may reasonably require to assure that Lender's interest in the Property and rights under this Security Instrument, and Borrower's obligation to pay the sums secured by this Security Instrument, shall continue unchanged. Lender may require that Borrower pay such reinstatement sums and expenses in one or more of the following forms, as selected by Lender: (a) cash; (b) money order; (c) certified check, bank check, treasurer's check or cashier's check, provided any such check is drawn upon an institution whose deposits are insured by a federal agency, instrumentality or entity; or (d) Electronic Funds Transfer. Upon reinstatement by Borrower, this Security Instrument and obligations secured hereby shall remain fully effective as if no acceleration had occurred. However, this right to reinstate shall not apply in the case of acceleration under Section 18.

Borrower: ____

20. Sale of Note; Change of Loan Servicer; Notice of Grievance. The Note or a partial interest in the Note (together with this Security Instrument) can be sold one or more times without prior notice to Borrower. A sale might result in a change in the entity (known as the "Loan Servicer") that collects Periodic Payments due under the Note and this Security Instrument and performs other mortgage loan servicing obligations under the Note, this Security Instrument, and Applicable Law. There also might be one or more changes of the Loan Servicer unrelated to a sale of the Note. If there is a change of the Loan Servicer, Borrower will be given written notice of the change which will state the name and address of the new Loan Servicer, the address to which payments should be made and any other information RESPA requires in connection with a notice of transfer of servicing. If the Note is sold and thereafter the Loan is serviced by a Loan Servicer other than the purchaser of the Note, the mortgage loan servicing obligations to Borrower will remain with the Loan Servicer or be transferred to a successor Loan Servicer and are not assumed by the Note purchaser unless otherwise provided by the Note purchaser.

Neither Borrower nor Lender may commence, join, or be joined to any judicial action (as either an individual litigant or the member of a class) that arises from the other party's actions pursuant to this Security Instrument or that alleges that the other party has breached any provision of, or any duty owed by reason of, this Security Instrument, until such Borrower or Lender has notified the other party (with such notice given in compliance with the requirements of Section 15) of such alleged breach and afforded the other party hereto a reasonable period after the giving of such notice to take corrective action. If Applicable Law provides a time period which must elapse before certain action can be taken, that time period will be deemed to be reasonable for purposes of this paragraph. The notice of acceleration and opportunity to cure given to Borrower pursuant to Section 22 and the notice of acceleration given to Borrower pursuant to Section 18 shall be deemed to satisfy the notice and opportunity to take corrective action provisions of this Section 20.

21. Hazardous Substances. As used in this Section 21: (a) "Hazardous Substances" are those substances defined as toxic or hazardous substances, pollutants, or wastes by Environmental Law and the following substances: gasoline, kerosene, other flammable or toxic petroleum products, toxic pesticides and herbicides, volatile solvents, materials containing asbestos or formaldehyde, and radioactive materials; (b) "Environmental Law" means federal laws and laws of the jurisdiction where the Property is located that relate to health, safety or environmental protection; (c) "Environmental Cleanup" includes any response action, remedial action, or removal action, as defined in Environmental Law; and (d) an "Environmental Condition" means a condition that can cause, contribute to, or otherwise trigger an Environmental Cleanup.

Borrower shall not cause or permit the presence, use, disposal, storage, or release of any Hazardous Substances, or threaten to release any Hazardous Substances, on or in the Property. Borrower shall not do, nor allow anyone else to do, anything affecting the Property (a) that is in violation of any Environmental Law, (b) which creates an Environmental Condition, or (c) which, due to the presence, use, or release of a Hazardous Substance, creates a condition that adversely affects the value of the Property. The preceding two sentences shall not apply to the presence, use, or storage on the Property of small quantities of Hazardous Substances that are generally recognized to be appropriate to normal residential uses and to maintenance of the Property (including, but not limited to, hazardous substances in consumer products).

Borrower shall promptly give Lender written notice of (a) any investigation, claim, demand, lawsuit or other action by any governmental or regulatory agency or private party involving the Property and any Hazardous Substance or Environmental Law of which Borrower has actual knowledge, (b) any Environmental Condition, including but not limited to, any spilling, leaking, discharge, release or threat of release of any Hazardous Substance, and (c) any condition caused by the presence, use or release of a Hazardous Substance which adversely affects the value of the Property. If Borrower learns, or is notified by any governmental or regulatory authority, or any private party, that any removal or other remediation of any Hazardous Substance affecting the Property is necessary, Borrower shall promptly take all necessary remedial actions in accordance with Environmental Law. Nothing herein shall create any obligation on Lender for an Environmental Cleanup.

NON-UNIFORM COVENANTS. Borrower and Lender further covenant and agree as follows:

22. Acceleration; Remedies. Lender shall give notice to Borrower prior to acceleration following Borrower's breach of any covenant or agreement in this Security Instrument (but not prior to acceleration under Section 18 unless Applicable Law provides otherwise). The notice shall specify: (a) the default; (b) the action

Borrower: ____

required to cure the default; (c) a date, not less than 30 days from the date the notice is given to Borrower, by which the default must be cured; and (d) that failure to cure the default on or before the date specified in the notice may result in acceleration of the sums secured by this Security Instrument and sale of the Property. The notice shall further inform Borrower of the right to reinstate after acceleration and the right to bring a court action to assert the non-existence of a default or any other defense of Borrower to acceleration and sale. If the default is not cured on or before the date specified in the notice, Lender at its option may require immediate payment in full of all sums secured by this Security Instrument without further demand and may invoke the power of sale and any other remedies permitted by Applicable Law. Lender shall be entitled to collect all expenses incurred in pursuing the remedies provided in this Section 22, including, but not limited to, reasonable attorneys' fees and costs of title evidence.

If Lender invokes the power of sale, Lender shall execute or cause Trustee to execute a written notice of the occurrence of an event of default and of Lender's election to cause the Property to be sold. Trustee shall cause this notice to be recorded in each county in which any part of the Property is located. Lender or Trustee shall mail copies of the notice as prescribed by Applicable Law to Borrower and to the other persons prescribed by Applicable Law. Trustee shall give public notice of sale to the persons and in the manner prescribed by Applicable Law. After the time required by Applicable Law, Trustee, without demand on Borrower, shall sell the Property at public auction to the highest bidder at the time and place and under the terms designated in the notice of sale in one or more parcels and in any order Trustee determines. Trustee may postpone sale of all or any parcel of the Property by public announcement at the time and place of any previously scheduled sale. Lender or its designee may purchase the Property at any sale.

Trustee shall deliver to the purchaser Trustee's deed conveying the Property without any covenant or warranty, expressed or implied. The recitals in the Trustee's deed shall be prima facie evidence of the truth of the statements made therein. Trustee shall apply the proceeds of the sale in the following order: (a) to all expenses of the sale, including, but not limited to, reasonable Trustee's and attorneys' fees; (b) to all sums secured by this Security Instrument; and (c) any excess to the person or persons legally entitled to it.

23. **Reconveyance.** Upon payment of all sums secured by this Security Instrument, Lender shall request Trustee to reconvey the Property and shall surrender this Security Instrument and all notes evidencing debt secured by this Security Instrument to Trustee. Trustee shall reconvey the Property without warranty to the person or persons legally entitled to it. Lender may charge such person or persons a reasonable fee for reconveying the Property, but only if the fee is paid to a third party (such as the Trustee) for services rendered and the charging of the fee is permitted under Applicable Law. If the fee charged does not exceed the fee set by Applicable Law, the fee is conclusively presumed to be reasonable.

24. **Substitute Trustee.** Lender, at its option, may from time to time appoint a successor trustee to any Trustee appointed hereunder by an instrument executed and acknowledged by Lender and recorded in the office of the Recorder of the county in which the Property is located. The instrument shall contain the name of the original Lender, Trustee and Borrower, the book and page where this Security Instrument is recorded and the name and address of the successor trustee. Without conveyance of the Property, the successor trustee shall succeed to all the title, powers and duties conferred upon the Trustee herein and by Applicable Law. This procedure for substitution of trustee shall govern to the exclusion of all other provisions for substitution.

25. **Statement of Obligation Fee.** Lender may collect a fee not to exceed the maximum amount permitted by Applicable Law for furnishing the statement of obligation as provided by Section 2943 of the Civil Code of California.

Borrower: _____

CALIFORNIA--Single Family--Fannie Mae/Freddie Mac UNIFORM INSTRUMENT - MERS
Form 3005 01/01   Page 12 of 14

BY SIGNING BELOW, Borrower accepts and agrees to the terms and covenants contained in this Security Instrument and in any Rider executed by Borrower and recorded with it.

The undersigned Borrower requests that a copy of any Notice of Default and any Notice of Sale under this Security Instrument be mailed to Borrower at the address set forth above.

_____ (Seal)
RICHARD WILLIAM ROGERS   -Borrower

_____ (Seal)
-Borrower

_____ (Seal)
-Borrower

_____ (Seal)
-Borrower

_____ (Seal)
-Borrower

_____ (Seal)
-Borrower

Witness: Witness:

_____   _____

CALIFORNIA--Single Family--Fannie Mae/Freddie Mac UNIFORM INSTRUMENT - MERS
Form 3005 01/01   Page 13 of 14

state and county where signing appoinment takes place ↘

——————————— [Space Below This Line For Acknowledgment] ———————————

State of California   )
) ss.
County of _____)

On _____ before me, _____

personally appeared ___ RICHARD WILLIAM ROGERS _____

_____

_____ ,

who proved to me on the basis of satisfactory evidence to be the person(s) whose name(s) is/are subscribed to the within instrument and acknowledged to me that he/she/they executed the same in his/her/their authorized capacity(ies), and that by his/her/their signature(s) on the instrument the person(s), or the entity upon behalf of which the person(s) acted, executed the instrument.

I certify under PENALTY OF PERJURY under the laws of the State of California that the foregoing paragraph is true and correct.

WITNESS my hand and official seal.

_____
NOTARY SIGNATURE

_____
(Typed Name of Notary)

NOTARY SEAL

↑ *Typed means printed*

CALIFORNIA--Single Family--Fannie Mae/Freddie Mac UNIFORM INSTRUMENT - MERS
Form 3005 01/01   Page 14 of 14

Loan Number: 1234567890

CONDOMINIUM RIDER

THIS CONDOMINIUM RIDER is made this   day of 13th   MARCH, 20XX
, and is incorporated into and shall be deemed to amend and supplement the Mortgage, Deed of Trust, or Security Deed (the "Security Instrument") of the same date given by the undersigned (the "Borrower") to secure Borrower's Note to   TRISTAR FINANCE GROUP., A CALIFORNIA CORPORATION
(the "Lender") of the same date and covering the Property described in the Security Instrument and located at:

8624 OAKLAWN AVENUE, MODESTO, CALIFORNIA 95355
[Property Address]

The Property includes a unit in, together with an undivided interest in the common elements of, a condominium project known as:

OAK CREEK CONDOMINIUMS
[Name of Condominium Project]

(the "Condominium Project"). If the owners association or other entity which acts for the Condominium Project (the "Owners Association") holds title to property for the benefit or use of its members or shareholders, the Property also includes Borrower's interest in the Owners Association and the uses, proceeds and benefits of Borrower's interest.

CONDOMINIUM COVENANTS. In addition to the covenants and agreements made in the Security Instrument, Borrower and Lender further covenant and agree as follows:

A. Condominium Obligations. Borrower shall perform all of Borrower's obligations under the Condominium Project's Constituent Documents. The "Constituent Documents" are the: (i) Declaration or any other document which creates the Condominium Project; (ii) by-laws; (iii) code of regulations; and (iv) other equivalent documents. Borrower shall promptly pay, when due, all dues and assessments imposed pursuant to the Constituent Documents.

B. Property Insurance. So long as the Owners Association maintains, with a generally accepted insurance carrier, a "master" or "blanket" policy on the Condominium Project which is satisfactory to Lender and which provides insurance coverage in the amounts (including deductible levels), for the periods, and against loss by fire, hazards included within the term "extended coverage," and any other hazards, including, but not limited to, earthquakes and floods, from which Lender requires insurance, then: (i) Lender waives the provision in Section 3 for the Periodic Payment to Lender of the yearly premium installments for property insurance on the Property; and (ii) Borrower's obligation under Section 5 to maintain property insurance coverage on the Property is deemed satisfied to the extent that the required coverage is provided by the Owners Association policy.

What Lender requires as a condition of this waiver can change during the term of the loan.

MULTISTATE CONDOMINIUM RIDER
Single Family--Fannie Mae/Freddie Mac UNIFORM INSTRUMENT
Form 3140 1/01   Page 1 of 3

Us3140.rid.xml

Borrower shall give Lender prompt notice of any lapse in required property insurance coverage provided by the master or blanket policy.

In the event of a distribution of property insurance proceeds in lieu of restoration or repair following a loss to the Property, whether to the unit or to common elements, any proceeds payable to Borrower are hereby assigned and shall be paid to Lender for application to the sums secured by the Security Instrument, whether or not then due, with the excess, if any, paid to Borrower.

C. Public Liability Insurance. Borrower shall take such actions as may be reasonable to insure that the Owners Association maintains a public liability insurance policy acceptable in form, amount, and extent of coverage to Lender.

D. Condemnation. The proceeds of any award or claim for damages, direct or consequential, payable to Borrower in connection with any condemnation or other taking of all or any part of the Property, whether of the unit or of the common elements, or for any conveyance in lieu of condemnation, are hereby assigned and shall be paid to Lender. Such proceeds shall be applied by Lender to the sums secured by the Security Instrument as provided in Section 11.

E. Lender's Prior Consent. Borrower shall not, except after notice to Lender and with Lender's prior written consent, either partition or subdivide the Property or consent to: (i) the abandonment or termination of the Condominium Project, except for abandonment or termination required by law in the case of substantial destruction by fire or other casualty or in the case of a taking by condemnation or eminent domain; (ii) any amendment to any provision of the Constituent Documents if the provision is for the express benefit of Lender; (iii) termination of professional management and assumption of self-management of the Owners Association; or (iv) any action which would have the effect of rendering the public liability insurance coverage maintained by the Owners Association unacceptable to Lender.

F. Remedies. If Borrower does not pay condominium dues and assessments when due, then Lender may pay them. Any amounts disbursed by Lender under this paragraph F shall become additional debt of Borrower secured by the Security Instrument. Unless Borrower and Lender agree to other terms of payment, these amounts shall bear interest from the date of disbursement at the Note rate and shall be payable, with interest, upon notice from Lender to Borrower requesting payment.

MULTISTATE CONDOMINIUM RIDER
Single Family--Fannie Mae/Freddie Mac UNIFORM INSTRUMENT
Form 3140 1/01   Page 2 of 3

Us3140.rid.xml

BY SIGNING BELOW, Borrower accepts and agrees to the terms and covenants contained in this Condominium Rider.

_____ (Seal)
RICHARD WILLIAM ROGERS -Borrower

_____ (Seal)
-Borrower

_____ (Seal)
-Borrower

_____ (Seal)
-Borrower

_____ (Seal)
-Borrower

_____ (Seal)
-Borrower

MULTISTATE CONDOMINIUM RIDER
Single Family--Fannie Mae/Freddie Mac UNIFORM INSTRUMENT
Form 3140 1/01   Page 3 of 3

Us3140.rid.xml

OCCUPANCY AND FINANCIAL STATUS AFFIDAVIT

STATE OF CALIFORNIA   )
) ss:

COUNTY OF STANISLAUS   )

BEFORE ME, the undersigned authority duly authorized to take acknowledgments and administer oaths, personally appeared
RICHARD WILLIAM ROGERS

(the "Borrower"),

who upon being duly sworn on oath, certified as follows:

1. **Material Inducement:** Borrower understands and agrees that the statements contained herein are given as a material inducement to TRISTAR FINANCE GROUP, INC

(the "Lender"),

and Lender is relying upon such statements, to make a mortgage loan (the "Loan") to Borrower, repayment of which is secured by a Mortgage, Deed of Trust, Security Deed or other instrument of security (the "Security Instrument") on certain real property located at 8624 OAKLAWN AVENUE, MODESTO, CALIFORNIA 95355

(the "Property").

2. **Occupancy:** [check one box only]

   [X] **Principal Residence.** Borrower either currently occupies and uses the Property as Borrower's principal residence, or Borrower will occupy and use the Property as Borrower's principal residence within 60 days after Borrower signs the Security Instrument. Borrower will continue to occupy and use the Property as Borrower's principal residence for at least one (1) year from the date that Borrower first occupies the Property. However, Borrower will not have to occupy and use the Property as Borrower's principal residence within the time frames set forth above if Lender agrees in writing that Borrower does not have to do so. Lender may not refuse to agree unless the refusal is reasonable. Borrower will also not have to occupy and use the Property as Borrower's principal residence within the time frames set forth above if extenuating circumstances exist which are beyond Borrower's control.

   [ ] **Second Home.** Borrower will occupy, and will use, the Property as Borrower's second home. Borrower will keep the Property available for Borrower's exclusive use and enjoyment at all times, and will not subject the Property to any timesharing or other shared ownership arrangement or to any rental pool or agreement that requires Borrower either to rent the Property or give a management firm or any other person any control over the occupancy or use of the Property.

   [ ] **Investment.** The Property is owned and held by Borrower as an investment property. Borrower does not now occupy or use the property, and has no present intention to occupy or use the Property in the future, either as Borrower's principal residence or second home. Borrower now occupies and uses other property or properties as Borrower's principal residence and/or second home.

3. **Financial Status:** Borrower understands that Lender is making the Loan based upon statements and representations contained in, or made in connection with, the residential mortgage loan application given by Borrower to Lender (the "Loan Application"). Borrower hereby certifies that the information provided by Borrower contained in, or made in connection with, the Loan Application related to Borrower's financial status (such as Borrower's employment, income, available cash, debts, expenses, credit obligations, and the like), has not changed significantly and that such information accurately reflects Borrower's current financial status. Borrower certifies further that Borrower has not received a layoff notice or otherwise have knowledge of a pending layoff, and Borrower, to the best of Borrower's knowledge and belief, is unaware of any events or circumstances in the foreseeable future that would impair or have an adverse effect on Borrower's ability to fulfill Borrower's Loan obligations, including, but not limited to Borrower's obligation to make required periodic payments.

4. **False, Misleading or Inaccurate Statements:** Borrower understands that Borrower will be in default under the terms of the Security Instrument if, during the application process for the Loan, Borrower or any persons or entities acting at the direction of Borrower or with Borrower's knowledge or consent gave materially false, misleading or inaccurate information or statements to Lender (or failed to provide Lender with material information) in connection with the Loan, including, but not limited to, representations concerning Borrower's occupancy of the Property and Borrower's financial status. Borrower understands further that any intentional or negligent misrepresentation(s) of the information contained in, or made in connection with, the Loan Application may result in severe civil and/or criminal penalties, including, but not limited to, fine or imprisonment or both under the provisions of Title 18, United States Code, Section 1001, et seq. and liability for monetary damages to the Lender, its agents, successors and assigns, insurers and any other person who may suffer any loss due to reliance upon any misrepresentation(s) which Borrower has made on or in connection with the Loan Application.

LoanNumber: 1234567890

Borrower RICHARD WILLIAM ROGERS   Date _____   Borrower _____ Date _____

Borrower _____ Date _____   Borrower _____ Date _____

Borrower _____ Date _____   Borrower _____ Date _____

State of CALIFORNIA
County of

Subscribed and sworn to (or affirmed) before me on this   day of   , by
RICHARD WILLIAM ROGERS

proved to me on the basis of satisfactory evidence to be the person(s) who appeared before me.

      (seal)   Signature _____

SIGNATURE AFFIDAVIT AND AKA STATEMENT

SIGNATURE AFFIDAVIT

I, RICHARD WILLIAM ROGERS
this is my true and correct signature:

RICHARD WILLIAM ROGERS
Borrower

_____
Sample Signature

AKA STATEMENT

I, RICHARD WILLIAM ROGERS
further certify that I am also known as:

RICHARD WILLIAM ROGERS
Name Variation (Print)

_____
Sample Signature (Variation)

RICHARD ROGERS
Name Variation (Print)

_____
Sample Signature (Variation)

RICK ROGERS
Name Variation (Print)

_____
Sample Signature (Variation)

RICK W. ROGERS
Name Variation (Print)

_____
Sample Signature (Variation)

RW ROGERS
Name Variation (Print)

_____
Sample Signature (Variation)

RICKY ROGERS
Name Variation (Print)

_____
Sample Signature (Variation)

R WILLY ROGERS
Name Variation (Print)

_____
Sample Signature (Variation)

State of

County of

Subscribed and sworn to (or affirmed) before me on this   day of
by RICHARD WILLIAM ROGERS

proved to me on the basis of satisfactory evidence to be the person(s) who appeared before me.

Signature _____

(seal)

SIGNATURE AFFIDAVIT AND AKA STATEMENT
CAAKA.LSR 01/08/08

Date Prepared: February 12, 20XX

LIMITED POWER OF ATTORNEY

The Undersigned hereby appoints TRISTAR FINANCE GROUP and/or its assignees, to be my attorney in fact/Agent (hereinafter referred to as Agent), to act for me only as to the matters stated below.

Loan Number: 1234567890

Property Address: 8624 Oaklawn Avenue,MODESTO, CA 95355

Legal Description: REFER TO SECURITY INSTRUMENT

Document Date: February 12, 20XX

Borrower Name: Richard William Rogers

All spaces must be filled in

POWERS:

In the event a clerical or typographical error is discovered on any document pertaining to this transaction, my agent and/or assignees, is hereby authorized to correct any clerical or typographical error and to initial, sign, seal and deliver as my act, any instrument to which my agent determines to be necessary to effectuate the correction. Specifically, my agent may make a correction limited to the matters stated below on an original document, and is authorized to rerecord that original document where appropriate. The undersigned declares that any and all corrections made by my agent shall be as valid as if they had been initialed, signed and delivered by me personally. The undersigned ratifies whatsoever my said agent shall lawfully do or cause to be done in the correction of clerical and typographical errors as limited below.

LIMITATIONS:

My agent is authorized to correct clerical and typographical errors as to the names of the parties to this transaction; the legal description; county or street address of the real property which is the subject of this transaction; and the date of any document.

My agent is not authorized to make any changes or corrections as to the interest rate stated on the deed of trust or promissory notes; the amount of principal indebtedness stated on the deed of trust or promissory note; or the amount of consideration on the Deed.

This Power of Attorney is made of my own free will for the purpose of facilitating necessary corrections. The undersigned understands that signing this Power of Attorney is not mandatory.

_____

Borrower: RICHARD WILLIAM ROGERS   Date

Page 1 of 2

LIMITED POWER OF ATTORNEY

ACKNOWLEDGMENT

State of _____)
County of _____)

On _____ before me, _____
(here insert name and title of the officer)

personally appeared

<u>RICHARD WILLIAM ROGERS</u>, who proved to me on the basis of satisfactory evidence to be the person(s) whose name(s) is/are subscribed to the within instrument and acknowledged to me that he/she/they executed the same in his/her/their authorized capacity(ies), and that by his/her/their signature(s) on the instrument the person(s), or the entity upon behalf of which the person(s) acted, executed the instrument.

WITNESS my hand and official seal.

Signature _____   (Seal)

COMPLIANCE AGREEMENT

STATE OF CALIFORNIA   )
) SS:

COUNTY OF STANISLAUS   )

Loan Number: 1234567890

Seller(s):

Lender: TRISTAR FINANCE GROUP, INC

Borrower(s): RICHARD WILLIAM ROGERS

Property: 8624 OAKLAWN AVENUE, MODESTO, CALIFORNIA 95355

The undersigned borrower(s) for and in consideration of the above referenced Lender this date funding the closing of this loan agrees, if requested by Lender or Closing Agent for Lender, to fully cooperate and adjust for clerical errors, any or all loan closing documentation if deemed necessary or desirable in the reasonable discretion of Lender to enable Lender to sell, convey, seek guaranty or market said loan to any entity, including but not limited to, an investor, Fannie Mae, Freddie Mac, Federal Housing Authority, the Department of Veterans Affairs or any municipal bonding authority.

The undersigned borrower(s) agree(s) to comply with all above noted requests by Lender or Closing Agent for Lender within 5   days from the date of mailing said requests. Borrower(s) agree(s) to assume all costs including, by way of illustration and not limitation, actual expenses, legal fees and marketing losses, for failing to comply with correction requests in such   5 day time period.

The undersigned borrower(s) do hereby so agree and covenant in order to assure that the loan documentation executed this date will conform and be acceptable in the market place in the instance of transfer, sale or conveyance by Lender or its interest in and to said loan documentation.

Dated effective

RICHARD WILLIAM ROGERS   _____   _____

_____   _____

_____   _____

State of   _____)
) ss.
County of _____)

On _____ before me RICHARD WILLIAM ROGERS _____ personally appeared _____

_____

_____ ,

who proved to me on the basis of satisfactory evidence to be the person(s) whose name(s) is/are subscribed to the within instrument and acknowledged to me that he/she/they executed the same in his/her/their authorized capacity(ies), and that by his/her/their signature(s) on the instrument the person(s), or the entity upon behalf of which the person(s) acted, executed the instrument.

WITNESS my hand and official seal.

_____
NOTARY SIGNATURE

_____
(Typed Name of Notary)

NOTARY SEAL

CALIFORNIA COMPLIANCE AGREEMENT
CACOMP.MSC 08/05/11

Uniform Residential Loan Application

This application is designed to be completed by the applicant(s) with the Lender's assistance. Applicants should complete this form as [...] as applicable. Co-Borrower information must also be provided (and the appropriate box checked) when ☒ the income or assets of a per[son] (including the Borrower's spouse) will be used as a basis for loan qualification or ☐ the income or assets of the Borrower's spouse or othe[r] property rights pursuant to state law will not be used as a basis for loan qualification, but his or her liabilities must be considered becaus[e] has community property rights pursuant to applicable law and Borrower resides in a community property state, the security property is loca[ted in a community property] state, or the Borrower is relying on other property located in a community property state as a basis for repayment of the loan.

If this is an application for joint credit, Borrower and Co-Borrower each agree that we intend to apply for joint credit (sign below):

[Handwritten note: If there is a co-borrower listed, they both need to sign here]

Borrower _____   Co-Borrower _____

I. TYPE OF MORTGAGE AND TERMS OF LOAN

Mortgage Applied for:	☐ VA ☒ FHA	☐ Conventional ☐ USDA/Rural Housing Service	☐ Other (explain):	Agency Case Number 000-5555555-000	Lender Case Number 1234567890

Amount $205,631.00	Interest Rate 3.250 %	No. of Months 360	Amortization Type:	☒ Fixed Rate ☐ GPM	☐ Other (explain): ☐ ARM (type):

II. PROPERTY INFORMATION AND PURPOSE OF LOAN

Subject Property Address (street, city, state & ZIP) 8624 OAKLAWN AVENUE, MODESTO, CALIFORNIA 95355	No. of Units 1

Legal Description of Subject Property (attach description if necessary) LOT 10, BLOCK 55555 OF VILLAGE HIGHLANDS PHASE III, AS PER MAP FILED DECEMBER 9, 19XX IN VOLUME 02 OF MAPS, PAGE 55 STANISLAUS COUNTY RECORDS.	Year Built 2000

Purpose of Loan	☐ Purchase ☒ Refinance	☐ Construction ☐ Construction-Permanent	☐ Other (explain):	Property will be: ☒ Primary Residence ☐ Secondary Residence ☐ Investment

Complete this line if construction or construction-permanent loan.

Year Lot Acquired	Original Cost $	Amount Existing Liens $	(a) Present Value of Lot $	(b) Cost of Improvements $	Total (a+b) $

Complete this line if this is a refinance loan.

Year Acquired 2000	Original Cost $168,000.00	Amount Existing Liens $203,000.00	Purpose of Refinance Change In Rate Term	Describe Improvements ☐ made ☐ to be made Cost: $

Title will be held in what Name(s) RICHARD WILLIAM ROGERS	Manner in which Title will be held To be determined in escrow	Estate will be held in: ☒ Fee Simple ☐ Leasehold (show expiration date)

Source of Down Payment, Settlement Charges, and/or Subordinate Financing (explain)

III. BORROWER INFORMATION

Borrower	Co-Borrower
or Sr. if applicable) RICHARD WILLIAM ROGERS	Co-Borrower's Name (include Jr. or Sr. if applicable)

Social Security Number	Home Phone (incl. area code) (209)555-5555	DOB (mm/dd/yyyy) 09/05/1966	Yrs. School 12	Social Security Number	Home Phone (incl. area code)	DOB (mm/dd/yyyy)	Yrs. School

☐ Married ☒ Unmarried (include single, divorced, widowed) ☐ Separated	Dependents (not listed by Co-Borrower) no.0 ages	☐ Married ☐ Unmarried (include single, divorced, widowed) ☐ Separated	Dependents (not listed by Borrower) no. ages

Present Address (street, city, state, ZIP) ☒ Own ☐ Rent 12 No. Yrs. 8624 OAKLAWN AVENUE MODESTO, CA 95355	Present Address (street, city, state, ZIP) ☐ Own ☐ Rent ____ No. Yrs.

Mailing Address, if different from Present Address	Mailing Address, if different from Present Address

Fannie Mae Form 1003 6/09
Freddie Mac Form 65 6/09   Borrower: _____   Page 1

[Right margin vertical text: Sample Document for National Notary Association Signing Agent Certification Study Guide]

If residing at present address for less than two years, complete the following:

Former Address (street, city, state, ZIP) ☐ Own ☐ Rent _____ No. Yrs.	Former Address (street, city, state, ZIP) ☐ Own ☐ Rent _____ No. Yrs.

Borrower	IV. EMPLOYMENT INFORMATION	Co-Borrower

Name & Address of Employer ☐ Self Employed	Yrs. on this job	Name & Address of Employer ☐ Self Employed	Yrs. on this job
Turn-Key Transportation Inc 4029 Leckron Road Modesto, CA 95357	21 yrs 6 mos Yrs. employed in this line of work/profession 21		Yrs. employed in this line of work/profession

Position/Title/Type of Business Fleet Property Manager	Business Phone (incl. area code) (555) 555-5555	Position/Title/Type of Business	Business Phone (incl. area code)

If employed in current position for less than two years or if currently employed in more than one position, complete the following:

Name & Address of Employer ☐ Self Employed	Dates (from - to) Monthly Income $	Name & Address of Employer ☐ Self Employed	Dates (from - to) Monthly Income $
Position/Title/Type of Business	Business Phone (incl. area code)	Position/Title/Type of Business	Business Phone (incl. area code)
Name & Address of Employer ☐ Self Employed	Dates (from - to) Monthly Income $	Name & Address of Employer ☐ Self Employed	Dates (from - to) Monthly Income $
Position/Title/Type of Business	Business Phone (incl. area code)	Position/Title/Type of Business	Business Phone (incl. area code)

V. MONTHLY INCOME AND COMBINED HOUSING EXPENSE INFORMATION						
Gross Monthly Income	Borrower	Co-Borrower	Total	Combined Monthly Housing Expense	Present	Proposed
Base Empl. Income*	$ .00	$	$ .00	Rent	$	
Overtime				First Mortgage (P&I)	969.23	$ 894.92
Bonuses				Other Financing (P&I)		
Commissions				Hazard Insurance	77.00	48.33
Dividends/Interest				Real Estate Taxes	196.65	196.65
Net Rental Income				Mortgage Insurance	195.48	200.25
Other (before completing, see the notice in "describe other income," below)				Homeowner Assn. Dues		
				Other:		
Total	$ .00	$	$ .00	Total	$ 1,438.36	$ 1,340.15

* Self Employed Borrower(s) may be required to provide additional documentation such as tax returns and financial statements.

Describe Other Income *Notice:* Alimony, child support, or separate maintenance income need not be revealed if the Borrower (B) or Co-Borrower (C) does not choose to have it considered for repaying this loan.

B/C		Monthly Amount
		$

Fannie Mae Form 1003 6/09
Freddie Mac Form 65 6/09   Borrower: _____   Page 2

VI. ASSETS AND LIABILITIES

This Statement and any applicable supporting schedules may be completed jointly by both married and unmarried Co-Borrowers if their assets and liabilities are sufficiently joined so that the Statement can be meaningfully and fairly presented on a combined basis; otherwise, separate Statements and Schedules are required. If the Co-Borrower section was completed about a non-applicant spouse or other person, this Statement and supporting schedules must be completed about that spouse or other person also.

Completed ☐ Jointly ☒ Not Jointly

ASSETS	Cash or Market Value	Liabilities and Pledged Assets. List the creditor's name, address and account number for all outstanding debts, including automobile loans, revolving charge accounts, real estate loans, alimony, child support, stock pledges, etc. Use continuation sheet, if necessary. Indicate by (*) those liabilities, which will be satisfied upon sale of real estate owned or upon refinancing of the subject property.		
Description				
Cash deposit toward purchase held by:	$			

List checking and savings accounts below		LIABILITIES	Monthly Payment & Months Left to Pay	Unpaid Balance
Name and address of Bank, S&L, or Credit Union CHASE PO BOX 555555, SAN ANTONIO, TX 78265		Name and address of Company QUICKEN LOANS	$ Payment/Months 1,438.00 * 142	$ 203,929.00
Acct. no. 55544444	$ 2,112.26	Acct. no. 8673304839629		
Name and address of Bank, S&L, or Credit Union CHASE PO BOX 555555, SAN ANTONIO, TX 78265		Name and address of Company THE GOLDEN 1 CREDIT UN	$ Payment/Months 419.00 54	$ 22,383.00
Acct. no. 44455555	$ 1,700.77	Acct. no. 136771601		
Name and address of Bank, S&L, or Credit Union		Name and address of Company CHASE	$ Payment/Months 158.00 R	$ 7,556.00
Acct. no.	$	Acct. no. 4388576048210002		
Name and address of Bank, S&L, or Credit Union		Name and address of Company KOHLS/CAPONE	$ Payment/Months 25.00 R	$ 259.00
Acct. no.	$	Acct. no. 6393050455483016		

Fannie Mae Form 1003 6/09
Freddie Mac Form 65 6/09

Borrower: _____   Page 3

VI. ASSETS AND LIABILITIES (cont'd)				
Stocks & Bonds (Company name/number & description)	$	Name and address of Company	$ Payment/Months	$
		Acct. no.		
Life Insurance net cash value	$	Name and address of Company	$ Payment/Months	$
Face amount: $				
Subtotal Liquid Assets	$ 3,813.03			
Real estate owned (enter market value from schedule of real estate owned)	$ 215,000.00			
Vested interest in retirement fund	$			
Net worth of business(es) owned (attach financial statement)	$	Acct. no.		
Automobiles owned (make and year)	$	Alimony/Child Support/Separate Maintenance Payments Owed to:	$	
Other Assets (itemize)	$	Job-Related Expense (child care, union dues, etc.)	$	
		Total Monthly Payments	$ 602.00	
Total Assets a. $ 218,813.03		Net Worth ▶ (a minus b) $ 188,615.03	**Total Liabilities b.** $ 30,198.00	

Schedule of Real Estate Owned (If additional properties are owned, use continuation sheet.)

Property Address (enter S if sold, PS if pending sale or R if rental being held for income) ▼	Type of Property	Present Market Value	Amount of Mortgages & Liens	Gross Rental Income	Mortgage Payments	Insurance, Maintenance, Taxes & Misc.	Net Rental Income
3321 Southgrove Ave, Modesto, CA 95355	SFR	$ 215,000.00	$ 203,405.00	$	$ 969.00	$ 469.00	$ 0.00
Totals		$ 215,000.00	$ 203,405.00	$	$ 969.00	$ 469.00	$ 0.00

List any additional names under which credit has previously been received and indicate appropriate creditor name(s) and account number(s):

Alternate Name	Creditor Name	Account Number

Fannie Mae Form 1003 6/09
Freddie Mac Form 65 6/09   Borrower: _____   Page 4

VII. DETAILS OF TRANSACTION		VIII. DECLARATIONS					

				Borrower		Co-Borrower	
		If you answer "Yes" to any questions a through i, please use continuation sheet for explanation.		Yes	No	Yes	No
a.	Purchase price	$ .00					
b.	Alterations, improvements, repairs	.00	a. Are there any outstanding judgments against you?	☐	☒	☐	☐
c.	Land (if acquired separately)		b. Have you been declared bankrupt within the past 7 years?	☐	☒	☐	☐
d.	Refinance (incl. debts to be paid off)	203,929.00	c. Have you had property foreclosed upon or given title or deed in lieu thereof in the last 7 years?	☐	☒	☐	☐
e.	Estimated prepaid items	1,800.00	d. Are you a party to a lawsuit?	☐	☒	☐	☐
f.	Estimated closing costs	1,583.19	e. Have you directly or indirectly been obligated on any loan which resulted in foreclosure, transfer of title in lieu of foreclosure, or judgment?	☐	☒	☐	☐
g.	PMI, MIP, Funding Fee	3,536.66	(This would include such loans as home mortgage loans, SBA loans, home improvement loans, educational loans, manufactured (mobile) home loans, any mortgage, financial obligation, bond, or loan guarantee. If "Yes," provide details, including date, name and address of Lender, FHA or VA case number, if any, and reasons for the action.)				
h.	Discount (if Borrower will pay)						
i.	Total costs (add items a through h)	210,848.85					

				Borrower		Co-Borrower	
			If you answer "Yes" to any questions a through i, please use continuation sheet for explanation.	Yes	No	Yes	No
j.	Subordinate financing	0.00					
k.	Borrower's closing costs paid by Seller	.00	f. Are you presently delinquent or in default on any Federal debt or any other loan, mortgage, financial obligation, bond, or loan guarantee?	☐	☒	☐	☐
l.	Other Credits (explain) OTHER	1,102.01 1,028.16	g. Are you obligated to pay alimony, child support, or separate maintenance?	☐	☒	☐	☐
			h. Is any part of the down payment borrowed?	☐	☒	☐	☐
			i. Are you a co-maker or endorser on a note?	☐	☒	☐	☐
m.	Loan amount (exclude PMI, MIP, Funding Fee financed)	202,095.00	j. Are you a U.S. citizen?	☒	☐	☐	☐
n.	PMI, MIP, Funding Fee financed	3,536.00	k. Are you a permanent resident alien?	☐	☒	☐	☐
o.	Loan amount (add m & n)	205,631.00	**l. Do you intend to occupy the property as your primary residence?** If "Yes," complete question m below.	☒	☐	☐	☐
p.	Cash from/to Borrower (subtract j, k, l & o from i)	3,087.68	m Have you had an ownership interest in a property in the last three years?	☒	☐	☐	☐
			(1) What type of property did you own - principal residence (PR), second home (SH), or investment property (IP)?	PR			
			(2) How did you hold title to the home - by yourself (S), jointly with your spouse (SP), or jointly with another person (O)?	S			

IX.   ACKNOWLEDGMENT AND AGREEMENT

Each of the undersigned specifically represents to Lender and to Lender's actual or potential agents, brokers, processors, attorneys, insurers, servicers, successors and assigns and agrees and acknowledges that: (1) the information provided in this application is true and correct as of the date set forth opposite my signature and that any intentional or negligent misrepresentation of this information contained in this application may result in civil liability, including monetary damages, to any person who may suffer any loss due to reliance upon any misrepresentation that I have made on this application, and/or in criminal penalties including, but not limited to, fine or imprisonment or both under the provisions of Title 18, United States Code, Sec. 1001, et. seq.; (2) the loan requested pursuant to this application (the "Loan") will be secured by a mortgage or deed of trust on the property described in this application; (3) the property will not be used for any illegal or prohibited purpose or use; (4) all statements made in this application are made for the purpose of obtaining a residential mortgage loan; (5) the property will be occupied as indicated in this application; (6) the Lender, its servicers, successors or assigns may retain the original and/or an electronic record of this application, whether or not the Loan is approved; (7) the Lender and its agents, brokers, insurers, servicers, successors and assigns may continuously rely on the information contained in the application, and I am obligated to amend and/or supplement the information provided in this application if any of the material facts that I have represented herein should change prior to closing of the Loan; (8) in the event that my payments on the Loan become delinquent, the Lender, its servicers, successors or assigns may, in addition to any other rights and remedies that it may have relating to such delinquency, report my name and account information to one or more consumer reporting agencies; (9) ownership of the Loan and/or administration of the Loan account may be transferred with such notice as may be required by law; (10) neither Lender nor its agents, brokers, insurers, servicers, successors or assigns has made any representation or warranty, express or implied, to me regarding the property or the condition or value of the property; and (11) my transmission of this application as an "electronic record" containing my "electronic signature," as those terms are defined in applicable federal and/or state laws (excluding audio and video recordings), or my facsimile transmission of this application containing a facsimile of my signature, shall be as effective, enforceable and valid as if a paper version of this application were delivered containing my original written signature.

Acknowledgment. Each of the undersigned hereby acknowledges that any owner of the Loan, its servicers, successors and assigns, may verify or reverify any information contained in this application or obtain any information or data relating to the Loan, for any legitimate business purpose through any source, including a source named in this application or a consumer reporting agency.

Borrower's Signature	Date	Co-Borrower's Signature	Date
X		X	

Fannie Mae Form 1003 6/09
Freddie Mac Form 65 6/09   Page 5

X. INFORMATION FOR GOVERNMENT MONITORING PURPOSES

The following information is requested by the Federal Government for certain types of loans related to a dwelling in order to monitor the lender's compliance with equal credit opportunity, fair housing and home mortgage disclosure laws. You are not required to furnish this information, but are encouraged to do so. The law provides that a lender may not discriminate either on the basis of this information, or on whether you choose to furnish it. If you furnish the information, please provide both ethnicity and race. For race, you may check more than one designation. If you do not furnish ethnicity, race, or sex, under Federal regulations, this lender is required to note the information on the basis of visual observation and surname if you have made this application in person. If you do not wish to furnish the information, please check the box below. (Lender must review the above material to assure that the disclosures satisfy all requirements to which the lender is subject under applicable state law for the particular type of loan applied for.)

BORROWER ☐ I do not wish to furnish this information	CO-BORROWER ☐ I do not wish to furnish this information
Ethnicity: ☐ Hispanic or Latino ☒ Not Hispanic or Latino	**Ethnicity:** ☐ Hispanic or Latino ☐ Not Hispanic or Latino
Race: ☐ American Indian or Alaska Native ☐ Asian ☐ Black or African American ☐ Native Hawaiian or Other Pacific Islander ☒ White	**Race:** ☐ American Indian or Alaska Native ☐ Asian ☐ Black or African American ☐ Native Hawaiian or Other Pacific Islander ☐ White
Sex: ☒ Female ☐ Male	**Sex:** ☐ Female ☐ Male

To be Completed by Loan Originator:

This information was provided:
☐ In a face-to-face interview
☒ In a telephone interview
☐ By the applicant and was submitted by fax or mail
☐ By the applicant and submitted via e-mail or the Internet

Loan Originator's Signature X	Date
Loan Originator's Name (print or type) Amir Kumar	Loan Originator Identifier 333333	Loan Originator's Phone Number (including area code) (916) 555-5555
Loan Origination Company's Name Property Financial Center Inc - Roseville, CA	Loan Origination Company Identifier 123456	Loan Origination Company's Address 555 55TH ST STE 208, MODESTO, CALIFORNIA 95816

Fannie Mae Form 1003 6/09
Freddie Mac Form 65 6/09   Borrower: _____   Page 6

CONTINUATION SHEET/RESIDENTIAL LOAN APPLICATION

Use this continuation sheet if you need more space to complete the Residential Loan Application. Mark **B** for Borrower or **C** for Co-Borrower	Borrower: RICHARD WILLIAM ROGERS	Agency Case Number: 000-5555555-000
	Co-Borrower:	Lender Case Number: 1234567890

Additional Names under which credit has been received

Alternate Name	Creditor Name	Account Number

Under California Civil Code 1812.30(j) "Credit applications for the obtainment of money, goods, labor, or services shall clearly specify that the applicant, if married, may apply for a separate account."

I/We fully understand that it is a Federal crime punishable by fine or imprisonment, or both, to knowingly make any false statements concerning any of the above facts as applicable under the provisions of Title 18, United States Code, Section 1001, et seq.

Borrower's Signature	Date	Co-Borrower's Signature	Date
X		X	

Fannie Mae Form 1003 6/09
Freddie Mac Form 65 6/09

Page 7

Read instructions carefully

Loan Number: 1234567890

Lender: TRISTAR FINANCE GROUP, INC

USA PATRIOT ACT
CUSTOMER IDENTIFICATION VERIFICATION
IMPORTANT INFORMATION ABOUT PROCEDURES FOR OPENING A NEW ACCOUNT

To help the government fight the funding of terrorism and money laundering activities, Federal law requires all financial institutions to obtain, verify, and record information that identifies each person who opens an account. What this means for you: When you open an account, we will ask for your name, address, date of birth, and other information that will allow us to identify you. We may also ask to see your driver's license or other identifying documents.

INSTRUCTIONS TO INDIVIDUAL COMPLETING THIS VERIFICATION
The named individual must present at least two (2) forms of identifying documents for review; at least one (1) of the identifying documents must be an unexpired government-issued document bearing a photograph of the named individual. Other identifying documents not specifically listed below must, at a minimum, bear the individual's name. Examples of other acceptable identifying documents include:

Current government-issued visa; Medicare card; student identification card; voter registration card; recent property tax or utility bill; most recent W-2 or signed federal or state tax returns; bank statements; and proof of car/house/renter's insurance coverage. Please contact the above-named Lender if you have any questions regarding the acceptability of any identifying document.

Borrower's Name: RICHARD WILLIAM ROGERS   Date of Birth: SEPTEMBER 5, 1966

[X] Residential or [ ] Business Address:* 8624 OAKLAWN AVENUE
MODESTO, CA 95355

Taxpayer Identification Number (SSN):** 555-55-5555

Identifying Documents	Place of Issuance	ID Number	Date of Birth	Issue/Expiration Date(s)	Photo?
[ ] State/Foreign Driver's License				------------------	[ ] Yes [ ] No
[ ] State/Foreign ID Card		'		------------------	[ ] Yes [ ] No
[ ] U.S./Foreign Passport				------------------	[ ] Yes [ ] No
[ ] Military ID				------------------	[ ] Yes [ ] No
[ ] Resident Alien Card				------------------	[ ] Yes [ ] No
[ ] Social Security Card				------------------	
[ ] Birth Certificate				------------------	
[ ] Other:				------------------	[ ] Yes [ ] No
[ ] Other:				------------------	[ ] Yes [ ] No

The signing Agent will complete this section with applicable ID info

*For an individual without a residential or business address, provide an APO or FPO box number, or the residential or business address of next of kin or another contact person.

**For non-U.S. persons without a tax identification number, provide a passport number and country of issuance; an alien identification card number, or the number and country of issuance of any other government-issued document evidencing nationality or residence and bearing a photograph or similar safeguard.

CUSTOMER IDENTIFICATION VERIFICATION
31 CFR 1020.220
CIV.MSC 03/06/13   Page 1 of 2

ADDITIONAL COMMENTS

(e.g., please note any discrepancies in the borrower's identifying documents): _____

_____

_____

CERTIFICATION

I, the undersigned, hereby certify that: (i) I have personally examined the identifying documents indicated above presented to me by the named individual, (ii) I have accurately recorded the information appearing in the identifying documents I examined, and (iii) except as may be indicated above, each of the indicated identifying documents appears to be genuine, the information contained in the identifying documents is consistent in all respects with the information provided by the named individual, and, where applicable, the photograph appears to be that of the named individual.

Signing Agent Signature and Date →

_____   _____
Signature   Date

_____
Name and Title

Title should be: Signing Agent

Loan Number: 1234567890

BORROWER'S CERTIFICATION AND AUTHORIZATION

CERTIFICATION

The undersigned certify the following:

1. I/We have applied for a mortgage loan from TRISTAR FINANCE GROUP, INC. INC. ("Lender"). In applying for the loan, I/we completed a loan application containing various information on the purpose of the loan, the amount and source of the downpayment, employment and income information, and assets and liabilities. I/We certify that all of the information is true and complete. I/We made no misrepresentations in the loan application or other documents, nor did I/we omit any pertinent information.

2. I/We understand and agree that Lender reserves the right to change the mortgage loan review process. This may include verifying the information provided on the application with the employer and/or the financial institution.

3. I/We fully understand that it is a Federal crime punishable by fine or imprisonment, or both, to knowingly make any false statements when applying for this mortgage, as applicable under the provisions of Title 18, United States Code, Section 1014.

4. I/We provided Lender with verbal and/or written authorization to order a consumer credit report and verify other credit information, including past and present mortgage and landlord references in connection with my/our application for this loan.

AUTHORIZATION TO RELEASE INFORMATION

To Whom It May Concern:

1. I/We have applied for a mortgage loan from Lender. As part of the application process, Lender and the mortgage guaranty insurer (if any), may verify information contained in my/our loan application and in other documents required in connection with the loan, either before the loan is closed or as part of its quality control program.

2. I/We authorize you to provide to Lender and to any investor to whom you may sell my mortgage, and to the mortgage guaranty insurer (if any), any and all information and documentation that they request. Such information includes, but is not limited to, employment history and income; bank, money market, and similar account balances; credit history; and copies of income tax returns.

3. I/We further authorize Lender to order a consumer credit report and verify other credit information, including past and present mortgage and landlord references.

4. Lender or any investor that purchases the mortgage, or the mortgage guaranty insurer (if any), may address this authorization to any party named in the loan application.

5. A copy of this authorization may be accepted as an original.

6. Your prompt reply to Lender, the investor that purchased the mortgage, or the mortgage guaranty insurer (if any) to their requests in connection with your mortgage loan application is appreciated.

7. Mortgage guaranty insurer (if any):
    N/A

BORROWER'S CERTIFICATION AND AUTHORIZATION
TDC.LSR 01/05/12   Page 1 of 2

Right of Financial Privacy Act of 1978 Notice- The Department of Housing and Urban Development (HUD) and the Department of Veterans Affairs (VA) have the right to access financial information held by a financial institution in determining whether to qualify a prospective applicant under their respective loan programs. If you are applying for HUD or VA loan, your financial records will be made available to the requesting government agency without further notice to or authorization from you; such financial information will not be disclosed or released outside the requesting agency except as required or permitted by law. Prior to the time that your financial records are disclosed, you may revoke this authorization at any time; however, your refusal to provide the information may cause your application to be delayed or rejected. If you believe that your financial records have been disclosed improperly, you may have legal rights under the Right to Financial Privacy Act of 1978 (12 USC 3400 **et seq**.).

555-55-5555
Borrower RICHARD WILLIAM ROGERS   Date   Social Security Number

Make sure SSN is there

Borrower _____ Date   Social Security Number _____

Borrower _____ Date   Social Security Number _____

Borrower _____ Date   Social Security Number _____

Borrower _____ Date   Social Security Number _____

Borrower _____ Date   Social Security Number _____

BORROWER'S CERTIFICATION AND AUTHORIZATION
TDC.LSR 01/05/12   Page 2 of 2

Loan Number: 1234567890

Form **4506-T**

(Rev. January 2012)

Department of the Treasury
Internal Revenue Service

Request for Transcript of Tax Return

▶ **Request may be rejected if the form is incomplete or illegible.**

OMB No. 1545-1872

Tip: Use Form 4506-T to order a transcript or other return information free of charge. See the product list below. You can quickly request transcripts by using our automated self-help service tools. Please visit us at IRS.gov and click on "Order a Transcript" or call 1-800-908-9946. If you need a copy of your return, use **Form 4506, Request for Copy of Tax Return.** There is a fee to get a copy of your return.

1a	Name shown on tax return. If a joint return, enter the name shown first. RICHARD WILLIAM ROGERS	**1b**	First social security number on tax return, individual taxpayer identification number, or employer identification number (see instructions) 555-55-5555
2a	If a joint return, enter spouse's name shown on tax return.	**2b**	Second social security number or individual taxpayer identification number if joint tax return

3   Current name, address (including apt., room, or suite no.), city, state, and ZIP code (See instructions) RICHARD WILLIAM ROGERS
8624 OAKLAWN AVENUE, MODESTO, CALIFORNIA 95355

4   Previous address shown on the last return filed if different from line 3 (See instructions)

Have borrower confirm all information is accurate

5   If the transcript or tax information is to be mailed to a third party (such as a mortgage company), enter the third party's name, address, and telephone number.
TRISTAR FINANCE, INC., 1000 MAIN STREET LOS ANGELES, CALIFORNIA
~~STREET, SUITE 250, CENTENNIAL, COLORADO 80112~~

Caution: If the tax transcript is being mailed to a third party, ensure that you have filled in lines 6 through 9 before signing. Sign and date the form once you have filled in these lines. Completing these steps helps to protect your privacy. Once the IRS discloses your IRS transcript to the third party listed on line 5, the IRS has no control over what the third party does with the information. If you would like to limit the third party's authority to disclose your transcript information, you can specify this limitation in your written agreement with the third party.

6   **Transcript requested.** Enter the tax form number here (1040, 1065, 1120, etc.) and check the appropriate box below. Enter only one tax form number per request. ▶ 1040

- **a**   **Return Transcript,** which includes most of the line items of a tax return as filed with the IRS. A tax return transcript does not reflect changes made to the account after the return is processed. Transcripts are only available for the following returns: Form 1040 series, Form 1065, Form 1120, Form 1120A, Form 1120H, Form 1120L, and Form 1120S. Return transcripts are available for the current year and returns processed during the prior 3 processing years. Most requests will be processed within 10 business days . . . . [X]

- **b**   **Account Transcript,** which contains information on the financial status of the account, such as payments made on the account, penalty assessments, and adjustments made by you or the IRS after the return was filed. Return information is limited to items such as tax liability and estimated tax payments. Account transcripts are available for most returns. Most requests will be processed within 30 calendar days . . [ ]

- **c**   **Record of Account,** which provides the most detailed information as it is a combination of the Return Transcript and the Account Transcript. Available for current year and 3 prior tax years. Most requests will be processed within 30 calendar days . . . . [ ]

7   **Verification of Nonfiling,** which is proof from the IRS that you **did not** file a return for the year. Current year requests are only available after June 15th. There are no availability restrictions on prior year requests. Most requests will be processed within 10 business days . . . . . . [ ]

8   **Form W-2, Form 1099 series, Form 1098 series, or Form 5498 series transcript.** The IRS can provide a transcript that includes data from these information returns. State or local information is not included with the Form W-2 information. The IRS may be able to provide this transcript information for up to 10 years. Information for the current year is generally not available until the year after it is filed with the IRS. For example, W-2 information for 2010, filed in 2011, will not be available from the IRS until 2012. If you need W-2 information for retirement purposes, you should contact the Social Security Administration at 1-800-772-1213. Most requests will be processed within 45 days . . . . [ ]

Caution: If you need a copy of Form W-2 or Form 1099, you should first contact the payer. To get a copy of the Form W-2 or Form 1099 filed with your return, you must use Form 4506 and request a copy of your return, which includes all attachments.

9   **Year or period requested.** Enter the ending date of the year or period, using the mm/dd/yyyy format. If you are requesting more than four years or periods, you must attach another Form 4506-T. For requests relating to quarterly tax returns, such as Form 941, you must enter each quarter or tax period separately.   12/31/20XX   12/31/20XX

Check this box if you have notified the IRS or the IRS has notified you that one of the years for which you are requesting a transcript involved **identity theft** on your federal tax return . . . . ▶ [ ]

Caution. Do not sign this form unless all applicable lines have been completed.

Signature of taxpayer(s). I declare that I am either the taxpayer whose name is shown on line 1a or 2a, or a person authorized to obtain the tax information requested. If the request applies to a joint return, **either** husband or wife must sign. If signed by a corporate officer, partner, guardian, tax matters partner, executor, receiver, administrator, trustee, or party other than the taxpayer, I certify that I have the authority to execute Form 4506-T on behalf of the taxpayer.
Note: For transcripts being sent to a third party, this form must be received within 120 days of signature date.

Phone number of taxpayer on line 1a or 2a
(555) 555-5555

Sign Here ▶ _____
Signature (see instructions)   Date

▶ _____
Title (if line 1a above is a corporation, partnership, estate, or trust)

▶ _____
Spouse's signature   Date

For Privacy Act and Paperwork Reduction Act Notice, see page 2.   Cat. No. 37667N   Form **4506-T** (Rev. 1-2012)

Page 1 of 2

Form 4506-T (Rev. 1-2012)

Section references are to the Internal Revenue Code unless otherwise noted.

What's New

The IRS has created a page on IRS.gov for information about Form 4506-T at *www.irs.go v/form4506*. Information about any recent developments affecting Form 4506-T (such as legislation enacted after we released it) will be posted on that page.

General Instructions

CAUTION. *Do not sign this form unless all applicable lines have been completed.*

Purpose of form. Use Form 4506-T to request tax return information. You can also designate (on line 5) a third party to receive the information. Taxpayers using a tax year beginning in one calendar year and ending in the following year (fiscal tax year) must file Form 4506-T to request a return transcript.

Note. If you are unsure of which type of transcript you need, request the Record of Accoun t, as it provides the most detailed information.

Tip. Use Form 4506, Request for Copy of Tax Return, to request copies of tax returns.

Where to file. Mail or fax Form 4506-T to the address below for the state you lived in, or the state your business was in, when that return was filed. There are two address charts: one for individual transcripts (Form 1040 series and Form W-2) and one for all other transcripts.

If you are requesting more than one transcript or other product and the chart below shows two different addresses, send your request to the address based on the address of your most recent return.

Automated transcript request. You can quickly request transcripts by using our automated self help-service tools. Please visit us at IRS.gov and click on "Order a Transcript" or call 1-800-908-9946.

Chart for individual transcripts (Form 1040 series and Form W-2 and Form 1099)

If you filed an individual return and lived in:	Mail or fax to the "Internal Revenue Service" at:
Alabama, Kentucky, Louisiana, Mississippi, Tennessee, Texas, a foreign country, American Samoa, Puerto Rico, Guam, the Commonwealth of the Northern Mariana Islands, the U.S. Virgin Islands, or A.P.O. or F.P.O. address	RAIVS Team Stop 6716 AUSC Austin, TX 73301 512-460-2272
Alaska, Arizona, Arkansas, California, Colorado, Hawaii, Idaho, Illinois, Indiana, Iowa, Kansas, Michigan, Minnesota, Montana, Nebraska, Nevada, New Mexico, North Dakota, Oklahoma, Oregon, South Dakota, Utah, Washington, Wisconsin, Wyoming	RAIVS Team Stop 37106 Fresno, CA 93888 559-456-5876
Connecticut, Delaware, District of Columbia, Florida, Georgia, Maine, Maryland, Massachusetts, Missouri, New Hampshire, New Jersey, New York, North Carolina, Ohio, Pennsylvania, Rhode Island, South Carolina, Vermont, Virginia, West Virginia	RAIVS Team Stop 6705 P-6 Kansas City, MO 64999 816-292-6102

Chart for all other transcripts

If you lived in or your business was in:	Mail or fax to the "Internal Revenue Service" at:
Alabama, Alaska, Arizona, Arkansas, California, Colorado, Florida, Hawaii, Idaho, Iowa, Kansas, Louisiana, Minnesota, Mississippi, Missouri, Montana, Nebraska, Nevada, New Mexico, North Dakota, Oklahoma, Oregon, South Dakota, Texas, Utah, Washington, Wyoming, a foreign country, or A.P.O. or F.P.O. address	RAIVS Team P.O. Box 9941 Mail Stop 6734 Ogden, UT 84409 801-620-6922
Connecticut, Delaware, District of Columbia, Georgia, Illinois, Indiana, Kentucky, Maine, Maryland, Massachusetts, Michigan, New Hampshire, New Jersey, New York, North Carolina, Ohio, Pennsylvania, Rhode Island, South Carolina, Tennessee, Vermont, Virginia, West Virginia, Wisconsin	RAIVS Team P.O. Box 145500 Stop 2800 F Cincinnati, OH 45250 859-669-3592

Line 1b. Enter your employer identification number (EIN) if your request relates to a business return. Otherwise, enter the first social security number (SSN) or your individual taxpayer identification number (ITIN) shown on the return. For example, if you are requesting Form 1040 that includes Schedule C (Form 1040), enter your SSN.

Line 3. Enter your current address. If you use a P.O. box, include it on this line.

Line 4. Enter the address shown on the last return filed if different from the address entered on line 3.

Note. If the address on lines 3 and 4 are different and you have not changed your address with the IRS, file Form 8822, Change of Address.

Line 6. Enter only one tax form number per request.

Signature and date. Form 4506-T must be signed and dated by the taxpayer listed on line 1a or 2a. If you completed line 5 requesting the information be sent to a third party, the IRS must receive Form 4506-T within 120 days of the date signed by the taxpayer or it will be rejected. Ensure that all applicable lines are completed before signing.

Individuals. Transcripts of jointly filed tax returns may be furnished to either spouse. Only one signature is required. Sign Form 4506-T exactly as your name appeared on the original return. If you changed your name, also sign your current name.

Corporations. Generally, Form 4506-T can be signed by: (1) an officer having legal authority to bind the corporation, (2) any person designated by the board of directors or other governing body, or (3) any officer or employee on written request by any principal officer and attested to by the secretary or other officer.

Partnerships. Generally, Form 4506-T can be signed by any person who was a member of the partnership during any part of the tax period requested on line 9.

All others. See section 6103(e) if the taxpayer has died, is insolvent, is a dissolved corporation, or if a trustee, guardian, executor, receiver, or administrator is acting for the taxpayer.

Documentation. For entities other than individuals, you must attach the authorization document. For example, this could be the letter from the principal officer authorizing an employee of the corporation or the letters testamentary authorizing an individual to act for an estate.

Privacy Act and Paperwork Reduction Act Notice. We ask for the information on this form to establish your right to gain access to the requested tax information under the Internal Revenue Code. We need this information to properly identify the tax information and respond to your request. You are not required to request any transcript ; if you do request a transcript, sections 6103 and 6109 and their regulations require you to provide this information, including your SSN or EIN. If you do not provide this information, we may not be able to process your request. Providing false or fraudulent information may subject you to penalties.

Routine uses of this information include giving it to the Department of Justice for civil and criminal litigation, and cities, states, the District of Columbia, and U.S. commonwealths and possessions for use in administering their tax laws. We may also disclose this information to other countries under a tax treaty, to federal and state agencies to enforce federal nontax criminal laws, or to federal law enforcement and intelligence agencies to combat terrorism.

You are not required to provide the information requested on a form that is subject to the Paperwork Reductio n Act unless the form displays a valid OMB control number. Books or records relating to a form or its instructions must be retained as long as their contents may become material in the administration of any Internal Revenue law. Generally, tax retur ns and return information are confidential, as required by section 6103.

The time needed to complete and file Form 4506-T will vary depending on individual circumstances. The estimated average time is: **Learning about the law or the form,** 10 min.; **Preparing the form,** 12 min.; and **Copying, assembling, and sending the form to the IRS,** 20 min.

If you have comments concerning the accuracy of these time estimates or suggestions for making Form 4506-T simpler, we would be happy to hear from you. You can write to:

Internal Revenue Service
Tax Products Coordinating Committee
SEW:CAR:MP:T:M:S
1111 Constitution Ave. NW, IR-6526
Washington, DC 20224

Do not send the form to this address. Instead, see *Where to file* on this page.

For **Privacy Act and Paperwork Reduction Act Notice,** see page 2.   Cat. No. 37667N   Form **4506-T** (Rev. 1-2012)

Loan Number: 1234567890

Form W-9
(Rev. December 2011)
Department of the Treasury
Internal Revenue Service

Request for Taxpayer Identification Number and Certification

Give Form to the requester. Do not send to the IRS.

Name (as shown on your income tax return)

RICHARD WILLIAM ROGERS

Business name/disregarded entity name, if different from above

Check appropriate box for federal tax classification:

[X] Individual/sole proprietor [ ] C Corporation [ ] S Corporation [ ] Partnership [ ] Trust/estate

[ ] Limited liability company. Enter the tax classification (C= C corporation, S= S corporation, P= partnership) ▶ ----------

[ ] Other (see instructions) ▶

[ ] Exempt payee

Address (number, street, and apt. or suite no.)

8624 OAKLAWN AVENUE

City, state, and ZIP code

MODESTO, CALIFORNIA 95355

List account number(s) here (optional)

1234567890

Requester's name and address (optional) TRISTAR FINANCE GROUP, INC 1000 MAIN STREET LOS ANGELES, CALIFORNIA 91301

See Specific Instructions on page 2. / *Print or type*

Part I Taxpayer Identification Number (TIN)

Enter your TIN in the appropriate box. The TIN provided must match the name given on the "Name" line to avoid backup withholding. For individuals, this is your social security number (SSN). However, for a resident alien, sole proprietor, or disregarded entity, see the Part I instructions on page 3. For other entities, it is your employer identification number (EIN). If you do not have a number, see *How to get a TIN* on page 3.

Note. If the account is in more than one name, see the chart on page 4 for guidelines on whose number to enter.

Social security number

555-55-5555

Employer ide

Have borrower confirm information is accurate and complete

Part II Certification

Under penalties of perjury, I certify that:

1. The number shown on this form is my correct taxpayer identification number (or I am waiting for a number to be issued

2. I am not subject to backup withholding because: (a) I am exempt from backup withholding, or (b) I have not been no Revenue Service (IRS) that I am subject to backup withholding as a result of a failure to report all interest or dividend notified me that I am no longer subject to backup withholding, and

3. I am a U.S. citizen or other U.S. person (defined below).

Certification instructions. You must cross out item 2 above if you have been notified by the IRS that you are currently subject to backup withholding because you have failed to report all interest and dividends on your tax return. For real estate transactions, item 2 does not apply. For mortgage interest paid, acquisition or abandonment of secured property, cancellation of debt, contributions to an individual retirement arrangement (IRA), and generally, payments other than interest and dividends, you are not required to sign the certification, but you must provide your correct TIN. See the instructions on page 4.

Sign Here	Signature of U.S. person ▶	Date ▶

General Instructions

Section references are to the Internal Revenue Code unless otherwise noted.

Purpose of Form

A person who is required to file an information return with the IRS must obtain your correct taxpayer identification number (TIN) to report, for example, income paid to you, real estate transactions, mortgage interest you paid, acquisition or abandonment of secured property, cancellation of debt, or contributions you made to an IRA.

Use Form W-9 only if you are a U.S. person (including a resident alien), to provide your correct TIN to the person requesting it (the requester) and, when applicable, to:

1. Certify that the TIN you are giving is correct (or you are waiting for a number to be issued),

2. Certify that you are not subject to backup withholding, or

3. Claim exemption from backup withholding if you are a U.S. exempt payee. If applicable, you are also certifying that as a U.S. person, your allocable share of any partnership income from a U.S. trade or business is not subject to the withholding tax on foreign partners' share of effectively connected income.

Note. If a requester gives you a form other than Form W-9 to request your TIN, you must use the requester's form if it is substantially similar to this Form W-9.

Definition of a U.S. person. For federal tax purposes, you are considered a U.S. person if you are:

■ An individual who is a U.S. citizen or U.S. resident alien,

■ A partnership, corporation, company, or association created or organized in the United States or under the laws of the United States,

■ An estate (other than a foreign estate) or

■ A domestic trust (as defined in Regulations section 301.7701-7).

Form **W-9** (Rev. 12-2011)

Cat. No. 10231X

Check for possible initial lines at bottom of document

Special rules for partnerships. Partnerships that conduct a trade or business in the United States are generally required to pay a withholding tax on any foreign partners' share of income from such business. Further, in certain cases where a Form W-9 has not been received, a partnership is required to presume that a partner is a foreign person, and pay the withholding tax. Therefore, if you are a U.S. person that is a partner in a partnership conducting a trade or business in the United States, provide Form W-9 to the partnership to establish your U.S. status and avoid withholding on your share of partnership income.

The person who gives Form W-9 to the partnership for purposes of establishing its U.S. status and avoiding withholding on its allocable share of net income from the partnership conducting a trade or business in the United States is in the following cases:

- The U.S. owner of a disregarded entity and not the entity,
- The U.S. grantor or other owner of a grantor trust and not the trust, and
- The U.S. trust (other than a grantor trust) and not the beneficiaries of the trust.

Foreign person. If you are a foreign person, do not use Form W-9. Instead, use the appropriate Form W-8 (see Publication 515, Withholding of Tax on Nonresident Aliens and Foreign Entities).

Nonresident alien who becomes a resident alien. Generally, only a nonresident alien individual may use the terms of a tax treaty to reduce or eliminate U.S. tax on certain types of income. However, most tax treaties contain a provision known as a "saving clause." Exceptions specified in the saving clause may permit an exemption from tax to continue for certain types of income even after the payee has otherwise become a U.S. resident alien for tax purposes.

If you are a U.S. resident alien who is relying on an exception contained in the saving clause of a tax treaty to claim an exemption from U.S. tax on certain types of income, you must attach a statement to Form W-9 that specifies the following five items:

1. The treaty country. Generally, this must be the same treaty under which you claimed exemption from tax as a nonresident alien.
2. The treaty article addressing the income.
3. The article number (or location) in the tax treaty that contains the saving clause and its exceptions.
4. The type and amount of income that qualifies for the exemption from tax.
5. Sufficient facts to justify the exemption from tax under the terms of the treaty article.

Example. Article 20 of the U.S.-China income tax treaty allows an exemption from tax for scholarship income received by a Chinese student temporarily present in the United States. Under U.S. law, this student will become a resident alien for tax purposes if his or her stay in the United States exceeds 5 calendar years. However, paragraph 2 of the first Protocol to the U.S.-China treaty (dated April 30, 1984) allows the provisions of Article 20 to continue to apply even after the Chinese student becomes a resident alien of the United States. A Chinese student who qualifies for this exception (under paragraph 2 of the first protocol) and is relying on this exception to claim an exemption from tax on his or her scholarship or fellowship income would attach to Form W-9 a statement that includes the information described above to support that exemption.

If you are a nonresident alien or a foreign entity not subject to backup withholding, give the requester the appropriate completed Form W-8.

What is backup withholding? Persons making certain payments to you must under certain conditions withhold and pay to the IRS a percentage of such payments. This is called "backup withholding."

Payments that may be subject to backup withholding include interest, tax-exempt interest, dividends, broker and barter exchange transactions, rents, royalties, nonemployee pay, and certain payments from fishing boat operators. Real estate transactions are not subject to backup withholding.

You will not be subject to backup withholding on payments you receive if you give the requester your correct TIN, make the proper certifications, and report all your taxable interest and dividends on your tax return.

Payments you receive will be subject to backup withholding if:

1. You do not furnish your TIN to the requester,
2. You do not certify your TIN when required (see the Part II instructions on page 4 for details),
3. The IRS tells the requester that you furnished an incorrect TIN,
4. The IRS tells you that you are subject to backup withholding because you did not report all your interest and dividends on your tax return (for reportable interest and dividends only), or
5. You do not certify to the requester that you are not subject to backup withholding under 4 above (for reportable interest and dividend accounts opened after 1983 only).

Certain payees and payments are exempt from backup withholding. See the instructions below and the separate Instructions for the Requester of Form W-9.

Also see *Special rules for partnerships* on this page.

Updating Your Information

You must provide updated information to any person to whom you claimed to be an exempt payee if you are no longer an exempt payee and anticipate receiving reportable payments in the future from this person. For example, you may need to provide updated information if you are a C corporation that elects to be an S corporation, or if you no longer are tax exempt. In addition, you must furnish a new Form W-9 if the name or TIN changes for the account, for example, if the grantor of a grantor trust dies.

Penalties

Failure to furnish TIN. If you fail to furnish your correct TIN to a requester, you are subject to a penalty of $50 for each such failure unless your failure is due to reasonable cause and not to willful neglect.

Civil penalty for false information with respect to withholding. If you make a false statement with no reasonable basis that results in no backup withholding, you are subject to a $500 penalty.

Criminal penalty for falsifying information. Willfully falsifying certifications or affirmations may subject you to criminal penalties including fines and/or imprisonment.

Misuse of TINs. If the requester discloses or uses TINs in violation of federal law, the requester may be subject to civil and criminal penalties.

Specific Instructions

Name

If you are an individual, you must generally enter the name shown on your income tax return. However, if you have changed your last name, for instance, due to marriage without informing the Social Security Administration of the name change, enter your first name, the last name shown on your social security card, and your new last name.

If the account is in joint names, list first, and then circle, the name of the person or entity whose number you entered in Part I of the form.

Form **W-9** (Rev. 12-2011)   Cat. No. 10231X

Sole proprietor. Enter your individual name as shown on your income tax return on the "Name" line. You may enter your business, trade, or "doing business as (DBA)" name on the "Business name/disregarded entity name" line.

Partnership, C Corporation, or S Corporation. Enter the entity's name on the "Name" line and any business, trade, or "doing business as (DBA) name" on the "Business name/disregarded entity name" line.

Disregarded entity. Enter the owner's name on the "Name" line. The name of the entity entered on the "Name" line should never be a disregarded entity. The name on the "Name" line must be the name shown on the income tax return on which the income will be reported. For example, if a foreign LLC that is treated as a disregarded entity for U.S. federal tax purposes has a domestic owner, the domestic owner's name is required to be provided on the "Name" line. If the direct owner of the entity is also a disregarded entity, enter the first owner that is not disregarded for federal tax purposes. Enter the disregarded entity's name on the "Business name/disregarded entity name" line. If the owner of the disregarded entity is a foreign person, you must complete an appropriate Form W-8.

Note. Check the appropriate box for the federal tax classification of the person whose name is entered on the "Name" line (Individual/sole proprietor, Partnership, C Corporation, S Corporation, Trust/estate).

Limited Liability Company (LLC). If the person identified on the "Name" line is an LLC, check the "Limited liability company" box only and enter the appropriate code for the tax classification in the space provided. If you are an LLC that is treated as a partnership for federal tax purposes, enter "P" for partnership. If you are an LLC that has filed a Form 8832 or a Form 2553 to be taxed as a corporation, enter "C" for C corporation or "S" for S corporation. If you are an LLC that is disregarded as an entity separate from its owner under Regulation section 301.7701-3 (except for employment and excise tax), do not check the LLC box unless the owner of the LLC (required to be identified on the "Name" line) is another LLC that is not disregarded for federal tax purposes. If the LLC is disregarded as an entity separate from its owner, enter the appropriate tax classification of the owner identified on the "Name" line.

Other entities. Enter your business name as shown on required federal tax documents on the "Name" line. This name should match the name shown on the charter or other legal document creating the entity. You may enter any business, trade, or DBA name on the "Business name/disregarded entity name" line.

Exempt Payee

If you are exempt from backup withholding, enter your name as described above and check the appropriate box for your status, then check the "Exempt payee" box in the line following the "Business name/disregarded entity name," sign and date the form.

Generally, individuals (including sole proprietors) are not exempt from backup withholding. Corporations are exempt from backup withholding for certain payments, such as interest and dividends.

Note. If you are exempt from backup withholding, you should still complete this form to avoid possible erroneous backup withholding.

The following payees are exempt from backup withholding:

1. An organization exempt from tax under section 501(a), any IRA, or a custodial account under section 403(b)(7) if the account satisfies the requirements of section 401(f)(2),

2. The United States or any of its agencies or instrumentalities,

3. A state, the District of Columbia, a possession of the United States, or any of their political subdivisions or instrumentalities,

4. A foreign government or any of its political subdivisions, agencies, or instrumentalities, or

5. An international organization or any of its agencies or instrumentalities.

Other payees that may be exempt from backup withholding include:

6. A corporation,

7. A foreign central bank of issue,

8. A dealer in securities or commodities required to register in the United States, the District of Columbia, or a possession of the United States,

9. A futures commission merchant registered with the Commodity Futures Trading Commission,

10. A real estate investment trust,

11. An entity registered at all times during the tax year under the Investment Company Act of 1940,

12. A common trust fund operated by a bank under section 584(a),

13. A financial institution,

14. A middleman known in the investment community as a nominee or custodian, or

15. A trust exempt from tax under section 664 or described in section 4947.

The following chart shows types of payments that may be exempt from backup withholding. The chart applies to the exempt payees listed above, 1 through 15.

IF the payment is for . . .	THEN the payment is exempt for . . .
Interest and dividend payments	All exempt payees except for 9
Broker transactions	Exempt payees 1 through 5 and 7 through 13. Also, C corporations.
Barter exchange transactions and patronage dividends	Exempt payees 1 through 5
Payments over $600 required to be reported and direct sales over $5,000 [1]	Generally, exempt payees 1 through 7 [2]

[1] See Form 1099-MISC, Miscellaneous Income, and its instructions.

[2] However, the following payments made to a corporation and reportable on Form 1099-MISC are not exempt from backup withholding: medical and health care payments, attorneys' fees, gross proceeds paid to an attorney, and payments for services paid by a federal executive agency.

Part I. Taxpayer Identification Number (TIN)

Enter your TIN in the appropriate box. If you are a resident alien and you do not have and are not eligible to get an SSN, your TIN is your IRS individual taxpayer identification number (ITIN). Enter it in the social security number box. If you do not have an ITIN, see *How to get a TIN* below.

If you are a sole proprietor and you have an EIN, you may enter either your SSN or EIN. However, the IRS prefers that you use your SSN.

If you are a single-member LLC that is disregarded as an entity separate from its owner (see *Limited Liability Company (LLC)* on page 3), enter the owner's SSN (or EIN, if the owner has one). Do not enter the disregarded entity's EIN. If the LLC is classified as a corporation or partnership, enter the entity's EIN.

Note. See the chart on page 4 for further clarification of name and TIN combinations.

How to get a TIN. If you do not have a TIN, apply for one immediately. To apply for an SSN, get Form SS-5, Application for a Social Security Card, from your local Social Security Administration office or get this form online at *www.ssa.gov*. You may also get this form by calling 1-800-772-1213. Use Form W-7, Application for IRS Individual Taxpayer Identification Number, to apply for an ITIN, or Form SS-4, Application for Employer Identification Number, to apply for an EIN. You can apply for an EIN online by accessing the IRS website at *www.irs.gov/businesses* and clicking on Employer Identification Number (EIN) under Starting a Business. You can get Forms W-7 and SS-4 from the IRS by visiting IRS.gov or by calling 1-800-TAX-FORM (1-800-829-3676).

If you are asked to complete Form W-9 but do not have a TIN, write "Applied For" in the space for the TIN, sign and date the form, and give it to the requester. For interest and dividend payments, and certain payments made with respect to readily tradable instruments, generally you will have 60 days to get a TIN and give it to the requester before you are subject to backup withholding on payments. The 60-day rule does not apply to other types of payments. You will be subject to backup withholding on all such payments until you provide your TIN to the requester.

Note. Entering "Applied For" means that you have already applied for a TIN or that you intend to apply for one soon.

Caution: *A disregarded domestic entity that has a foreign owner must use the appropriate Form W-8.*

Part II. Certification

To establish to the withholding agent that you are a U.S. person, or resident alien, sign Form W-9. You may be requested to sign by the withholding agent even if items 1, 4 and 5 below indicate otherwise.

For a joint account, only the person whose TIN is shown in Part I should sign (when required). In the case of a disregarded entity, the person identified on the "Name" line must sign. Exempt payees, see *Exempt Payee* on page 3.

Signature requirements. Complete the certification as indicated in items 1 through 5, below.

1. Interest, dividend, and barter exchange accounts opened before 1984 and broker accounts considered active during 1983. You must give your correct TIN, but you do not have to sign the certification.

2. Interest, dividend, broker, and barter exchange accounts opened after 1983 and broker accounts considered inactive during 1983. You must sign the certification or backup withholding will apply. If you are subject to backup withholding and you are merely providing your correct TIN to the requester, you must cross out item 2 in the certification before signing the form.

3. Real estate transactions. You must sign the certification. You may cross out item 2 of the certification.

4. Other payments. You must give your correct TIN, but you do not have to sign the certification unless you have been notified that you have previously given an incorrect TIN. "Other payments" include payments made in the course of the requester's trade or business for rents, royalties, goods (other than bills for merchandise), medical and health care services (including payments to corporations), payments to a nonemployee for services, payments to certain fishing boat crew members and fishermen, and gross proceeds paid to attorneys (including payments to corporations).

5. Mortgage interest paid by you, acquisition or abandonment of secured property, cancellation of debt, qualified tuition program payments (under section 529), IRA, Coverdell ESA, Archer MSA or HSA contributions or distributions, and pension distributions. You must give your correct TIN, but you do not have to sign the certification.

What Name and Number To Give the Requester

For this type of account:	Give name and SSN of:
1. Individual	The individual
2. Two or more individuals (joint account)	The actual owner of the account or, if combined funds, the first individual on the account [1]
3. Custodian account of a minor (Uniform Gift to Minors Act)	The minor [2]
4. a. The usual revocable savings trust (grantor is also trustee)	The grantor-trustee [1]
b. So-called trust account that is not a legal or valid trust under state law	The actual owner [1]
5. Sole proprietorship or disregarded entity owned by an individual	The owner [3]
6. Grantor trust filing under Optional Form 1099 Filing Method 1 (see Regulation section 1.671-4(b)(2)(i)(A))	The grantor*

For this type of account:	Give name and EIN of:
7. Disregarded entity not owned by an individual	The owner
8. A valid trust, estate, or pension trust	Legal entity [4]
9. Corporate or LLC electing corporate status on Form 8832 or Form 2553	The corporation
10. Association, club, religious, charitable, educational, or other tax-exempt organization	The organization
11. Partnership or multi-member LLC	The partnership
12. A broker or registered nominee	The broker or nominee
13. Account with the Department of Agriculture in the name of a public entity (such as a state or local government, school district, or prison) that receives agricultural program payments	The public entity
14. Grantor trust filing under the Form 1041 Filing Method or the Optional Form 1099 Filing Method 2 (see Regulation section 1.671-4(b)(2)(i)(B))	The trust

[1] List first and circle the name of the person whose number you furnish. If only one person on a joint account has an SSN, that person's number must be furnished.
[2] Circle the minor's name and furnish the minor's SSN.
[3] You must show your individual name and you may also enter your business or "DBA" name on the "Business name/disregarded entity" name line. You may use either your SSN or EIN (if you have one), but the IRS encourages you to use your SSN.
[4] List first and circle the name of the trust, estate, or pension trust. (Do not furnish the TIN of the personal representative or trustee unless the legal entity itself is not designated in the account title.) Also see *Special rules for partnerships* on page 2.
* **Note.** Grantor also must provide a Form W-9 to trustee of trust.

Note. If no name is circled when more than one name is listed, the number will be considered to be that of the first name listed.

Secure Your Tax Records from Identity Theft

Identity theft occurs when someone uses your personal information such as your name, social security number (SSN), or other identifying information, without your permission, to commit fraud or other crimes. An identity thief may use your SSN to get a job or may file a tax return using your SSN to receive a refund.

To reduce your risk:
- Protect your SSN,
- Ensure your employer is protecting your SSN, and
- Be careful when choosing a tax preparer.

If your tax records are affected by identity theft and you receive a notice from the IRS, respond right away to the name and phone number printed on the IRS notice or letter.

If your tax records are not currently affected by identity theft but you think you are at risk due to a lost or stolen purse or wallet, questionable credit card activity or credit report, contact the IRS Identity Theft Hotline at 1-800-908-4490 or submit Form 14039.

For more information, see Publication 4535, Identity Theft Prevention and Victim Assistance.

Victims of identity theft who are experiencing economic harm or a system problem, or are seeking help in resolving tax problems that have not been resolved through normal channels, may be eligible for Taxpayer Advocate Service (TAS) assistance. You can reach TAS by calling the TAS toll-free case intake line at 1-877-777-4778 or TTY/TDD 1-800-829-4059.

Protect yourself from suspicious emails or phishing schemes. Phishing is the creation and use of email and websites designed to mimic legitimate business emails and websites. The most common act is sending an email to a user falsely claiming to be an established legitimate enterprise in an attempt to scam the user into surrendering private information that will be used for identity theft.

The IRS does not initiate contacts with taxpayers via emails. Also, the IRS does not request personal detailed information through email or ask taxpayers for the PIN numbers, passwords, or similar secret access information for their credit card, bank, or other financial accounts.

If you receive an unsolicited email claiming to be from the IRS, forward this message to *phishing@irs.gov*. You may also report misuse of the IRS name, logo, or other IRS property to the Treasury Inspector General for Tax Administration at 1-800-366-4484. You can forward suspicious emails to the Federal Trade Commission at: *spam@uce.gov* or contact them at *www.ftc.gov/idtheft* or 1-877-IDTHEFT (1-877-438-4338).

Visit IRS.gov to learn more about identity theft and how to reduce your risk.

Privacy Act Notice

Section 6109 of the Internal Revenue Code requires you to provide your correct TIN to persons (including federal agencies) who are required to file information returns with the IRS to report interest, dividends, or certain other income paid to you; mortgage interest you paid; the acquisition or abandonment of secured property; the cancellation of debt; or contributions you made to an IRA, Archer MSA, or HSA. The person collecting this form uses the information on the form to file information returns with the IRS, reporting the above information. Routine uses of this information include giving it to the Department of Justice for civil and criminal litigation and to cities, states, the District of Columbia, and U.S. possessions for use in administering their laws. The information also may be disclosed to other countries under a treaty, to federal and state agencies to enforce civil and criminal laws, or to federal law enforcement and intelligence agencies to combat terrorism. You must provide your TIN whether or not you are required to file a tax return. Under section 3406, payers must generally withhold a percentage of taxable interest, dividend, and certain other payments to a payee who does not give a TIN to the payer. Certain penalties may also apply for providing false or fraudulent information.

Sample Document for National Notary Association Signing Agent Certification Study Guide

Loan Number: 1234567890

HUD/VA Addendum to Uniform Residential Loan Application

OMB Approval No. VA: 2900-0144
HUD: 1234-1234 (exp. 02/28/20 XX)

Part I - Identifying Information (mark the type of application)	2. Agency Case No. (include any suffix)	3. Lender's Case No.	4. Section of the Act (for HUD cases)
1. ☐ VA Application for Home Loan Guaranty ☒ HUD/FHA Application for Insurance under the National Housing Act	000-5555555-000	1234567890	203B

5. Borrower's Name & Present Address (include zip code)	7. Loan Amount (include the UFMIP if for HUD or Funding Fee if for VA)	8. Interest Rate	9. Proposed Maturity
RICHARD WILLIAM ROGERS 8624 OAKLAWN AVENUE MODESTO, CALIFORNIA 95355	$205,631.00	3.250 %	30 yrs. mos.

6. Property Address (including name of subdivision, lot & block no. & zip code)	10. Discount Amount (only if borrower is permitted to pay)	11. Amount of Up Front Premium	12a. Amount of Monthly Premium	12b. Term of Monthly Premium
8624 OAKLAWN AVENUE, MODESTO, CALIFORNIA 95355		$3,536.66	$200.25 /mo.	63 months

13. Lender's I.D. Code	14. Sponsor/Agent I.D. Code
2294400215	2294400215

15. Lender's Name & Address (include zip code)	16. Name & Address of Sponsor/Agent
TRISTAR FINANCE GROUP, INC 1000 MAIN STREET LOS ANGELES, CALIFORNIA 91301 **Type or Print all entries clearly**	TRISTAR FINANCE GROUP, INC 1000 MAIN STREET LOS ANGELES, CALIFORNIA 91301 17. Lender's Telephone Number (555) 555-5555

VA: The veteran and the lender hereby apply to the Secretary of Veterans Affairs for Guaranty of the loan described here under Section 3710, Chapter 37, Title 38, United States Code, to the full extent permitted by the veteran's entitlement and severally agree that the Regulations promulgated pursuant to Chapter 37, and in effect on the date of the loan shall govern the rights, duties, and liabilities of the parties.

18. First Time Homebuyer?	19. VA Only Title will be Vested in:	20. Purpose of Loan (blocks 9-12 are for VA loans only)
a. ☐ Yes b. ☒ No	☐ Veteran ☐ Veteran & Spouse ☐ Other (specify)	1) ☐ Purchase Existing Home Previously Occupied 7) ☐ Construct Home (proceeds to be paid out during construction) 2) ☐ Finance Improvements to Existing Property 8) ☐ Finance Co-op Purchase 3) ☒ Refinance (Refi.) 9) ☐ Purchase Permanently Sited Manufactured Home 4) ☐ Purchase New Condo. Unit 10) ☐ Purchase Permanently Sited Manufactured Home & Lot 5) ☐ Purchase Existing Condo. Unit 11) ☐ Refi. Permanently Sited Manufactured Home to Buy Lot 6) ☐ Purchase Existing Home Not Previously Occupied 12) ☐ Refi. Permanently Sited Manufactured Home/Lot Loan

Part II - Lender's Certification

21. The undersigned lender makes the following certifications to induce the Department of Veterans Affairs to issue a certificate of commitment to guarantee the subject loan or a Loan Guaranty Certificate under Title 38, U.S. Code, or to induce the Department of Housing and Urban Development - Federal Housing Commissioner to issue a firm commitment for mortgage insurance or a Mortgage Insurance Certificate under the National Housing Act.

A. The loan terms furnished in the Uniform Residential Loan Application and this Addendum are true, accurate and complete.

B. The information in the Uniform Residential Loan Application and this Addendum was obtained directly from the borrower by a employee of the undersigned lender or its duly authorized agent and is true to the best of the lender's knowledge and belief.

C. The credit report submitted on the subject borrower (and co-borrower, if any) was ordered by the undersigned lender or its duly authorized agent directly from the credit bureau which prepared the report and was received directly from said credit bureau.

D. The verification of employment and verification of deposits were requested and received by the lender or its duly authorized agent without passing through the hands of any third persons and are true to the best of the lender's knowledge and belief.

E. The Uniform Residential Loan Application and this Addendum were signed by the borrower after all sections were completed.

F. This proposed loan to the named borrower meets the income and credit requirements of the governing law in the judgment of the undersigned.

G. To the best of my knowledge and belief, I and my firm and its principals: **(1)** are not presently debarred, suspended, proposed for debarment, declared ineligible, or voluntarily excluded from covered transactions by any Federal department or agency; **(2)** have not, within a three-year period preceding this proposal, been convicted of or had a civil judgment rendered against them for (a) commission of fraud or a criminal offense in connection with obtaining, attempting to obtain, or performing a public (Federal, State or local) transaction or contract under a public transaction; (b) violation of Federal or State antitrust statutes or commission of embezzlement, theft, forgery, bribery, falsification or destruction of records, making false statements, or receiving stolen property; **(3)** are not presently indicted for or otherwise criminally or civilly charged by a governmental entity (Federal, State or local) with commission of any of the offenses enumerated in paragraph G(2) of this certification; and **(4)** have not, within a three-year period preceding this application/proposal, had one or more public transactions (Federal, State or local) terminated for cause or default.

Items "H" through "J" are to be completed as applicable for VA loans only.

H. The names and functions of any duly authorized agents who developed on behalf of the lender any of the information or supporting credit data submitted are as follows:

Name & Address	Function (e.g., obtained information on the Uniform Residential Loan Application, ordered credit report, verifications of employment, deposits, etc.)

If no agent is shown above, the undersigned lender affirmatively certifies that all information and supporting credit data were obtained directly by the lender.

I. The undersigned lender understands and agrees that it is responsible for the omissions, errors, or acts of agents identified in item H as to the functions with which they are identified.

J. The proposed loan conforms otherwise with the applicable provisions of Title 38, U.S. Code, and of the regulations concerning guaranty or insurance of loans to veterans.

Signature of Officer of Lender	Title of Officer of Lender	Date (mm/dd/yyyy)

Initial: _____

form **HUD-92900-A** (09/2010)
VA Form **26-1802a**

Page 1 of 5

Part III - Notices to Borrowers. Public reporting burden for this collection of information is estimated to average 6 minutes per response, including the time for reviewing instructions, searching existing data sources, gathering and maintaining the data needed, and completing and reviewing the collection of information. This agency may not conduct or sponsor, and a person is not required to respond to, a collection of information unless that collection displays a valid OMB control number can be located on the OMB Internet page at http://www.whitehouse.gov/omb/library/OMBINV.LIST.OF.AGENCIES.html#LIST_OF_AGENCIES.

Privacy Act Information. The information requested on the Uniform Residential Loan Application and this Addendum is authorized by 38 U.S.C. 3710 (if for DVA) and 12 U.S.C. 1701 et seq. (if for HUD/FHA). The Debt Collection Act of 1982, Pub. Law 97-365, and HUD's Housing and Community Development Act of 1987, 42 U.S.C. 3543, require persons applying for a federally insured or guaranteed loan to furnish his/her social security number (SSN). You must provide all the requested information, including your SSN. HUD and/or VA may conduct a computer match to verify the information you provide. HUD and/or VA may disclose certain information to Federal, State and local agencies when relevant to civil, criminal, or regulatory investigations and prosecutions. It will not otherwise be disclosed or released outside of HUD or VA, except as required and permitted by law. The information will be used to determine whether you qualify as a mortgagor. Any disclosure of information outside VA or HUD/FHA will be made only as permitted by law. Failure to provide any of the requested information, including SSN, may result in disapproval of your loan application. This is notice to you as required by the Right to Financial Privacy Act of 1978 that VA or HUD/FHA has a right of access to financial records held by financial institutions in connection with the consideration or administration of assistance to you. Financial records involving your transaction will be available to VA and HUD/FHA without further notice or authorization but will not be disclosed or released by this institution to another Government Agency or Department without your consent except as required or permitted by law.

Caution. Delinquencies, defaults, foreclosures and abuses of mortgage loans involving programs of the Federal Government can be costly and detrimental to your credit, now and in the future. The lender in this transaction, its agents and assigns as well as the Federal Government, its agencies, agents and assigns, are authorized to take any and all of the following actions in the event loan payments become delinquent on the mortgage loan described in the attached application: (1) Report your name and account information to a credit bureau; (2) Assess additional interest and penalty charges for the period of time that payment is not made; (3) Assess charges to cover additional administrative costs incurred by the Government to service your account; (4) Offset amounts owed to you under other Federal programs; (5) Refer your account to a private attorney, collection agency or mortgage servicing agency to collect the amount due, foreclose the mortgage, sell the property and seek judgment against you for any deficiency; (6) Refer your account to the Department of Justice for litigation in the courts; (7) If you are a current or retired Federal employee, take action to offset your salary, or civil service retirement benefits; (8) Refer your debt to the Internal Revenue Service for offset against any amount owed to you as an income tax refund; and (9) Report any resulting written-off debt of yours to the Internal Revenue Service as your taxable income. All of these actions can and will be used to recover any debts owed when it is determined to be in the interest of the lender and/or the Federal Government to do so.

Part IV - Borrower Consent for Social Security Administration to Verify Social Security Number

I authorize the Social Security Administration to verify my Social Security number to the Lender identified in this document and HUD/FHA, through a computer match conducted by HUD/FHA.

I understand that my consent allows no additional information from my Social Security records to be provided to the Lender, and HUD/FHA and that verification of my Social Security number does not constitute confirmation of my identity. I also understand that my Social Security number may not be used for any other purpose than the one stated above, including resale or redisclosure to other parties. The only other redisclosure permitted by this authorization is for review purposes to ensure that HUD/FHA complies with SSA's consent requirements.

I am the individual to whom the Social Security number was issued or that person's legal guardian. I declare and affirm under the penalty of perjury that the information contained herein is true and correct. I know that if I make any representation that I know is false to obtain information from Social Security records, I could be punished by a fine or imprisonment or both.

This consent is valid for 180 days from the date signed, unless indicated otherwise by the individual(s) named in this loan application.

Read consent carefully. Review accuracy of social security number(s) and birth dates provided on this application.

Signature(s) of Borrower(s)	Date Signed	Signature(s) of Co-Borrower(s)	Date signed

Part V - Borrower Certification

22. Complete the following for a HUD/FHA Mortgage.

	Is it to be sold?	22b. Sales Price	22c. Original Mortgage Amt.
22a. Do you own or have you sold **other** real estate within the past 60 months on which there was a HUD/FHA mortgage? ☐ Yes ☒ No	☐ Yes ☒ No	$	$

22d. Address

22e. If the dwelling to be covered by this mortgage is to be rented, is it a part of, adjacent or contiguous to any project subdivision or group of concentrated rental properties involving eight or more dwelling units in which you have any financial interest? ☐ Yes ☒ No   If "Yes" give details.

22f. Do you own more than four dwellings? ☐ Yes ☒ No   If "Yes" submit form HUD-92561.

23. Complete for VA-Guaranteed Mortgage. Have you ever had a VA home Loan? ☐ Yes ☐ No

24. Applicable for Both VA & HUD. As a home loan borrower, you will be legally obligated to make the mortgage payments called for by your mortgage loan contract. The fact that you dispose of your property after the loan has been made **will not relieve you of liability for making these payments. Payment of the loan in full is ordinarily the way liability on a mortgage note is ended.** Some home buyers have the mistaken impression that if they sell their homes when they move to another locality, or dispose of it for any other reasons, they are no longer liable for the mortgage payments and that liability for these payments is solely that of the new owners. Even though the new owners may agree in writing to assume liability for your mortgage payments, this assumption agreement will not relieve you from liability to the holder of the note which you signed when you obtained the loan to buy the property. Unless you are able to sell the property to a buyer who is acceptable to VA or to HUD/FHA and who will assume the payment of your obligation to the lender, you will not be relieved from liability to repay any claim which VA or HUD/FHA may be required to pay your lender on account of default in your loan payments. **The amount of any such claim payment will be a debt owed by you to the Federal Government.** This debt will be the object of established collection procedures.

25. I, the Undersigned Borrower(s) Certify that: (1) I have read and understand the foregoing concerning my liability on the loan

form **HUD-92900-A** (09/2010)
VA Form **26-1802a**   Page 2 of 5

and Part III Notices to Borrowers.

(2) Occupancy: (for VA only -- mark the applicable box)

☒ **(a)** I now actually occupy the above-described property as my home or intend to move into and occupy said property as my home within a reasonable period of time or intend to reoccupy it after the completion of major alterations, repairs or improvements.

☐ **(b)** My spouse is on active military duty and in his or her absence, I occupy or intend to occupy the property securing this loan as my home.

☐ **(c)** I previously occupied the property securing this loan as my home. (for interest rate reductions)

☐ **(d)** While my spouse was on active military duty and unable to occupy the property securing this loan, I previously occupied the property that is securing this loan as my home. (for interest rate reduction loans)

Note: If box **2b** or **2d** is checked, the veteran's spouse must also sign below.

(3) Mark the applicable box (not applicable for Home Improvement or Refinancing Loan) I have been informed that ($ N/A   ) is:

☐ the reasonable value of the property as determined by VA or;

☐ the statement of appraised value as determined by HUD/FHA.

Note: If the contract price or cost exceeds the VA "Reasonable Value" or HUD/FHA "Statement of Appraised Value", mark either item (a) or item (b), whichever is applicable.

☐ **(a)** I was aware of this valuation when I signed my contract and I have paid or will pay in cash from my own resources at or prior to loan closing a sum equal to the difference between the contract purchase price or cost and the VA or HUD/FHA established value. I do not and will not have outstanding after loan closing any unpaid contractual obligation on account of such cash payment;

☐ **(b)** I was not aware of this valuation when I signed my contract but have elected to complete the transaction at the contract purchase price or cost. I have paid or will pay in cash from my own resources at or prior to loan closing a sum equal to the difference between contract purchase price or cost and the VA or HUD/FHA established value. I do not and will not have outstanding after loan closing any unpaid contractual obligation on account of such cash payment.

(4) Neither I, nor anyone authorized to act for me, will refuse to sell or rent, after the making of a bona fide offer, or refuse to negotiate for the sale or rental of, or otherwise make unavailable or deny the dwelling or property covered by his/her loan to any person because of race, color, religion, sex, handicap, familial status or national origin. I recognize that any restrictive covenant on this property relating to race, color, religion, sex, handicap, familial status or national origin is illegal and void and civil action for preventive relief may be brought by the Attorney General of the United States in any appropriate U.S. District Court against any person responsible for the violation of the applicable law.

(5) All information in this application is given for the purpose of obtaining a loan to be insured under the National Housing Act or guaranteed by the Department of Veterans Affairs and the information in the Uniform Residential Loan Application and this Addendum is true and complete to the best of my knowledge and belief. Verification may be obtained from any source named herein.

(6) For HUD Only (for properties constructed prior to 1978) I have received information on lead paint poisoning.

☐ Yes ☒ Not Applicable

(7) I am aware that neither HUD/FHA nor VA warrants the condition or value of the property.

Signature(s) of Borrower(s) -- **Do not sign** unless this application is fully completed. Read the certifications carefully & review accuracy of this application.

Signature(s) of Borrower(s)	Date Signed	Signature(s) of Co-Borrower(s)	Date Signed

(Borrowers Must Sign Both Parts IV & V) Federal statutes provide severe penalties for any fraud, intentional misrepresentation, or criminal connivance or conspiracy purposed to influence the issuance of any guaranty or insurance by the VA Secretary or the HUD/FHA Commissioner.

Direct Endorsement Approval for a HUD/FHA-Insured Mortgage

Part I - Identifying Information (mark the type of application)

	2. Agency Case No. (include any suffix)	3. Lender's Case No.	4. Section of the Act (for HUD cases)
1. [X] **HUD/FHA** Application for Insurance under the National Housing Act	000-5555555-000	1234567890	203B

5. Borrower's Name & Present Address (include zip code)	7. Loan Amount (include the UFMIP)	8. Interest Rate	9. Proposed Maturity
RICHARD WILLIAM ROGERS 8624 OAKLAWN AVENUE MODESTO, CALIFORNIA 95355	$205,631.00	3.250 %	30 yrs. mos.

6. Property Address (including name of subdivision, lot & block no. & zip code)	10. Discount Amount (only if borrower is permitted to pay)	11. Amount of Up Front Premium	12a. Amount of Monthly Premium	12b. Term of Monthly Premium
8624 OAKLAWN AVENUE, MODESTO, CALIFORNIA 95355		$ 3,536.66	$ 200.25 /mo.	63 months

13. Lender's I.D. Code	14. Sponsor/Agent I.D. Code
123456789	2345678999

15. Lender's Name & Address (include zip code)	16. Name & Address of Sponsor/Agent
TRISTAR FINANCE GROUP, INC 1000 MAIN STREET LOS ANGELES, CALIFORNIA 91301 **Type or Print all entries clearly**	TRISTAR FINANCE GROUP, INC 1000 MAIN STREET LOS ANGELES, CALIFORNIA 91301 17. Lender's Telephone Number (555)555-5555

Sponsored Originations	Name of Loan Origination Company	Tax ID of Loan Origination Company	NMLS ID of Loan Origination Company
	Property Financial Center Inc - Roseville, CA	55-0000000	123456

[X] **Approved:** Approved subject to the additional conditions stated below, if any.

Date Mortgage Approved FEBRUARY 13, 2013   Date Approval Expires MARCH 1, 20XX

[ ] **Modified & Approved as follows:**	Loan Amount (include UFMIP)	Interest Rate	Proposed Maturity	Monthly Payment	Amount of Up Front Premium	Amount of Monthly Premium	Term of Monthly Premium
	$	%	Yrs. Mos	$	$	$	months

Additional Conditions:

[ ] If this is proposed construction, the builder has certified compliance with HUD requirements on form HUD-92541.
[ ] If this is new construction, the lender certifies that the property is 100% complete (both on site and off site improvements) **and** the property meets HUD's minimum property standards and local building codes.
[ ] Form HUD-92544, Builder's Warranty is required.
[ ] The property has a 10-year warranty.
[ ] Owner-Occupancy **Not** required (item (b) of the Borrower's Certificate does not apply).
[ ] The mortgage is a high loan-to-value ratio for non-occupant mortgagor in military.

[ ] Other: (specify)

[ ] This mortgage was rated as an "accept" or "approve" by FHA's Total Mortgage Scorecard. As such, the undersigned representative of the mortgagee certifies to the integrity of the data supplied by the lender used to determine the quality of the loan, that a Direct Endorsement Underwriter reviewed the appraisal (if applicable) and further certifies that this mortgage is eligible for HUD mortgage insurance under the Direct Endorsement program. I hereby make all certifications required for this mortgage as set forth in HUD Handbook 4000.4.

Mortgagee Representative _____

[ ] This mortgage was rated as a "refer" by FHA's Total Mortgage Scorecard, and/or was manually underwritten by a Direct Endorsement underwriter. As such, the undersigned Direct Endorsement underwriter certifies that I have personally reviewed the appraisal report (if applicable), credit application, and all associated documents and have used due diligence in underwriting this mortgage. I find that this mortgage is eligible for HUD mortgage insurance under the Direct Endorsement program and I hereby make all certifications required for this mortgage as set forth in HUD Handbook 4000.4.

Direct Endorsement Underwriter _____ DE's CHUMS ID Number _____

The Mortgagee, its owners, officers, employees or directors [ ] do [X] do not **have a financial interest in or a relationship, by affiliation or ownership, with the builder or seller involved in this transaction.**

Initial: _____

form **HUD-92900-A** (09/2010)
VA Form **26-1802a**   Page 4 of 5

Borrower's Certificate:

The undersigned certifies that:

(a) I will not have outstanding any other unpaid obligations contracted in connection with the mortgage transaction or the purchase of the said property except obligations which are secured by property or collateral owned by me independently of the said mortgaged property, or obligations approved by the Commissioner;

(b) One of the undersigned intends to occupy the subject property, (note: this item does not apply if owner-occupancy is not required by the commitment);

(c) All charges and fees collected from me as shown in the settlement statement have been paid by my own funds, and no other charges have been or will be paid by me in respect to this transaction;

(d) Neither I, nor anyone authorized to act for me, will refuse to sell or rent, after the making of a bona fide offer, or refuse to negotiate for the sale or rental of or otherwise make unavailable or deny the dwelling or property covered by this loan to any person because of race, color, religion, sex, handicap, familial status or national origin. I recognize that any restrictive covenant on this property relating to race, color, religion, sex, handicap, familial status or national origin is illegal and void and any such covenant is hereby specifically disclaimed. I understand that civil action for preventative relief may be brought by the Attorney General of the United States in any appropriate U.S. District Court against any person responsible for a violation of this certificate.

Borrower(s) Signature(s) & Date

Lender's Certificate:

The undersigned certifies that to the best of its knowledge:

(a) The statements made in its application for insurance and in this Certificate are true and correct;

(b) The conditions listed above or appearing in any outstanding commitment issued under the above case number have been fulfilled;

(c) Complete disbursement of the loan has been made to the borrower, or to his/her creditors for his/her account and with his/her consent;

(d) The security instrument has been recorded and is a good and valid first lien on the property described;

(e) No charge has been made to or paid by the borrower except as permitted under HUD regulations;

(f) The copies of the credit and security instruments which are submitted herewith are true and exact copies as executed and filed for record;

(g) It has not paid any kickbacks, fee or consideration of any type, directly or indirectly, to any party in connection with this transaction except as permitted under HUD regulations and administrative instructions.

I, the undersigned, as authorized representative of   TRISTAR FINANCE GROUP, INC.   mortgagee at this time of closing of , this mortgage loan, certify that I have personally reviewed the mortgage loan documents, closing statements, application for insurance endorsement, and all accompanying documents. I hereby make all certifications required for this mortgage as set forth in HUD Handbook 4000.4.

Lender's Name TRISTAR FINANCE GROUP, INC		**Note:** If the approval is executed by an agent in the name of lender, the agent must enter the lender's code number and type.	
Title of Lender's Officer			
Signature of Lender's Officer	Date	Code Number (5 digits)	Type

IMPOUND AUTHORIZATION
AND FIRST PAYMENT NOTIFICATION

Loan Number: 1234567890   Date: MARCH 13, 20XX

Lender: TRISTAR FINANCE GROUP, INC

Borrower(s): RICHARD WILLIAM ROGERS

Property Address: 8624 OAKLAWN AVENUE, MODESTO, CALIFORNIA 95355

Loan Amount: $205,631.00

We are fully aware of our obligation to the above lender as evidenced by a Note, secured by a Security Instrument on real property commonly known by the above address, and executed on the above date.

We understand that:

CHECK BOX IF APPLICABLE

☒   Regulations require the lender to establish an impound account for taxes, insurance premiums, assessments, or other items relating to the property.

☒   The lender requires, as a condition of the loan being made to us, an impound account for taxes, insurance premiums, assessments, or other items relating to the property.

☐   An impound account is not required by the lender as a condition of the loan being made to us. We want the lender to establish an impound account for taxes, insurance premiums, assessments, or other items relating to the property.

☐   An impound account is not required by the lender. We do not want the lender to establish an impound account. We agree to make timely payments to the appropriate agents when bills for taxes, insurance premiums, assessments, or other items relating to the property become due.

We authorize the lender to collect monthly impounds, if applicable, in the manner detailed below to pay for taxes, insurance premiums, assessments, or other items relating to the property on our behalf. We understand that funds so impounded are subject to all provisions of the Note and Security Instrument securing this loan. Our failure to pay these monthly impounds constitutes a default under the obligation to the lender as evidenced by said Note and Security Instrument. We understand this authorization is being executed under the provisions of the Laws within the State of   CALIFORNIA   , as amended.

We are fully aware that the First Monthly Payment on the Note is due and payable on MAY 1, 2013 and must be paid within the grace period as set forth in the note to avoid a late charge.

We understand the monthly payment consists of the following:

PRINCIPAL AND INTEREST	894.92
MORTGAGE INSURANCE	200.25
HAZARD INSURANCE	48.33
COUNTY PROPERTY TAX	196.65

TOTAL PAYMENT   1,340.15

The amount of each monthly impound to be collected is determined by the lender. The amounts are subject to adjustment from time to time. We agree to pay these modified impounded amounts along with each monthly payment of principal and interest.

RICHARD WILLIAM ROGERS	Date		Date
	Date		Date
	Date		Date

IMPOUND AUTHORIZATION AND FIRST PAYMENT NOTIFICATION
05/03/06

TRISTAR FINANCE GROUP, INC
1000 MAIN STREET
LOS ANGELES, CALIFORNIA 91301

Loan Number: 1234567890

SERVICING DISCLOSURE STATEMENT

NOTICE TO FIRST LIEN MORTGAGE LOAN APPLICANTS
THE RIGHT TO COLLECT YOUR MORTGAGE LOAN PAYMENTS MAY BE TRANSFERRED

Date: MARCH 13, 20XX

You are applying for a mortgage loan covered by the Real Estate Settlement Procedures Act (RESPA) (12 U.S.C. 2601 et seq.). RESPA gives you certain rights under Federal law. This statement describes whether the servicing for this loan may be transferred to a different loan servicer. "Servicing" refers to collecting your principal, interest, and escrow payments, if any, as well as sending any monthly or annual statements, tracking account balances, and handling other aspects of your loan. You will be given advance notice before a transfer occurs.

Check the appropriate box under "Servicing Transfer Information."

SERVICING TRANSFER INFORMATION

☐ We may assign, sell, or transfer the servicing of your loan while the loan is outstanding.

or

☒ We do not service mortgage loans of the type for which you applied. We intend to assign, sell, or transfer the servicing of your mortgage loan before the first payment is due.

or

☐ The loan for which you have applied will be serviced at this financial institution and we do not intend to sell, transfer, or assign the servicing of the loan.

SERVICING DISCLOSURE STATEMENT
12 U.S.C. 2605; 12 CFR 1024.21(b); Model Form MS-1
LSDS.MSC 12/30/11

Loan Number: 200911000

NOTICE OF ASSIGNMENT, SALE OR
TRANSFER OF SERVICING RIGHTS

You are hereby notified that the servicing of your mortgage loan, that is, the right to collect payments   from you, is being assigned, sold or transferred from TRISTAR FINANANCE GROUP. to JPMORGAN CHASE BANK, N.A., P.O. BOX 8000, MONROE, LA 71211 , effective APRIL 1, 20XX

The assignment, sale or transfer of the servicing of the mortgage loan does not affect any term or condition of the mortgage instruments, other than terms directly related to the servicing of your loan.

Except in limited circumstances, the law requires that your present servicer send you this notice at least 15 days before the effective date of transfer, or at closing. Your new servicer must also send you this notice no later than 15 days after this effective date or at closing. In this case, all necessary information is combined in this one notice.

Your present servicer is TRISTAR FINANCE GROUP
If you have any questions relating to the transfer of servicing from your present servicer call (555) 555-5555
between 8:30 a.m. and 5:00 p.m. on the following days: MONDAY – FRIDAY .
This is a ☐ toll-free or ☒ collect call number.

Your new servicer will be JPMORGAN CHASE BANK, N.A. C/O CHASE HOME .
FINANCE, LLC
The business address for your new servicer is: P.O. BOX 79046, PHOENIX, ARIZONA
85062-9046 .

The ☒ toll-free or ☐ collect call telephone number of your new servicer is (800)888-8888 .
If you have any questions relating to the transfer of servicing to your new servicer call CUSTOMER RESEARCH
at (800)848-0000   between 7:00 a.m.
and 7:00 p.m. on the following days: MONDAY – FRIDAY

The date that your present servicer will stop accepting payments from you is APRIL 1, 2010 .
The date that your new servicer will start accepting payments from you is APRIL 1, 2010
Send all payments due on or after that date to your new servicer.

You should also be aware of the following information, which is set out in more detail in Section 6 of the Real Estate Settlement Procedures Act (RESPA) (12 U.S.C. 2605):

During the 60-day period following the effective date of the transfer of the loan servicing, a loan payment received by your old servicer before its due date may not be treated by the new loan servicer as late, and a late fee may not be imposed on you.

Section 6 of RESPA (12 U.S.C. 2605) gives you certain consumer rights. If you send a "qualified written request" to your loan servicer concerning the servicing of your loan, your servicer must provide you with a written   acknowledgment within 20 Business Days of receipt of your request. A "qualified written request" is a written correspondence, other than notice on a payment coupon or other payment medium supplied by the servicer, which includes your name and account number, and your reasons for the request. If you want to send   a "qualified written request" regarding the servicing of your loan, it must be sent to this address:

JPMORGAN CHASE BANK, N.A. C/O CHASE HOME FINANCE, LLC

P.O. BOX 77777, PHOENIX, ARIZONA 85060

Not later than 60 Business Days after receiving your request, your servicer must   make any appropriate corrections to your account, and must provide you with a written clarification regarding any dispute. During this 60-Business Day period, your servicer may not provide information to a consumer reporting agency concerning any overdue payment related to such period or qualified written request. However, this does not prevent the servicer from initiating foreclosure if proper grounds exist under the mortgage documents.

A Business Day is a day on which the offices of the business entity are open to the public for carrying on substantially all of its business functions.

Section 6 of RESPA also provides for damages and costs for individuals or classes of individuals in circumstances where servicers are shown to have violated the requirements of that Section. You should seek legal advice if you believe your rights have been violated.

BORROWER ACKNOWLEDGMENT
I/We have read this disclosure form, and understand its contents, as evidenced by my/our loan signature(s) below.

Borrower RICHARD WILLIAM ROGERS Date	Borrower Date
Borrower Date	Borrower Date
Borrower Date	Borrower Date

PAYOFF SCHEDULE

Loan No.: 1234567890

Borrower(s): RICHARD WILLIAM ROGERS

The following accounts <u>must</u> be paid off through escrow as a condition of the attached loan approval:

PAYOFF to QUICKEN LOANS   203,929.00

TOTAL: 203,929.00

<u>RICHARD WILLIAM ROGERS</u>

PAYOFFSCHEDULE
PSL.MSC 05/18/12

Sample Document for National Notary Association Signing Agent Certification Study Guide

Save this Loan Estimate to compare with your Closing Disclosure.

Loan Estimate

DATE ISSUED	3/13/20XX
APPLICANTS	Richard Williams Rogers
	8624 Oaklawn Ave.
	Modesto, CA 95355
PROPERTY	8624 Oaklawn Ave., Modesto, CA 95355
SALE PRICE	$280,000

LOAN TERM	30 years
PURPOSE	Refinance
PRODUCT	Fixed Rate
LOAN TYPE	☒ Conventional ☐ FHA ☐ VA ☐ _____
LOAN ID #	
RATE LOCK	☐ NO ☒ YES, until 4/16/20XX at 5:00 pm. EDT

Before closing, your interest rate, points, and lender credits can change unless you lock the interest rate. All other estimated closing costs expire on 3/4/20XX at 5:00 p.m. EDT

Loan Terms

Loan Terms		Can this amount increase after closing?
Loan Amount	$205,631.00	**NO**
Interest Rate	3.25%	**NO**
Monthly Principal & Interest *See Projected Payments below for your Estimated Total Monthly Payment*	$894.92	**NO**

		Does the loan have these features?
Prepayment Penalty		**NO**
Balloon Payment		**NO**

Projected Payments

Payment Calculation	Years 1–4	Years 5–30
Principal & Interest	$894.92	$894.92
Mortgage Insurance	+ 82	+ —
Estimated Escrow *Amount can increase over time*	$445.23	$445.23
Estimated Total Monthly Payment	**$1,340.15**	**$1,340.15**

Estimated Taxes, Insurance & Assessments *Amount can increase over time*	$445.23 a month	**This estimate includes** ☒ Property Taxes ☒ Homeowner's Insurance ☐ Other: *See Section G on page 2 for escrowed property costs. You must pay for other property costs separately.*	**In escrow?** **YES** **YES**

Costs at Closing

Estimated Closing Costs	Includes ___ in Loan Costs + ___ in Other Costs – ___ in Lender Credits. *See page 2 for details.*
Estimated Cash to Close	$2,555.92	Includes Closing Costs. *See Calculating Cash to Close on page 2 for details.* ☐ From ☒ To Borrower

Visit **www.consumerfinance.gov/mortgage-estimate** for general information and tools.

LOAN ESTIMATE

PAGE 1 OF 3 · LOAN ID #

Additional Information About This Loan

LENDER	Tristar Finance Group
NMLS/__LICENSE ID	
LOAN OFFICER	Joe Smith
NMLS/ LICENSE ID	12345
EMAIL	mortgagebroker@tristarfin.com
PHONE	310-321-4567

MORTGAGE BROKER	
NMLS/ LICENSE ID	
LOAN OFFICER	
NMLS/___LICENSE ID	
EMAIL	
PHONE	

Comparisons
Use these measures to compare this loan with other loans.

In 5 Years	$51,932	Total you will have paid in principal, interest, mortgage insurance, and loan costs.
	$13,788	Principal you will have paid off.
Annual Percentage Rate (APR)	3.94%	Your costs over the loan term expressed as a rate. This is not your interest rate.
Total Interest Percentage (TIP)	67.28%	The total amount of interest that you will pay over the loan term as a percentage of your loan amount.

Other Considerations

Appraisal
We may order an appraisal to determine the property's value and charge you for this appraisal. We will promptly give you a copy of any appraisal, even if your loan does not close. You can pay for an additional appraisal for your own use at your own cost.

Assumption
If you sell or transfer this property to another person, we
☐ will allow, under certain conditions, this person to assume this loan on the original terms.
☒ will not allow assumption of this loan on the original terms.

Homeowner's Insurance
This loan requires homeowner's insurance on the property, which you may obtain from a company of your choice that we find acceptable.

Late Payment
If your payment is more than ___ days late, we will charge a late fee of _____

Refinance
Refinancing this loan will depend on your future financial situation, the property value, and market conditions. You may not be able to refinance this loan.

Servicing
We intend
☐ to service your loan. If so, you will make your payments to us.
☒ to transfer servicing of your loan.

Confirm Receipt
By signing, you are only confirming that you have received this form. You do not have to accept this loan because you have signed or received this form.

_____   _____   _____   _____
Applicant Signature   Date   Co-Applicant Signature   Date

LOAN ESTIMATE   PAGE 3 OF 3 • LOAN ID #

OMB Approval No. 2502-0265

Good Faith Estimate (GFE)

Name of Originator	Tristar Financial Corp		Borrower	Richard William Rogers

Originator Address	1000 Main Street Los Angeles, CA 91301		Property Address	8624 Oaklawn Avenue, Modesto, CA 95355

Originator Phone Number	(310) 321-4567

Originator Email	mortgagebroker@tristarfin.com

Date of GFE	1/20/20XX

Purpose
This GFE gives you an estimate of your settlement charges and loan terms if you are approved for this loan. For more information, see HUD's *Special Information Booklet* on settlement charges, your *Truth-in-Lending Disclosures*, and other consumer information at www.hud.gov/respa. If you decide you would like to proceed with this loan, contact us.

Shopping for your loan
Only you can shop for the best loan for you. Compare this GFE with other loan offers, so you can find the best loan. Use the shopping chart on page 3 to compare all the offers you receive.

Important dates
1. The interest rate for this GFE is available through   1/20/2010 1:23 pm . After this time, the interest rate, some of your loan Origination Charges, and the monthly payment shown below can change until you lock your interest rate.

2. This estimate for all other settlement charges is available through   2/1/2010   .

3. After you lock your interest rate, you must go to settlement within ☐ days (your rate lock period) to receive the locked interest rate.

4. You must lock the interest rate at least ☐ days before settlement.

Summary of your loan

Your initial loan amount is	$ 205,631.00
Your loan term is	30 years
Your initial interest rate is	3.25 %
Your initial monthly amount owed for principal, interest, and any mortgage insurance is	$ 894.92 per month
Can your interest rate rise?	☒ No ☐ Yes, it can rise to a maximum of %. The first change will be in
Even if you make payments on time, can your loan balance rise?	☒ No ☐ Yes, it can rise to a maximum of $
Even if you make payments on time, can your monthly amount owed for principal, interest, and any mortgage insurance rise?	☒ No ☐ Yes, the first increase can be in and the monthly amount owed can rise to $. The maximum it can ever rise to is $
Does your loan have a prepayment penalty?	☒ No ☐ Yes, your maximum prepayment penalty is $.
Does your loan have a balloon payment?	☒ No ☐ Yes, you have a balloon payment of $ due in years.

Escrow account information

Some lenders require an escrow account to hold funds for paying property taxes or other property-related charges in addition to your monthly amount owed of $ 894.92 .
Do we require you to have an escrow account for your loan?
☐ No, you do not have an escrow account. You must pay these charges directly when due.
☒ Yes, you have an escrow account. It may or may not cover all of these charges. Ask us.

Summary of your settlement charges

A	Your Adjusted Origination Charges *(See page 2.)*	$	3,310.00
B	Your Charges for All Other Settlement Services *(See page 2.)*	$	7,086.33
A + B	Total Estimated Settlement Charges	$	10,396.33

Good Faith Estimate (HUD-GFE)   1

Understanding your estimated settlement charges

Some of these charges can change at settlement. See the top of page 3 for more information.

Your Adjusted Origination Charges

1. Our origination charge This charge is for getting this loan for you.	$0.00
2. Your credit or charge (points) for the specific interest rate chosen ☐ The credit or charge for the interest rate of ☐ % is included in "Our origination charge." (See item 1 above.) ☐ You receive a credit of $ ☐ for this interest rate of ☐ %. This credit **reduces** your settlement charges. ☐ You pay a charge of $ ☐ for this interest rate of ☐ %. This charge (points) **increases** your total settlement charges. The tradeoff table on page 3 shows that you can change your total settlement charges by choosing a different interest rate for this loan.	$5936.08
A Your Adjusted Origination Charges	$ 5936.08

Your Charges for All Other Settlement Services

3. Required services that we select These charges are for services we require to complete your settlement. We will choose the providers of these services.	$1078.16

Service	Charge
Re-Appraisal Fee	$375.00
Appraisal and Appraisal Review Fee	$415.00
HOA Cert	$90.00

4. Title services and lender's title insurance This charge includes the services of a title or settlement agent, for example, and title insurance to protect the lender, if required.	$3536.00
5. Owner's title insurance You may purchase an owner's title insurance policy to protect your interest in the property.	$0.00
6. Required services that you can shop for These charges are for other services that are required to complete your settlement. We can identify providers of these services or you can shop for them yourself. Our estimates for providing these services are below.	$0.00

Service	Charge
Association Transfer Fee	

7. Government recording charges These charges are for state and local fees to record your loan and title documents.	$110.00
8. Transfer taxes These charges are for state and local fees on mortgages and home sales.	$1,179.90
9. Initial deposit for your escrow account This charge is held in an escrow account to pay future recurring charges on your property and includes ☒ all property taxes, ☐ all insurance, and ☒ other HO6 Insurance .	$2,011.50
10. Daily interest charges This charge is for the daily interest on your loan from the day of your settlement until the first day of the next month or the first day of your normal mortgage payment cycle. This amount is $ 28.36 per day for 11 days (if your settlement is 2/12/2010).	$256.33
11. Homeowner's insurance This charge is for the insurance you must buy for the property to protect from a loss, such as fire.	$241.65

Policy	Charge
HO6 Insurance	

B Your Charges for All Other Settlement Services	$ 8,838.54
A + **B** Total Estimated Settlement Charges	$ $9227.12

 Good Faith Estimate (HUD-GFE)   2

Instructions

Understanding which charges can change at settlement

This GFE estimates your settlement charges. At your settlement, you will receive a HUD-1, a form that lists your actual costs. Compare the charges on the HUD-1 with the charges on this GFE. Charges can change if you select your own provider and do not use the companies we identify. (See below for details.)

These charges **cannot increase** at settlement:	The total of these charges **can increase up to 10%** at settlement:	These charges **can change** at settlement:
▪ Our origination charge ▪ Your credit or charge (points) for the specific interest rate chosen *(after you lock in your interest rate)* ▪ Your adjusted origination charges *(after you lock in your interest rate)* ▪ Transfer taxes	▪ Required services that we select ▪ Title services and lender's title insurance *(if we select them or you use companies we identify)* ▪ Owner's title insurance *(if you use companies we identify)* ▪ Required services that you can shop for *(if you use companies we identify)* ▪ Government recording charges	▪ Required services that you can shop for *(if you do not use companies we identify)* ▪ Title services and lender's title insurance *(if you do not use companies we identify)* ▪ Owner's title insurance *(if you do not use companies we identify)* ▪ Initial deposit for your escrow account ▪ Daily interest charges ▪ Homeowner's insurance

Using the tradeoff table

In this GFE, we offered you this loan with a particular interest rate and estimated settlement charges. However:

- If you want to choose this same loan with **lower settlement charges,** then you will have a **higher interest rate.**
- If you want to choose this same loan with a **lower interest rate,** then you will have **higher settlement charges.**

If you would like to choose an available option, you must ask us for a new GFE.

Loan originators have the option to complete this table. Please ask for additional information if the table is not completed.

	The loan in this GFE	The same loan with lower settlement charges	The same loan with a lower interest rate
Your initial loan amount	$ 205,631.00	$ 205,631.00	$ 205,631.00
Your initial interest rate[1]	3.25 %	%	%
Your initial monthly amount owed	$ 814.00	$	$
Change in the monthly amount owed from this GFE	No change	You will pay $ **more** every month	You will pay $ **less** every month
Change in the amount you will pay at settlement with this interest rate	No change	Your settlement charges will be **reduced** by $	Your settlement charges will **increase** by $
How much your total estimated settlement charges will be	$ 10,396.33	$ 10,396.33	$

[1] For an adjustable rate loan, the comparisons above are for the initial interest rate before adjustments are made.

Using the shopping chart

Use this chart to compare GFEs from different loan originators. Fill in the information by using a different column for each GFE you receive. By comparing loan offers, you can shop for the best loan.

	This loan	Loan 2	Loan 3	Loan 4
Loan originator name				
Initial loan amount	$205,631.00			
Loan term	30 years			
Initial interest rate	3.250%			
Initial monthly amount owed	$894.92			
Rate lock period				
Can interest rate rise?	No			
Can loan balance rise?	No			
Can monthly amount owed rise?	No			
Prepayment penalty?	No			
Balloon payment?	No			
Total Estimated Settlement Charges	$9227.12			

If your loan is sold in the future

Some lenders may sell your loan after settlement. Any fees lenders receive in the future cannot change the loan you receive or the charges you paid at settlement.

 Good Faith Estimate (HUD-GFE) 3

FROM: TRISTAR FINANCE GROUP, INC
      1000 MAIN STREET
      LOS ANGELES, CALIFORNIA 91301
      Phone: (555)555-5555
TO: STALLWART TITLE OF MODESTO
      5555 CASANDRA BLVD., SUITE 2
      MODESTO, CALIFORNIA 95822
      (222)222-2222
ATTN:

RE: Borrower(s): RICHARD WILLIAM ROGERS

Property Address: 8624 OAKLAWN AVENUE
MODESTO, CALIFORNIA 95355

Document Date: MARCH 13, 20XX

Closing Date: MARCH 13, 20XX

Disbursement: MARCH 18, 20XX

Case No.: 000-5555555-000

Loan No.: 1234567890

App. No.:

Order No.: LP-55555555-ST

Escrow No.: LP-55555555-ST

GENERAL CLOSING INSTRUCTIONS

Do not close or fund this loan unless **ALL** conditions in these closing instructions and any supplemental closing instructions have been satisfied. The total consideration in this transaction except for our loan proceeds and approved secondary financing must pass to you in the form of cash. Do not close or fund this loan if you have knowledge of a concurrent or subsequent transaction which would transfer the subject property.

You must follow these instructions exactly. These closing instructions can only be modified with our advance written approval. You shall be deemed to have accepted and to be bound by these closing instructions if you fail to notify us in writing to the contrary within 48 hours of your receipt hereof or if you disburse any funds to or for the account of the Borrower(s).

All documents with the exception of those to be recorded (Security Instrument, Riders, Corporation Assignment(s), Grant Deed, Quit Claim, Power of Attorney, etc.) must be returned to our office within 48 HOURS of the signing. Please return certified copies of those documents that are to be recorded. Failure to comply with these instructions may delay funding.

EXECUTION OF DOCUMENTS:

1. Each Borrower must sign all documents exactly as his or her name appears on the blank line provided for his or her signature. All signatures must be witnessed if required or customary. All signature acknowledgements must be executed by a person authorized to take acknowledgements in the state of closing.

2. Any correction to loan documents must be approved in writing by us in advance. **No white-out permitted.** Approved deletion should be made by marking a single line through the language being deleted. All additions and deletions must be initialed by all borrowers.

3. All Powers of Attorney must be provided to and approved by us in advance. If approved, the Power of Attorney must be recorded in the same county(ies) in which the Security Instrument is recorded, a certified copy provided to us.

RESCISSION:

1. If the transaction is subject to rescission, provide **each** Borrower and **each** person having any ownership interest in the security property with **two (2) copies** of the completed Notice of Right to Cancel. The Notice of Right to Cancel must be properly completed (including all dates) and each borrower and person given two notices must execute an acknowledgement of receipt. Your failure to properly complete and provide the Notices of Right to Cancel to each person entitled to receive them will delay this closing.

2. No Borrower or other person having an ownership interest in the Security Property may modify or waive his or her right to rescind without our prior written consent.

3. If any Borrower or other person having an ownership interest in the security property indicates that he or she wishes to cancel this transaction, contact us immediately for further instructions.

SURVEYS:

1. A valid survey dated within 90 days of closing is required in areas where surveys are customary.

2. The survey must contain all relevant and customary information and certifications and the legal description, lot size and street must agree with the appraisal and closing documents.

HAZARD INSURANCE:

1. The Borrower(s) must provide satisfactory evidence of hazard insurance coverage and flood insurance coverage if the Property is located in a special flood hazard area.

2. Dwelling coverage must be equal to the lesser of the loan amount or the full replacement value of the property improvements, and must extend for either a term of at least one (1) year after the closing date for purchase transactions or six (6) months after the closing date for refinance transactions.

3. Loss payee/mortgagee clause to read: TRISTAR FINANCE GROUP IT'S SUCCESSORS AND/OR ASSIGNS
      1000 MAIN STREET
      LOS ANGELES, CALIFORNIA 91301
      Loan Number: 1234567890

ACKNOWLEDGED AND AGREED: _____
                                   Settlement Agent

GENERAL CLOSING INSTRUCTIONS
04/26/06

FROM: TRISTAR FINANCE GROUP, INC
1000 MAIN STREET
LOS ANGELES, CALIFORNIA 91301
Phone: (555) 555-5555

TO: STALLWART TITLE OF MODESTO
5555 CASANDRA BLVD., SUITE 2
MODESTO, CALIFORNIA 95822
Phone: (222) 222-2222

ATTN:

RE: Borrower(s): RICHARD WILLIAM ROGERS

Property Address: 8624 OAKLAWN AVENUE
MODESTO, CALIFORNIA 95355

Document Date: MARCH 13, 20XX

Closing Date: MARCH 13, 20XX

Disbursement: MARCH 18, 20XX

Case No.: 000-5555555-000

Loan No.: 1234567890

App. No.:

Order No.: LP-55555555-ST

Escrow No.: LP-55555555-ST

SPECIFIC CLOSING INSTRUCTIONS

LOAN DOCUMENTS:

We enclose the following documents necessary to complete the above referenced loan transaction:

(X) Note
(X) Deed of Trust
(X) Settlement Statement Cert.
(X) Itemization of amt fin.
(X) Payment Letter
(X) Hazard Ins. Req.

(X) Initial Escrow Acct. Disc.
Stmt.
(X) Rescission Notice
(X) Closing Inst. Addendum
(X) Affidavit and Agrmnt.
(X)

(X) Program Disclosure
(X) Servicing Disclosure
Statement
(X) Worksheets
(X) Loan Application
(X) Patriot Act

Deliver one (1) copy of all loan documents to the Borrower(s); deliver one (1) copy of the Federal Truth-In-Lending Disclosure Statement to **each** Borrower.

LOAN TERMS:

Loan Amount: 205,631.00
Initial Advance:
Sales Price:
Term (Months): 360
Interest Rate: 3.250
Initial Payment: 894.92
First Payment Date: 05/01/XX
Last Payment Date: 04/01/43

ARM Loan: ( ) Yes (X) No
Index:
Margin:
Periodic Rate Cap:
Lifetime Rate Cap:
Lifetime Rate Floor:
Interest Change Date:
Payment Change Date:
Loan Purpose: REFINANCE

PAYOFF REQUIREMENTS:

It is a condition to the funding of this loan that the following payoffs be made through this closing. Indicate payoffs on the HUD-1 Settlement Statement or provide other satisfactory evidence of payoff:
PAYOFF to QUICKEN LOANS $203,929.00

CONDITIONS TO BE SATISFIED PRIOR TO DISBURSEMENT OF LOAN PROCEEDS:

PTF - Funding VVOE within 5 days of funding for
all borrowers
PTF - 3-DAY RIGHT TO CANCEL
SEE ATTACHED ADDENDUM TO CLOSING INSTRUCTIONS

WE ARE TO BE AT NO EXPENSE IN THIS TRANSACTION

TITLE INSURANCE REQUIREMENTS:

You are authorized to use funds for the account of the Borrowers and to record all instruments when you comply with the following:

1. THIS LOAN MUST RECORD IN 1ST LIEN POSITION ON OR PRIOR TO THE DISBURSEMENT DATE NOTED ABOVE. PROVIDE DUPLICATE ORIGINALS OF THE ALTA TITLE POLICY.

2. Vesting to read: RICHARD WILLIAM ROGERS, AN UNMARRIED MAN

3. Title Policy must contain the following endorsements (or their equivalents): 100, 116, 8.1

4. ALTA Title Policy must be free from liens, encumbrances, easements, encroachments and other title matters except (i) the lien of our loan in the amount of our loan on the property described herein showing the Instrument or Document Number and the date of recording of the Security Instrument; (ii) general, specific, state, county, city, school or other taxes and assessments not yet due or payable: (BOTH INSTALLMENT OF TAXES TO BE PAID AT CLOSING)   ; (iii) other items as permitted by us; and (iv) the following items as shown on the preliminary title report, commitment, binder or equivalent dated   20XX

SECONDARY FINANCING:

Secondary financing in the amount of $ NONE   has been approved.

SPECIFIC CLOSING INSTRUCTIONS
SCI.MSC 10/08/10   Page 1 of 2

ESTIMATE OF FEES AND COSTS:

ITEM	AMOUNT	POC	PAID BY
Credit report to: Property Financial Center	$29.85	$0.00	Borrower
Inc PRMG Underwriting Fee to: PARAMOUNT	$333.19	$0.00	Borrower
RESIDENTI Originator Compensation - Lender	$4,112.62	$0.00	Lender
Paid to: Ass Wholesale LPC / Retail YSP (to	-$4,112.62	$0.00	Lender
line 802) to: MIP Refund to: HUD	-$1,102.01	$0.00	Borrower
Settlement or closing fee to: STALLWART	$400.00	$0.00	Borrower
TITLE O Lender's title insurance to:	$385.00	$0.00	Borrower
STALLWART TITLE OF Endorsements to:	$25.00	$0.00	Borrower
STALLWART TITLE OF MODESTO Notary fee to:	$175.00	$0.00	Borrower
STALLWART TITLE OF MODESTO OVERNIGHT to:	$35.00	$0.00	Borrower
STALLWART TITLE OF MODESTO WIRE FEE to:	$20.00	$0.00	Borrower
STALLWART TITLE OF MODESTO COUNTY TAXES	$1,179.90	$0.00	Borrower
to: Other	$110.00	$0.00	Borrower
Deed to: STALLWART TITLE OF MODESTO	$0.66	$0.00	Borrower
MIP (CASH) to: H U D	$3,536.00	$0.00	Borrower
MIP (FINANCED) to: H U D	-$1,142.82		Borrower
MIP (REFUND) to: Other			

PREMIUM PRICING AMOUNT* (Add to line 802) (0.500%) $1,028.16
*This amount MUST be applied as a credit towards the Borrower's Closing Costs. The combined total of this amount and
the "Lender Credit for Broker Comp" above,
should be entered on line 802 of the HUD I*   Subtotal of Estimated Fees and Costs: $ _____ 3,984.77

PER DIEM INTEREST:

From: 03/18/XX   To: 04/01/XX
                (Anticipated Closing Date)

__14__ days at $ _____ 18.3096 _____ per day   Subtotal of Per Diem Interest: $ _____ 256.33

IMPOUNDS/ESCROWS:

Impound/escrow checks should be made payable to and sent to us together with the original final HUD-1 Settlement Statement.

Mortgage Insurance	__0__ month(s) at $ __200.25__ per month = $ ____ .00		
HAZARD INSURANCE	__5__ month(s) at $ __48.33__ per month = $ ____ 241.65		
COUNTY PROPERTY TAX	__4__ month(s) at $ __196.65__ per month = $ ____ 786.60		
_____	____ month(s) at $ _____ per month = $ ____		
_____	____ month(s) at $ _____ per month = $ ____		
_____	____ month(s) at $ _____ per month = $ ____		

Aggregate Escrow Adjustment: $ _____ -293.27

Impound Subtotal: $ _____ 734.98
Mortgage Ins. Premium: $ _____
TOTAL OF FEES AND COSTS: $ _____ 4,976.08

HUD-1 SETTLEMENT STATEMENT:

The **final** HUD-1 Settlement Statement must be completed at settlement and must accurately reflect all receipts and disbursements indicated in these closing instructions and any amended closing instructions subsequent hereto. If any changes to fees occur documents may need to be re-drawn and re-signed. Fax a certified copy of the final HUD-1 Settlement Statement to TRISTAR FINANCE GROUP, INC
Attention: Quality Assurance. Send the original final HUD-1 Settlement Statement to us at the following address within 24 hours of settlement: 1000 MAIN ST, LOS ANGELES, CALIFORNIA 91301

ADDITIONAL INFORMATION: BORROWER MUST SIGN AND DATE THESE CLOSING INSTRUCTIONS.

If for any reason this loan does not close within 48 hours of your receipt of funds, immediately return all documents to Lender and wire all funds only to: TRISTAR FINANCE GROUP, INC
1000 MAIN ST, LOS ANGELES, CALIFORNIA 91301

If you have any questions regarding any of these instructions, please contact TRISTAR FINANCIAL MORTGAGE GROUP, INC.   at (555) 555-5555

BORROWER ACKNOWLEDGMENT: I/We have read and acknowledged receipt of these Closing Instructions.

Borrower   RICHARD WILLIAM ROGERS Date   Borrower   Date

Borrower   Date   Borrower   Date

Borrower   Date   Borrower   Date

ACKNOWLEDGED AND AGREED:
                                              Settlement Agent   Date

SPECIFIC CLOSING INSTRUCTIONS
SCI.MSC 10/08/10   Page 2 of 2

TAX INFORMATION SHEET

Loan Number: __1234567890__

Borrower(s) Name(s): **RICHARD WILLIAM ROGERS**

Street Address: __8624 OAKLAWN AVENUE, MODESTO, CALIFORNIA 95355__

New Construction? (Y/N) _____

ESCROW FOR TAXES? (Y/N) __N__ PAYMENT FREQUENCY _____

Please indicate below, the name(s) of the municipality to which taxes are payable.

COUNTY (if any) _____

Taxes paid through: (MM/YY) _____

Address: _____

Last Amount paid or Estimated Amount of next disbursement: _____

Next tax payment due: (MM/YY) _____

Property Identification Number (i.e. parcel number): _____

CITY, TOWNSHIP OR ~~_____~~

Taxes paid through: (MM/YY)

Address:

Last Amount paid or Estim

Next tax payment due: (MM

Property Identification Nu

Signing Agent should not fill this out

SCHOOL (if any) _____

Taxes paid through: (MM/YY) _____

Address: _____

Last Amount paid or Estimated Amount of next disbursement: _____

Next tax payment due: (MM/YY) _____

Property Identification Number (i.e. parcel number): _____

Other (Assessments, etc.) _____

Taxes paid through: (MM/YY) _____

Address: _____

Last Amount paid or Estimated Amount of next disbursement: _____

Next tax payment due: (MM/YY) _____

Property Identification Number (i.e. parcel number): _____

TAX BILLS DUE WITHIN 30 DAYS OF CHASE'S PURCHASE OF THE LOAN **MUST BE PAID** BY THE CLOSING AGENT. FAILURE TO PAY TAXES DUE WITHIN 30 DAYS OF FUNDING WILL RESULT IN FUNDING DELAYS.

CLOSING AGENT: __STALLWORTH ESCROW__

ADDRESS: __1001 MAIN STREET, LOS ANGELES, CALIFORNIA 991301__

PHONE NUMBER: __(310)555-5555__ ESCROW/FILE #: __ML-00000__

BY: _____

_____   _____

DATE   NAME/TITLE

800-649-1362

NOTARIAL EVIDENCE FORM

Please print. Fully complete all fields below. Only one form is required per loan.

Include all borrower or signer information, as applicable, in Section 2 below. If multiple documents are notarized, include each document notarized for each borrower or signer in Section 3 below. Use additional sheets as required based on number of documents notarized.

SECTION 1 – NOTARY INFORMATION

Notary Name	
State of Notary Commission	
Notary Commission No.	
Notary Identification No. (if applicable)	
Commission Effective Date	
Commission Expiration Date	

SECTION 2 – BORROWER(S)/SIGNER(S) INFORMATION

Name and Address of all Borrowers/Signers Executing Notarized Documents. List exact name(s) used in the document(s) being notarized.

Borrower's/Signer's Name:	Borrower's/Signer's Address:

Method of Identification of Borrower/Signer (government issued ID, passport, personal knowledge, etc.)

Borrower's/Signer's Name:	Borrower's/Signer's Address:

Method of Identification of Borrower/Signer (government issued ID, passport, personal knowledge, etc.)

SECTION 3 – DETAILS FOR NOTARIZED DOCUMENTS

Loan Number	
Date of Notarization	
Time of Notarization	

Name or brief description of notarized document	Type of Notarization (oath, affirmation or acknowledgement)	Document Number of Pages
1.		
2.		
3.		
4.		
5.		
6.		
7.		
8.		
9.		

Positive Proof Identification and Notary Signature Affidavit

State of _____

Conty of _____

Notary Public please complete the following:

Notary's Name: _____

(please print)

Address _____

Phone: _____

I, the above described Notary Public, hereby certify that I have checked the identification of:
_____
those parties who have signed before me and I have attached copies of their driver(s) license(s) or other picture identification. I have verified them to be the same parties as those described in the instruments acknowledged by me.

WITNESS my hand and official seal In the County and State last aforesaid this _____ day of _____, 20_____.

_____
        Notary Public Signature

_____   Seal
        Print Name of Notary

My Commission Expires:_____

My Commission Number is: _____

Notary: Please make a copy of driver's license(s), passport, state issued ID card, or military ID card and return with documents.

Notary Identity Certification

Signer(s):   Nancy A.

           Jeffrey D.

The loan document signing occurred where no photo copy equipment was available. The signatory's/signatories' identification was presented and the information was recorded as indicated below.

In addition, I acknowledge that the signatory(ies) appeared before me at all points of notarization to acknowledge that he/she/they freely executed the required documents included in this package.

I, _____, the undersigned notary public commissioned in the State of _____, acknowledgments included in this package in the presence of the signatory(ies).

Notary Stamp as proof of commission:

Notary Public: _____

                     Signature

Nancy A.

Type of Identification: _____

Identification Number: _____   Expiration Date: _____

Jeffrey D.

Type of Identification: _____

Identification Number: _____   Expiration Date: _____

FLORIDA INDIVIDUAL ACKNOWLEDGMENT
F.S. 117.05(13)

State of Florida

County of _____ }

The foregoing instrument was acknowledged before me by means of

☐ Physical Presence,

— OR —

☐ Online Notarization,

this _____ day of _____, _____, by
　　　Date　　　　　　*Month*　　　*Year*

_____.
Name of Person Acknowledging

_____
Signature of Notary Public — State of Florida

_____
Name of Notary Typed, Printed or Stamped

☐ Personally known

☐ Produced Identification

Type of Identification Produced: _____

Place Notary Seal Stamp Above　　_____

――――――――― **OPTIONAL** ―――――――――

Completing this information can deter alteration of the document or
fraudulent reattachment of this form to an unintended document.

Description of Attached Document

Title or Type of Document: _____

Document Date: _____ Number of Pages: _____

Signer(s) Other Than Named Above: _____

©2020 National Notary Association

MIKOS ESCROW

OPA-396074

MIKOS ESCROW, INC
555 N. JUNE ST
MODESTO, CA 95963

SERVICE REQUEST

THIS form acts as your invoice and MUST be returned
with every package and fax/scan as the COVER PAGE.

SERVICE REQUESTED - Witness Closing
Order #: 555555
Requested By: lenderinfo@mikos.com

VENDOR INFORMATION
Vendor Charge:	$XXX.00
Vendor Number:	71219
Vendor Name:	MEGAN BRADY
Vendor Address:	58 W. 91ST STREET
	MODESTO CA, 95350
Vendor Office Phone:	(555) 606-4938
Vendor Fax:	
Vendor Cell:	
Vendor Email:	mbrady@sbcglobal.net
Projected Closing Date:	06/22/20XX 12:00:00

BORROWER INFORMATION
Borrowers Name(s):	RICHARD W. ROGERS
Borrower Home Phone:	(209) 555-5555
Borrower Office Phone:	
Borrower Cell Phone:	
Borrower Office Phone 2:	
Borrower Office Fax:	
Borrower Home Fax:	
Borrower Home Email:	

PROPERTY / LOAN INFORMATION
Property Address: 8624 OAKLAWN AVENUE
MODESTO, CA 95355
County: STANISLAUS   **Township:** MODESTO

CLOSING LOCATION

5555 GLORIETTA LANE
MODESTO, CA 95356
County: STANISLAUS   **Township:** MODESTO

REQUIREMENTS

1. In the closing documents, you will see a form called "SIGNING CONFIRMATION CHECKLIST" - it lists our special instructions that pertain to the lender for the loan. Please be sure to take the time and read it before you leave the signing table.

2.   Refer to the "Stacking Order" sheet when returning documents by FedEx/UPS.

3.   Confirm a closing:

     a. Go to www.mikos.com/vendor-closing (No login needed.)

     b. Fax this form over to: 555-555-8203

     c. Scan/email this form to Closings@mikos.com

If anything happened at the closing or did not happen, please be sure to give feedback so we can note the system and/or pass along to the lender.

COMMENTS FROM NOTARY:

?Q U E S T I O N S?

(General Questions) **During business hours** (M-F; 8am-5pm CST):
SCHEDULER:

(Looking for Documents / Document Questions)
CLOSER: Nicola Waters nwaters@mikos.com

At the Closing:
1st try the borrower's loan officer contact.
2nd try the Closer and/or Scheduler.
3rd try emergency number below (for after hours).

After Hours EMERGENCY - Closing Document Questions:
(M-F; 5pm-8pm and Saturday from 7am-8pm):
CLOSER/MANAGER on CALL:

After Hours EMERGENCY SCHEDULING Issues:
(M-F; 5pm-8pm CST and Saturday from 7am-8pm):
MAXIMA: 555-555-5555

About the Publisher

National Notary Association

The National Notary Association is the nation's premier organization dedicated to training, serving and supporting the nation's 4.4 million Notaries Public. Established in 1957, the NNA is committed to advancing the consumer protection role of Notaries Public as the global need for identity verification, fraud prevention and trust in transactions — both commercial and private — continues to surge.

A nonprofit professional organization, the NNA serves the nation's Notaries Public in several valuable and innovative ways. It provides:

❖ The nation's leading live and online training programs for new and renewing Notaries, mobile Notaries and Notary signing agents, and for businesses and corporations that employ Notaries.

❖ The highest quality equipment, guidebooks and custom state-based supply packages that meet the needs of every Notary in every U.S. geographic region.

❖ A membership program that offers Notaries the essential resources, support and connections they need to succeed in their public service role.

❖ The NNA® Hotline staffed with experts to answer questions and help solve notarization issues the moment they arise.

❖ The latest industry news, information and best practice guidance delivered through its online *Notary Bulletin* and its webinar series.

❖ A vibrant social media community of like-minded Notaries that discuss trends, practices and career-building strategies.

❖ A scalable suite of enterprise services that helps companies easily manage their Notary workforce and establish policies and custom training programs that ensure compliance with state laws and best practices.

❖ An annual conference where Notaries, industry leaders, state officials and other stakeholders in consumer protection converge for an unparalleled training and networking experience, and to discuss national events that directly impact their Notary practices.

A Notary's alliance with the NNA helps ensure that they are on top of the latest industry needs and trends; that they are properly equipped and trained to perform sound notarizations for their clients, employers and the public; and that they embrace the highest legal and ethical standards of conduct to both serve and protect the public trust. ■

Notes

Notes

Notes

Notes

Notes

Notes

Notes

Notes

Notes

Notes